THE LEGAL CULTURE OF NORTHERN NEW SPAIN,

1700–1810

❖ ❖ ❖ ❖ ❖

The Legal Culture of Northern New Spain, 1700–1810

Charles R. Cutter

University of New Mexico Press
ALBUQUERQUE

Chapter 2 draws substantially from my article
"Community and the Law in Northern New Spain,"
The Americas L (April 1994): 467–80.
Reproduced with permission.

Library of Congress Cataloguing-in-Publication Data

Cutter, Charles R., 1950–
The legal culture of northern New Spain, 1700–1810 /
Charles R. Cutter,—1st ed.
p.   cm.
Includes bibliographical references and index.
ISBN 0-8263-2775-3
1. Law—Southwest, New—History—18th century.
2. Law—Texas—History—18th century.
3. Law—New Spain—History—18th century.
I. Title.
KF361.C87 1995
349.764'09'033—dc20
[347.64009033]   95-4334
CIP

The publication of this book was made possible in part
by a grant from the program for Cultural Cooperation
Between Spain's Ministry of Culture
and United States' Universities.

For Susan,
querida compañera

❖ ❖ ❖

Contents

Illustrations

Figures

Maps

Acknowledgments

A number of individuals and entities have contributed in many ways to the completion of this work, and I am grateful for the time, money, and expertise that they have so generously shared. Travel for research in various foreign archives was facilitated by grants from the Fulbright Commission, the Ministerio de Cultura of the Spanish government, the trustees of the Dorothy Woodward Memorial Fellowship, the Colonial New Mexico Historical Foundation, the Student Research Allocation Committee of the University of New Mexico Graduate Student Association, and the Purdue Research Foundation.

I wish also to recognize the staffs at various libraries and archives where I carried out the bulk of my research: The Archivo General de Indias in Seville; the Archivo Histórico Nacional, Biblioteca Nacional, and Instituto Gonzalo Fernández de Oviedo in Madrid; the Archivo General de la Nación in Mexico City; and the Archivo de Instrumentos Públicos and Biblioteca del Estado de Jalisco in Guadalajara. In Albuquerque, the personnel at Special Collections at the University of New Mexico General Library extended every courtesy.

For their helpful comments and suggestions on the doctoral dissertation from which this book derives, I thank Richard Ellis and Elinore Barrett. Peter Bakewell, who guided my dissertation, and John Kessell continue to be sources of inspiration, and they have shown constant support for my professional endeavors. I am most grateful.

Special thanks are due Ana María Barrero García, now at the Universidad Autónoma de Madrid, and her erstwhile staff at the Instituto de Estudios Jurídicos in Madrid. While a Fulbrighter in Spain from 1985 to 1986, I enjoyed her professional camaraderie and the luxury of uncrowded research in a marvelous legal library. She

also extended to me the opportunity to participate at the IX Congreso del Instituto Internacional de Historia del Derecho Indiano,
held in Madrid in 1990. As a result of this and other meetings of the
IIHDI, I have had the chance not only to share my views but, more
important, to learn from some of the best in the field of Spanish
colonial legal history. From this group of scholars, I would like to
thank Víctor Tau Anzoátegui, Bernardino Bravo Lira, Guillermo
Margadant, Andrés Lira, and especially Abelardo Levaggi for their
counsel and encouragement.

Finally, I am fortunate to have a family—nuclear and otherwise—
that understands and appreciates what a historian does. I thank
them for that. In seeing this manuscript through to completion,
Susan Curtis, my wife, colleague, and editor *extraordinaire*, has
cheerfully shared in both the sublime and the ridiculous. I dedicate
this book to her.

THE LEGAL CULTURE OF NORTHERN NEW SPAIN,

1700–1810

Introduction

In December 1802, royal officials in Madrid sent a dispatch to the Real Audiencia of Mexico City. Concerned about the administration of justice and the "pernicious consequences" of a "multitude of lawyers" in the Indies, the crown requested that the tribunal prepare a report on the number of lawyers that existed in each district of the *audiencia*.[1] Earlier, the crown had made another such inquiry regarding the number of notaries (*escribanos*) in New Spain. Throughout the viceroyalty various local officials complied with the instructions and furnished the required information. The response must have been startling. Far from a parasitic "multitude" of lawyers and notaries that the court undoubtedly expected to hear about, a dearth of such professionals typified all but the major cities of New Spain.

José Maldonado, *juez subdelegado* of Coatepec Chalco, near Mexico City, reported that his jurisdiction had no *escribano* and only two lawyers—one, a secular clergyman (who would have been barred from practicing in a royal court); the other, a hacienda administrator who resided in the capital.[2] An important mining center—Real y Minas de Pachuca—had neither *escribano* nor *abogado*. The *subdelegado* of that district advised that he routinely acted in legal matters by delegated authority (*receptoría*) and simply used witnesses (*testigos de asistencia*) to countersign documents.[3] A similar situation existed in Acapulco, the most important Pacific port. Wrote Subdelegado José Barreyro y Quijano,

> not only in this city and territory under my command, but also throughout this extensive southern coast, there exist no *abogados;* nor do I have news that there are any in the interior as far as [Mexico City], which is more than one hundred leagues from this city. Thus, it is obvious that the administration of justice, the

public, and the King's service must necessarily experience great
harm by having so many *abogados* assembled in only one place, at
so great a distance.[4]

From Yucatán in the south to New Mexico in the north, the
problem was evident—legal professionals avoided the extensive
peripheral regions while, as Subdelegado Barreyro pointed out per-
ceptively, they abounded in the centers.[5] In the province of Mexico
alone, fifty-five of the total seventy-two *escribanos* plied their trade
in the capital city, while the rest were scattered among the remaining
forty-four districts.[6] Lawyers, too, tended to practice in large cities.
The Audiencia of Guadalajara, the judicial seat for the northern
frontier, reported that in the city of Guadalajara there were thirty-
one lawyers, only eighteen of whom were not disqualified in some
way from practicing law. Zacatecas province boasted five trained
lawyers, Durango three, and a handful of other settlements one each.
But the rest had none.[7] The situation within the Audiencia of Mexico
was similar—among the 210 practicing lawyers, well over half lived
in Mexico City.[8]

New Mexico and Texas, two provinces on the northern frontier of
New Spain, also experienced a lack of adequately trained legal
professionals. Governor Fernando Chacón communicated "that in
this province of New Mexico there are no, nor have there ever been,
legal advisers, lawyers, or notaries who can properly conduct a
[criminal] case."[9] Likewise, Texas Governor Juan Bautista de Elgue-
zábal disclosed that in his jurisdiction there were no lawyers.[10]

Many contemporaries believed that the lack of trained personnel
greatly hindered the efficiency and propriety of judicial administration in New Spain. The validity of this view is arguable, but the
absence of a trained judiciary certainly had an impact on legal
practice in New Spain. For modern scholars seeking to understand
the nature of the colonial regime, the absence of trained legal functionaries poses important questions. In a political structure that
rested upon an administrative judiciary, how did the crown maintain control outside the urban centers? How did non-experts handle
judicial affairs? Did legal proceedings in the peripheral areas conform to the juristic norm, or did they represent aberrations within
the larger system? An understanding of legal administration in
these neglected areas is essential for an accurate and balanced picture of Spanish law in the New World.

Law and the provision of justice figured prominently in the institutional makeup of the Spanish empire. Historians have long realized the importance of legal administration in Spanish colonial society and have written extensively on the subject. Two approaches characterize traditional historiography on Spanish colonial law. First, most older studies have made extensive use of the great compendia of the colonial era (most notably the *Recopilación de Indias* of 1681) in drawing conclusions about the nature of the colonial legal system. Often employing the technique of textual analysis, scholars of this historiographical bent contributed to our understanding of the juridical principles that formed the basis of the colonial regime, yet they frequently ignored the all-important questions of day-to-day implementation of the legal system.[11] In contrast, a younger generation of Latin American historians, eager to understand the economic and social structures of the colonial era, also have looked to the legal record as a historical source. But because their primary aim has been to explore social arrangements and patterns of economic exploitation, they rarely have sought to explicate the legal milieu from which these documents sprang.

Another characteristic of colonial legal historiography is the overwhelming focus on the heavily populated centers of empire.[12] In those areas the system boasted a full array of legal personnel. Perhaps on the assumption that these core areas best represent the colonial world, most legal historians have failed to consider regions that had no such abundance of trained functionaries. An understanding of legal practice in the northern borderlands provides a much-needed different point of view from which we can better assess the bigger picture of Spanish colonial legal practice.

Spanish colonial law encompassed more than the juridical principles of the state, the social and economic structures that it upheld, or the labor of legal professionals in the urban centers. Indeed, a distinct legal culture permeated the colonial world and served as the touchstone by which Spanish subjects understood and negotiated their relationship to the rest of society. While some Latin Americanists question the relevance of peripheral areas, a study of the legal culture of such regions can offer a way to understand the full range of the Spanish colonial legal culture.[13] Granted, to fully appreciate the distinctiveness of legal practice on the peripheries, one cannot afford to lose sight of the great urban centers. Yet many of the features of legal administration on the frontier must have been common throughout New Spain, if not the entire Hispanic world of the *antiguo régimen*. In many ways, judicial administration in New Mexico and Texas was more similar to the rest of New Spain than legal practice in the large metropolitan areas of Mexico City and Guadalajara. The centers, not the peripheries, were the exceptions.

The Spanish legal heritage has been particularly prominent in the American Southwest. Because of their distinctive histories, the states of New Mexico and Texas have retained some legal practices first established during the long period of Spanish sovereignty. Especially important has been the legacy of Hispanic law regarding property rights, inheritance, and land and water use. Regional historians have tended to treat the legal history of the Spanish colonial period in piecemeal fashion. As the need arose, a scholar or some other investigator might write a report dealing with one particular aspect of Spanish law.[14] To date, no comprehensive overview exists that gives a general picture of the workings of the Spanish legal system in the northern borderlands of New Spain. One purpose of this study is to fill such a need. My aim is to place a regional topic within the imperial context.

This book examines judicial procedure in two provinces located on the northern frontier of New Spain, roughly from 1700 to 1810. I have chosen these dates for several reasons. First, they represent convenient landmarks in colonial history—1700 marked the beginning of the Bourbon regime; 1810 is generally regarded as the start of the movement for independence in Mexico. Concurrent with the famous *grito de Dolores,* events on the peninsula combined to change the ideological outlook of the Hispanic world and undermine the political cohesion of the *antiguo régimen.* Another reason for focusing on the eighteenth and early nineteenth centuries is a practical one—few pertinent documents remain from earlier periods. Most local New Mexico documents from the seventeenth century were destroyed in 1680; civilians did not settle Texas until 1718. Thus, the historical record of colonial New Mexico and Texas is found largely within the period from 1700 to 1810.

Like other parts of the empire, New Mexico and Texas had parallel legal jurisdictions that operated simultaneously. I have restricted this study only to ordinary royal jurisdiction (*justicia real ordinaria*) and have not examined military or ecclesiastical jurisdictions. While important, military and ecclesiastical jurisdictions touched only select portions of the population. On the other hand, *justicia real ordinaria* affected almost all of the local inhabitants in New Mexico and Texas, and thus constituted the most prominent jurisdiction in those provinces.

While the influence of the church remained a considerable force throughout the entire colonial period, the eighteenth century was a time of slow but inexorable growth of secular over religious aspects of colonial administration. Legal administration mirrored the general trend, and in many ways it became the vehicle for the crown's attacks on the prerogatives of the church. Particularly important was the curtailment of a special legal jurisdiction that had long been one of the traditional sources of ecclesiastical autonomy, and through a series of decrees the church lost many of its privileges during the course of the century.[15] As the status of the clergy declined, the fortunes of the military soared.

The Bourbon accession to the throne portended an increased role for the military in the Indies. From 1708, for example, the governing regime in Nueva Galicia shifted from *letrado* rule to a military one.[16] Absent in early colonial times, the professional army grew in size and prestige from the time of its creation in 1762 until Independence. The *fuero militar,* which played a limited role in judicial matters early in the century, became one of the main privileges of those connected with the military. In some places, this privilege began to impinge upon ordinary royal jurisdiction.[17]

In the northern borderlands the clergy were clearly not marginal figures in the eighteenth century; but in keeping with the general trend of Bourbon rule, their role became increasingly subordinate to that of civil officials. Taking care to counter foreign presence on the North American continent, the crown's interest in New Spain's far north had more to do with imperial defense than with saving heathen souls. Imperial administrators recast the role of Texas, New Mexico, and the entire north to serve as a protective buffer for the rest of New Spain, by this time the crown's most precious overseas holding. Military affairs emerged as the central concern in provincial administration.

In order to avoid confusion, I should explain the orthographic conventions employed. When possible I have used English rather than Spanish words in the text, but only when a good equivalent exists (thus, the king; but, the *alcalde*). Proper nouns are Anglicized if well-known by those names (Philip II rather than Felipe II; Albuquerque, not Alburquerque). The present-day city of San Antonio comprised several different jurisdictions, each with different names, during the colonial period. In an effort to simplify and avoid confusion, I use the modern nomenclature for that urban area. Finally, when using Spanish, I have chosen to modernize the spelling and diacritical marks (José rather than Joseph; *gobernación* instead of *governazion*), except in bibliographic citations and in footnotes where, for the sake of identification, document titles retain the original orthography.

Mention should also be made of the sources used in this study, since to a large degree they shaped the methodology employed in research and analysis. In examining the legal system at a local level, I scrutinized some six hundred court cases, most of which came from the Spanish Archives of New Mexico (Series I and II), the Bexar Archives, and the Bexar County Archives. Special problems arose in dealing with each archive. Colonial documentation in New Mexico has suffered over the years from neglect and destruction. During the Pueblo Revolt of 1680, Indians destroyed most vestiges of the Spanish regime, including almost all of the local government documents. After Diego de Vargas's recolonization of New Mexico in the 1690s, government documents seem to have remained intact, if not particularly well cared for, throughout the remainder of the Spanish and Mexican periods until U.S. occupation.

The Territorial period of New Mexico history proved disastrous for the collection known as the "Spanish Archives" (which also included Mexican period documentation). This archive contains a broad range of provincial and municipal government documentation, including criminal proceedings and civil litigation. Pilfering, improper funding and storage, and some outright destruction quickly caused the collection to fall into disarray. Documents relative to property seem to have survived the calamity best—if nothing else, the newcomers recognized the value of property—but other documents "of no value" reportedly were thrown out of the governor's palace and sold to local merchants for wrapping paper. Not until the end of the nineteenth century did the Spanish Archives begin to receive the care and attention that they deserve.[18]

While the records for colonial Texas perhaps have not suffered such outright destruction, they, too, have experienced a precarious existence. The collection known as the Bexar Archives became dispersed throughout the state. Like the Spanish Archives of New

Mexico, the Bexar Archives are in essence the documents generated by the provincial government, plus much of the municipal record. Not until end-of-the-century scholars at the University of Texas recognized their value was the physical well-being of the Bexar Archives ensured.[19] Another collection of Texas documents, the Bexar County Archives, also went through a period of neglect until the 1920s, when Carlos E. Castañeda arranged them. This archive is limited almost exclusively to municipal records of San Antonio. The amount of material missing from each of the three collections of local documentation is impossible to determine.

The fate of the documents at the next jurisdictional level, the Comandancia General of the Provincias Internas, is even sadder. Most of the papers from this jurisdiction probably perished in 1941 when the Archivo General del Estado de Chihuahua went up in flames. One pertinent section of the general archive, the "Comandancia General," was totally destroyed. Another, the "Comandancia de las Provincias Internas," may have suffered the same bad luck, though some believe that portions of this group had been transferred elsewhere before the fire. Still, investigators have yet to discover its whereabouts.[20]

Even if all the colonial records had survived, these would not represent the full range of legal action pursued by Spanish subjects in Texas and New Mexico. In a number of instances, a magistrate undoubtedly brought the parties to some sort of verbal conciliation, since one aim of the Spanish legal system was to settle petty disputes without resorting to the courtroom.[21] How often this occurred we simply have no way of knowing because these cases did not generate written documentation. Thus we lose sight of an important facet of the Spanish legal system.

Likewise, petty crimes at times failed to produce any written record. Lope de la Vega, *alcalde ordinario* of the city of Chihuahua, for example, reported that in the last six months of 1809 not one criminal case had been prosecuted in his court because, "though in this period there have been several defendants in the royal jail at the expense of this same court, they have been for petty crimes, which do not require legal proceedings."[22] Apparently, not all crimes (not even those that were punished) generated documentation.

These documentary gaps pose problems for a historical study. First, detection of trends over time through statistical analysis is severely hampered. What does a drop-off in litigious activity, as happened in New Mexico in the 1770s, really mean? Did colonists suddenly enter into a new era of social harmony? Did local magistrates resort to a greater number of verbal judgments? Now that the Comandancia General existed, did governors routinely send legal paperwork south to the commandant's legal adviser? If so, why were so few documents returned to the provincial governor for sentencing? Or did the bundle of documents for the 1770s end up as wrapping paper for Santa Fe merchants nearly a century later? The significant lacunae in the documentary record make quantitative analysis risky.

I have not considered in my analysis cases of a purely military nature—insubordination, irregularities in presidial finances, desertion, and so forth. On the other hand, because of the prominent position of presidial forces and their intimate relations with the ordinary citizenry, I *have* considered those cases that involve members of the military and ordinary citizens, or even two military figures, which appear to have been adjudicated under the rubric of *justicia real ordinaria.*

If the documentary collections for colonial New Mexico and Texas are not conducive to quantitative history, they still have much to say about Spanish colonial society. The setting of the courtroom reveals to us the attitudes of settlers, their notions of right and wrong, the boundaries of social propriety, and the extent to which they assented to and legitimized the crown's role as arbiter. An examination of the legal record provides considerable insight into the values of this bygone era. To be sure, the judicial process imposed a conformity on the participants, who quite likely adopted speech and behavior that they believed to be appropriate to the setting. While procedural rules no doubt limited the amount of spontaneity in legal testimony, participants often managed to articulate their hopes, fears, and expectations during the course of a trial. Because of the juridical simplicity of New Mexico and Texas and the inherent flexibility of Spanish colonial law, most magistrates heard out the contending parties, sought equitable solutions, and avoided excessive legalism.

Other legal documents—wills, testaments, and conveyances— display more fidelity to protocol. Although the specialized jargon masks to some degree the true sentiments of the parties involved, these also serve as indicators of the society's values. The conformity to textual convention in these documents demonstrates the importance placed on the written word in a society that was largely semiliterate. A testator, for example, often sought the assistance of someone familiar with legal formula to ensure the validity of a will. Thus, trial records and other legal documents reveal the interplay between the material world of the settlers and the abstract world of legal principles, between the social setting and the cultural tools (or ideology) found in the Hispanic world of the eighteenth and early nineteenth centuries. In practice, the law not only shaped the outlook and expectations of society but also reflected them.[23]

PART ONE

Constructing a Legal Culture

❖ ❖ 1 ❖ ❖

The Geographic Setting

The contrasts between Mexico City and the far north of New Spain in the eighteenth century were staggering. Majestic, grandiose, and by far the largest urban center in all of the Americas, Mexico City ranked among the great cities of the world.[1] The hill of Chapultepec offered a breathtaking sight to the eighteenth-century observer. Broad, poplar-lined thoroughfares led travelers to this great metropolis bathed by Lake Texcoco, crisscrossed by canals and aqueducts, and teeming with monumental architecture and bustling marketplaces. Mexico City brought together the full range of colonial society, and it figured as the political, economic, and intellectual hub of New Spain—truly the crown jewel of Spain's overseas possessions.

Beyond the busy urban cluster a keen-eyed observer also might have spotted the Camino Real de Tierra Adentro that led to Querétaro and Zacatecas, then branched out into the vast interior of the far north. One road continued to Durango—the last sizeable city—passed through Chihuahua, and came to an end at the *villa* of Santa Fe, capital of the province of New Mexico. A secondary road ran in a northeasterly direction from just past Zacatecas to Saltillo. From there it continued to San Antonio de Béxar, in Texas, and the northeastern border of Spanish America. At trail's end, far from the splendor of the capital and amid harsh environments, lay the provinces of New Mexico and Texas, distant and "remote beyond compare."[2] Central Mexico and the peripheries of the far north differed in many ways. But the fundamental difference was that urban complexity gave way to rural simplicity.

Spaniards acquired at an early date some rudimentary geographic knowledge of what eventually became the provinces of Texas and New Mexico. As early as 1519 Alonso de Pineda had

NORTHERN NEW SPAIN
(drawn by Stephen Martin)

explored the Texas gulf coast, and the later wanderings of Alvar Núñez Cabeza de Vaca also brought attention to the region. In 1540, amid rumors of a sophisticated Indian culture to the north, Francisco Vázquez de Coronado headed a group of adventurer-soldiers who sought to verify these propitious reports.[3] Coronado and his men did not find fabulous riches, as they hoped, but their reports did contribute much to expanding the geographic knowledge of the Europeans. Authorities branded Coronado's expedition a failure, however, and the far north receded into the background of Spanish endeavors.[4]

Over the next half century, Spaniards consolidated their position in New Spain and began to refine the instruments of colonial control.[5] The crown found energetic and capable administrators in early viceroys such as Antonio de Mendoza (1535–50) and Luis de Velasco (1550–64). On steady footing, and with the wealth of the north beckoning, Spanish settlement spilled over the Valley of Mexico, past the rich Bajío, and into the arid Chihuahuan Desert. As the century waned, Spaniards once again set their sights on the far north.[6] The colonization of Juan de Oñate in 1598 extended Spanish sovereignty to the upper Rio Grande Valley of New Mexico. Son of a millionaire Zacatecas mining family with influential connections, Oñate hoped that la nueva méxico would render mineral wealth on a par with Zacatecas.[7] This was not to be, and he soon was relieved of his command and left the province. But religious motives—ever present in government policy—led the crown to keep New Mexico as a mission field.[8] With the appointment of Pedro de Peralta (1610–14) as provincial governor, the "kingdom" of New Mexico came under closer viceregal supervision, and Spaniards settled into a regime sustained economically by the encomienda system and complicated by frequent squabbles between civil and ecclesiastical authorities.[9]

Missionary zeal also contributed to the permanent occupation of Texas. While Franciscans had long urged the crown to sponsor this undertaking, the presence of René Robert Cavalier, Sieur de la Salle, and the establishment of Fort Saint Louis at Matagorda Bay prompted Spanish action. Responding to French intrusion, Captain Alonso de León and Father Damián Massanet founded in 1690 the first Spanish mission in East Texas. Although both Mission San Francisco de los Tejas and the French fort proved to be temporary, Texas now assumed the role it would play for the remainder of the

colonial period—a buffer against foreign presence in North America.[10] When French pressure resumed in the early eighteenth century, Spain countered with more mission activity in East Texas and
with the founding in 1718 of the first permanent settlement in the
province—the presidio at San Antonio de Béxar. In time the San
Antonio area became the heartland of Spanish Texas.

While the geographic extent of the province was always hazily
defined, Spanish Texas encompassed considerably less territory
than the present Lone Star State. Official correspondence reveals
the ambiguity not only about the extent but also the precise name
of this territory far to the north of the viceregal capital. Typical is a
1739 communiqué from the king to the Audiencia of Mexico. On
the margin, a royal functionary noted that the letter concerned "the
government of Los Adonais, today of Los Tejes [sic], or New Philippines."[11] So amorphous were the physical boundaries that the
identity problem continued throughout most of the eighteenth century. Generally, however, Spanish Texas lay between the Nueces,
Red, and Sabine rivers.[12] Occupation of Nacogdoches, at the eastern limit, held only strategic importance for the region. The real
core of Spanish settlement lay further west, along the San Antonio
River, in a region geographically and culturally distinct from the
Piney Woods of East Texas.[13] Nestled between the Edwards Pla-
teau to the northwest and the Coastal Prairie, San Antonio lies in a
fertile zone known geologically as the Black Prairie. Rainfall is
unpredictable, but the early settlers of San Antonio found the area
to be well-watered by the San Antonio River and several reliable
feeder creeks. Above all, the abundance of flora and fauna impressed colonial visitors. Writing in 1783, Fray Juan Agustín Morfi
extolled the virtues of the country.

> The fertility of the soil exceeds all exaggeration. . . . Nothing
> proves the fertility of the land and the richness of the soil more
> than the incredible number of wild horses and cattle found ev-
> erywhere. It is the multitude of rivers, creeks, and lakes that is
> responsible for its great fecundity.[14]

But others had a different view of the environment. Nicolás Lafora,
of the Spanish Royal Corps of Engineers, noted the irregular pre-
cipitation and the abundance of "so many flies of various kinds,
horse-flies, ticks, mites, and various other insects that they make it

uninhabitable." Lafora also believed that the unhealthful climate caused women to become "sterile."[15]

Like Texas, precise geographic boundaries of colonial New Mexico were elusive. Official claims aside, effective occupation of the province centered primarily along the Rio Grande, north to south from Taos to Socorro. Isolated downriver, and intermittently under the jurisdiction of Nueva Vizcaya, stood El Paso. From west to east, a narrow corridor of Spanish jurisdiction extended from the Indian pueblos of Zuni to Pecos. Because of scant annual rainfall, nearly all settlement in New Mexico—Spanish and Indian—occurred along the few reliable sources of water. The sedentary inhabitants vied with one another to control the arable land in the province, most of which hugged the banks of the Rio Grande and its tributaries.[16]

Spanish authorities intended that all New World urban settlement should conform to a rational pattern, essentially quadrangular, with government and church structures at the center. Embodied in the *Recopilación de Indias* and reiterated in subsequent legislation, the archetypical Spanish municipality served as the pattern for settlement throughout the Indies.[17] Indeed, in contrast to, say, English colonization, most Spanish settlers lived in urban clusters. It is no mere coincidence that considerable local power was often connected intimately with the municipality. As in other aspects of the colonial experience, however, New Mexico and Texas differed from the proposed ideal settlement pattern.

Rather than a carefully laid out rectangle, the centers of settlement in New Mexico constituted little more than a haphazard structural hodgepodge.[18] Top-level administrators frequently remarked on this anomaly. One observer noted in 1778 that the *villa* of Albuquerque, if reduced to proper form, "would be a medium-sized settlement" that might provide ample farmland and common lands. Instead, because of its "defective establishment" it occupied "more than twelve leagues along the Rio [Grande]."[19] The provincial capital at Santa Fe resembled more closely the Hispanic ideal, but only barely. Wrote Bishop Francisco Atanasio Domínguez,

> Its appearance, design, arrangement, and plan do not correspond to its status as a *villa*. . . . The Villa of Santa Fe (for the most part) consists of many small *ranchos* at various distances from one another, with no plan as to their location, for each owner built as he was able, wished to, or found convenient.[20]

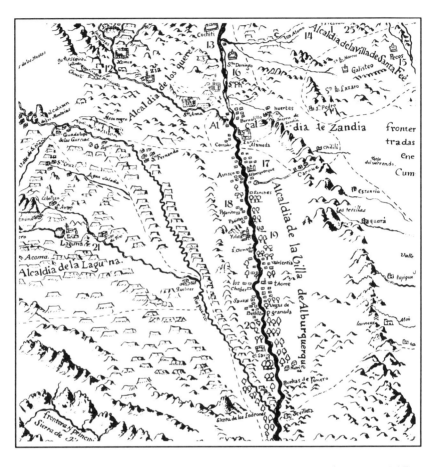

DETAIL OF BERNARDO DE MIERA Y PACHECO'S 1779 MAP,
SHOWING THE DISPERSED SETTLEMENT PATTERN
WITHIN THE ALCALDÍA OF ALBUQUERQUE

So dispersed was New Mexico's Spanish population that officials in the late eighteenth century attempted, unsuccessfully, to force settlers to concentrate in more easily protected clusters of population.[21]

Under normal circumstances, the municipality as a political unit carried with it certain rights and privileges associated with the administration of justice. The municipal corporation, or *cabildo*, had the power to choose magistrates from among its ranks to provide justice within its corresponding territorial limits.[22] In New Mexico, perhaps because of the aberrant settlement patterns as well as for political reasons, the *cabildo* failed to exist during most of the period covered in this study. Santa Fe boasted a *cabildo* until about the mid-1710s, but, because of this body's unending contentiousness, the city apparently lost this privilege. The remaining two *villas*, Albuquerque and Santa Cruz de la Cañada, at no time had municipal governments until established by virtue of early-nineteenth-century constitutional reform.[23] Government officials may have had in mind the trouble-prone Santa Fe *cabildo* when they failed to allow for the creation of similar institutions for Albuquerque and Santa Cruz. And surely the extended settlement pattern of both areas did little to create the impression of a cohesive urban unit.

San Antonio, the eventual provincial capital of Spanish Texas, conformed initially to the archetypical urban pattern. Maps and plans from the period indicate that Canary Islanders, who arrived in 1731, adhered to tradition and law in establishing the original Villa de San Fernando.[24] Here, the classic pattern of the town took root, with the *plaza mayor* at the center and all streets emanating at right angles from it. Perhaps San Antonio conformed to the norm more than the New Mexico counterparts because of the presence of the *isleños*. Determined to preserve their privileges as "first families," they may well have paid more attention to detail in matters of town planning. Yet over time, the Hispanic ideal of the well-situated urban hub simply failed to materialize. A later visitor, American officer Zebulon Montgomery Pike, saw past the obvious poverty and discerned the underlying intention. "The town," wrote Pike, "is laid out on a very grand plan."[25] Spaniards were less impressed. Teodoro de Croix in 1781 described the civil settlement of Béxar as consisting of "huts and little wooden houses."[26] Another interested observer of the northern frontier, Fray Juan Agustín Morfi, remarked in similar disparaging terms that the town consists of fifty-nine houses of stone and mud and seventy-nine of wood, but all poorly built, without any preconceived plan, so that the whole resembles more a poor village than a *villa*, capital of so pleasing a province. . . . The streets are tortuous and are filled with mud the minute it rains.[27]

Apparently, the less-than-opulent circumstances of the far north had diluted the good intentions of crown administrators and early settlers.

The economies of both provinces, particularly New Mexico, lagged behind much of the rest of New Spain. Despite repeated efforts, Spaniards failed to locate mineral deposits large enough to sustain steady economic growth and, thus, attract many settlers from the interior. If anything, the two provinces were an economic drag on the empire. Indeed, one scholar has estimated that for every peso extracted from pre-Revolt New Mexico, the crown invested ninety, an economic imbalance that changed little throughout the colonial period.[28] In these border provinces, afflicted with a chronic state of war, the tributary castes—Indians, blacks, and mulattoes—were exempt from economic obligation.[29] For the same reasons, the *alcabala* (sales tax) had no applicability in either New Mexico or Texas.[30] Threatened by imperial rivals, the far northern provinces stood as guardians of the wealthy interior. And, as strategic outposts, the crown maintained them at a high cost.

Propped up economically by the crown, the far north received most of its hard currency via government supply channels. The all important *situados* for presidial troops, and *sínodos* for missionaries, may have accounted for the limited amount of specie that circulated on the frontier. Just how much actually reached New Mexico and Texas is unclear, since many of these official payments arrived in the form of supplies.[31] Some believe that more specie circulated in the province than contemporary reports indicated, but the lack of hard currency cannot be discounted.[32] A perusal of the judicial records confirms the scarcity of this medium of exchange in New Mexico. As in the case of Agustín Sáez who in 1701 paid a penalty of forty pesos in "common goods and at customary prices," many courtroom transactions—fines, debts, court costs, and the like—were executed either in kind, or through the monetary fiction of *pesos de la tierra*.[33] Under this arrangement, locals suffered a considerable disadvantage when trading with merchants, who sold their wares at normal prices (based on *pesos de plata*), but who accepted local goods only at the discounted rate of the *pesos de la tierra*.[34] Not only the impoverished, but also the relatively well-to-do often satisfied courtroom obligations by paying in *pesos de la tierra*. Even as late as 1820, a fairly wealthy New Mexican, Luis María Cabeza de Baca, satisfied an *audiencia*-imposed penalty by supplying the Santa Fe presidio with eight mules.[35]

Lacking specie, most New Mexicans resorted to barter, or *cambalache*. At formally established fairs, such as the famous annual gathering at Taos, Spaniards, Pueblos, and *indios bárbaros* put aside immediate differences and exchanged items of value. As with so many aspects of colonial life, Spanish authorities scrutinized closely these trade fairs, setting opening dates, controlling prices, and keeping a watchful eye to curb black market operations.[36] Not only at trade fairs, but also on a daily basis colonial New Mexicans usually bartered for, rather than bought, what they needed or desired.[37]

In general, New Mexicans drew their sustenance from the land. Small irrigated family plots, geared to local markets, characterized land tenure in eighteenth-century New Mexico. According to the 1790 census, 55.8 percent of the 1,658 heads of families were farmers. Another 13.2 percent were day laborers—many of whom often worked in agriculture. A mere 6.7 percent figured as artisans.[38] Using methods similar to their Indian neighbors, Hispanic farmers raised crops principally of maize, frijoles, corn, wheat, and of course, chile. As the eighteenth century progressed, livestock production grew to be the most lucrative economic pursuit and became the mainstay of the limited export economy. Although only 6.8 percent of the heads of families were listed as stock raisers, another 13 percent—mostly in the Albuquerque area—made their living as carders, spinners, or weavers.[39] In New Mexico, the hardy *churro* variety of Iberian sheep proved to be adaptable to the harsh climatic conditions of its new environment.[40] By mid-century, several families, especially in the Albuquerque area, emerged as the first true *ricos* whose economic power depended upon the sheep business. The development of the *partido* system—under which a wealthy sheepowner provided another party with livestock and received in return a percentage of the increase—enlarged not only the flocks, but also, by extending networks of personal obligations, the economic, political, and social standing of the *ricos*.[41] New Mexico sheep reached many of the presidios in Nueva Vizcaya as well as the *villa* of Chihuahua, which became the principal trading center for New Mexico merchants.[42]

While a small segment of New Mexico's population enjoyed relative prosperity, the bulk of the inhabitants maintained a precarious existence. Court documents such as the *embargo de bienes* reveal that many New Mexicans possessed only the bare essentials for eking out a living—a small one- or two-room adobe house, sometimes nothing more substantial than a shack (*jacal*) of poles and adobe, a table, some utensils, perhaps a chair, and a pallet or a bed for sleeping.

The economic structure of Texas resembled that of New Mexico in many respects. Production for local consumption characterized agricultural activity.[43] The missions of Texas, however, assumed a greater role in the provincial economy than in New Mexico. Here, the mission resembled more closely the classic self-contained socioeconomic unit often described by historians.[44] Producing agricultural surpluses, the missionaries of Texas not only fed and clothed the neophytes under their charge, but also supplied the local military garrison and some of the Spanish population as well. Not surprisingly, conflicts erupted between *vecinos* and missionaries, as both groups sought to control the lifeblood of the far northern provinces—water. The arrival of the contentious Canary Islanders in 1731 only aggravated the situation. Friction between settlers and missionaries continued until secularization at the end of the eighteenth century, when mission lands were divided among local residents.[45]

Even more than New Mexico, Texas grew to depend upon livestock production to provide a marketable commodity for export. Instead of sheep, cattle and horses became the mainstays of Texas and eventually overshadowed other aspects of the economy. Indeed, so suited to the environment was ranching that the Anglo Americans who later arrived simply adopted most of the Hispanic techniques and practices in building their cattle kingdoms.[46] Unlike in other northern provinces, the great hacienda was not characteristic of livestock production in Texas. Instead of the self-sufficient *hacendados* described by François Chevalier, the ranchers of colonial Texas tended to live in San Antonio, or nearby, and to take an active part in local municipal life.[47] Driving herds of cattle and horses southward to Nuevo León and Coahuila, and eastward to Louisiana, often illegally, some colonial Texans achieved relative wealth.

To the south, Saltillo and Monterrey served as economic entrepôts for colonial Texas. Despite the importance of livestock raising, the censuses of 1777, 1792, and 1820 show, as Oakah Jones has noted, that most of the settlers in Texas were small farmers, day laborers, and artisans.[48]

In contrast to New Mexico, hard currency seems to have circulated more freely in Texas. In addition to an influx of coin via legal channels, the frequent contraband trade with French and Anglo Americans perhaps accounted for the presence of specie in the province. At any rate, officials did not remark on its absence, as they did in New Mexico, and the judicial records make no mention of *pesos de la tierra*.[49] Zebulon Pike noted that Texans traded for their needs with "specie, horses, and mules."[50] Still, the barter system may have characterized a good share of local commerce.

Despite the emergence of a limited *rico* class, both provinces maintained a somewhat egalitarian society conditioned by the generalized poverty. Discounting the presence of salaried government officials and of itinerant merchants, most settlers were day laborers or small farmers.[51] Since royal policy theoretically curtailed population movement, the possibility of relocating to a more favorable economic setting was often slight.[52] In Texas, a few—many of them offspring of the original Canary Island settlers—maintained a position of social and economic prominence in the community. New Mexico, too, had a nucleus of preeminent families who played, and continue to play, an important role in local affairs. Simple in their stratification, however, the colonial societies of the far north differed significantly from the multi-tiered hierarchies that developed throughout most of the large urban centers of Spanish America.[53]

Like the economic structure, racial designations also became simplified on the northern frontier of New Spain. Recent scholarship has called into question the issue of strict application of the racial caste system in other parts of the Spanish Indies.[54] As elsewhere, racial lines became blurred in colonial Texas and New Mexico.[55] Cultural identity, rather than strict biological criteria, became the prime determinant in racial classification. Predominantly European blood may have flowed through the veins of the *ricos* of New Mexico or the *isleños* of Texas, but here was a society composed of racial mixtures. Whether accurate in the strictest sense or not, most Hispanic settlers viewed themselves as *españoles*, probably in an effort to clarify who they were not. Since all classes on the frontier were exempt from civil taxation—whether *alcabala* or tribute—the designations carried no immediate financial obligation or privilege, but they did underscore a racially tinged social hierarchy.[56]

Contemporary judicial records often reveal the emotionally charged implications of racial epithets that permeated colonial slang. *"Perro indio," "mulato,"* even *"morisco"* appear in court testimony as the immediate cause of some altercations.[57] While deeper reasons no doubt existed for such conflict, these "fighting words" could bring resentments to a head. Outsiders, frequently *peninsulares,* pointed out the fallacy of viewing these societies strictly through a racial lens. As Morfi noted caustically, the term *español* in New Mexico included "even mulatos [and] coyotes." And he referred to the *cabildo* members of San Antonio, most of them *isleños,* as "a ragged lot, of every color."[58] For most New Mexicans and Texans, to live in the Spanish way, among other "Spaniards," was to be an *español.* It should be noted, however, that classification as *español* held no guarantee of social or economic prominence. Indeed, some 60 percent of San Antonio's native-born Spanish heads of household were landless day laborers and servants.[59] New Mexico, too, had its share of *españoles* who served and worked for others.[60]

The colonial milieu, however, consisted not simply of *españoles* and mixed-bloods. The Indian component was ever present, indeed crucial, in the Spanish colonial world. In a very real sense, the various Indian groups who inhabited the far north of New Spain contributed mightily to the Hispanic experience. In New Mexico one found the Pueblo Indians, sedentary groups who had a strong attachment to their particular locale.[61] Maintaining a clear self-identity, yet borrowing selectively from European culture, many Pueblos learned to live in both worlds and normally were peaceful subjects of the crown. In the late seventeenth century the Pueblos threw off the yoke of a particularly harsh Spanish regime. With Diego de Vargas's recolonization and reconquest of New Mexico in the 1690s, however, a new era of mutual accommodation began. Pueblos now partook actively in the economic, political, and most importantly, military life of the Spanish province.[62] Ironically, it was precisely this participation that allowed the Spaniards to retain New Mexico during the remainder of the colonial period.

From the time of initial contact, Spanish observers recognized the admirable qualities of the Pueblo people. Indeed, in many respects the external elements of Pueblo culture fit neatly the European ideals of a rational, sedentary existence. The chronicler of the Coronado expedition of 1540–42, Pedro Castañeda de Nájera, spoke with high regard for the modesty and sobriety of the various Pueblo groups with whom he had dealings.[63] Centuries later, other Spanish observers would comment in a similarly positive manner. Writing in the early eighteenth century, don Francisco Alvarez Barreiro, lieutenant colonel of infantry and chief engineer of the province of Texas, lauded the military prowess of the Pueblos and described them as

> better proportioned and better looking than the [Central] Mexicans and other nations in between; both men and women always go about clothed and with shoes. They are hard workers; not only women weave cotton and woolen blankets for their use, but also the men do this during the snow season, when they cannot cultivate the land. As a result, all these Indians are wealthy, and even the poorest have enough to live comfortably. All have food, tools, and equipment for the cultivation of the land, and cattle and sheep; the Indian who does not ride on horseback is considered very unfortunate. Drunkenness is unknown among them, and above all the good customs seen among them, they faithfully keep the ancient and praiseworthy one (which they were taught by the first missionaries) of greeting the Spaniards as well as each other with the sweet name of Ave María.[64]

For Fray Juan Agustín Morfi, the Pueblos served as a foil to underscore the perceived moral shortcomings and haphazard organization of the Spanish population.

> [The Indians] frequent mass and the sacraments. At the first sound of the drum or the bell, they gather to defend themselves or to give pursuit. The contiguity of their fields facilitates cultivation because of the speed of help in case of surprise. The pueblo's livestock and horse herds graze in common and with sufficient guard, and although they occasionally lose some, it is not as much or as often as the Spaniards. They know not robbery nor drunkenness. Simply by removing the ladder a bit, so that it is not in front of the door of the house, all know that the owner is not there and no one dares violate the public trust. They generally harvest their crops freely, and they live in abundance. Thus, it is clear that the only way the Spaniards might enjoy these benefits is to reduce their villages [poblazones] to a similar order.[65]

Genízaros—indigenous people usually of Plains Indian origin who had been captured or bought by Spaniards—also lived in New Mexico. Scattered throughout the province as servants, many *genízaros* adopted Christianity and a sedentary existence. Many maintained contact with Plains culture, however, and they distinguished themselves as scouts and hunters. Recognizing their military worth, Spanish officials allowed the establishment of several *genízaro* communities in locations vulnerable to incursions of the *indios bárbaros.*[66]

In stark contrast to the technological and cultural sophistication of the Pueblos stood the native inhabitants who formed the core of the Spanish mission system in Texas. Those who lived in the missions in and around San Antonio came mostly from Coahuiltecan and Karankawa origin. Reliable information from the protohistoric period is sparse, but these groups appear to have been hunter-gatherers who moved regularly in pursuit of their livelihood.[67] Under pressure from Spaniards and other Indian groups such as the Apaches and, later, the Comanches, the aboriginal bands faced considerable hardship in maintaining their traditional way of life. For the indigenous people of Texas, the missions often became institutions that, according to one scholar, "provided places of refuge for remnants of displaced and declining Indian populations."[68] While the mission may have been a haven for some, many did not survive the abrupt cultural changes that the mission regime imposed.[69]

Spanish authorities recognized the great cultural diversity among their indigenous subjects. Nevertheless, Spanish Indian policy generally demanded that Indians reside in permanent agricultural settlements where they might learn the rudiments of European culture. As a vehicle of acculturation, the mission system squared admirably with the aims of the crown. In northern New Spain, the mission had mixed success. New Mexico and Texas both had their particular versions of this institution. The Pueblos accepted the veneer of this system, not without some animosity toward individual clerics, and after the Pueblo Revolt, usually on their own terms.[70] In Texas, unable to withstand the pressure of Spanish presence, the coastal Indians accepted it perhaps as the only feasible alternative.

If the missions of the far north enjoyed uneven success among some Indian groups, they failed miserably with the *indios bárbaros,* who defied the fundamental notions of Spanish Indian policy. War-

riors and raiders, sometime trading partners, and more often re-
lentless foes, the mounted Indians of the borderlands challenged
not only the basis of Spanish Indian policy, but also the very existence of Spanish settlement in the north. Attempts to establish missions among these people went nowhere, and by the end of the
eighteenth century, royal authorities had begun to deal with these
groups in a much different way. Treaties and gift-giving, rather
than missions, seemed the most effective means to curb their hos-
tility.[71] The presence of the *indios bárbaros* tinged almost every aspect of daily existence in colonial New Mexico and Texas. The Utes
and Navajos intermittently waged war and lived at peace with the
Spaniards in New Mexico. In Texas the Nations of the North
proved to be troublesome. And, everywhere, all feared the Apaches
and Comanches.[72]

The presence of these mounted warriors hindered communication with the rest of New Spain. As Viceroy Antonio María Bucareli
noted, the far north lay "encircled everywhere by enemies who
wage war with tenacity."[73] Some believed that, above all else, the
perennial raiding of these groups caused the economic stagnation
of the northern provinces. Commandant General Felipe de Neve
wrote in 1783 that warfare was

> the true and only means by which those provinces might achieve
> this incomparable benefit [of peace]; to provide their inhabitants
> with the felicity and prosperity that the fertile lands and rich and
> abundant placers and mines promise; to establish on solid prin-
> ciples the proper order and rules that must be followed to rectify
> the administration of justice, to improve public order, and to
> increase the royal treasury. During the hostilities, agriculture,
> livestock raising, mining, and commerce—intimately related and
> mutually dependent—cannot flourish.[74]

In sum, frontier existence was harsh. The geographic setting of
northern New Spain posed considerable hardships for those who
inhabited the region. Distant from administrative centers, under-
developed economically, and threatened constantly by unfriendly
natives, Spanish subjects in Texas and New Mexico endured a rug-
ged environment characterized by material impoverishment and
institutional simplicity. Not surprisingly, legal confrontations reflected the physical reality and cultural values of their world. Disputes over scarce resources, commercial and labor grievances,

injury to one's person, prestige, or honor—these conflicts and others found in the legal system a venue for adjudication in this remote, but strategically important area.

The lack of wealth and sparse population of the north held little attraction for legal professionals, whose existence depended on a clientele who could afford their services. In the absence of real judicial expertise, royal administrators and informally trained local inhabitants shared in conducting the judicial affairs of the north. Certainly, because of its simplicity, the far north often lacked much of the institutional machinery and juridical sophistication that might be found in heavily populated areas of the empire. But this pattern held sway in many parts of New Spain and, for that matter, the rest of the empire. Thus, while judicial administration in the remote provinces of New Mexico and Texas did not conform to practice in the metropolis, neither was it the aberration that some have perceived. In this geographic setting, physical reality and political ideology confronted one another. Both helped shape the legal culture of the far north of New Spain. Because of its inherent flexibility, Spanish colonial law proved adaptable to the geographic circumstances.

The Construction and Spirit of
Derecho Indiano

Spanish colonists who arrived in the far north brought with them not only their material possessions but also their cultural values, which included their political ideology. The cornerstone of Spain's colonial regime was a legal system rooted in medieval European tradition and modified by New World circumstances that provided the basis for the political and social ordering of the Indies. This was a government of judges, where nearly every appointed official exercised some sort of judicial authority. Although the Bourbon monarchs assumed a more active role in other spheres of activity, many in the eighteenth-century Hispanic world held dear the traditional notion that, above all else, the prime function of the monarchy was to dispense justice. "The true occupation of the king," as Lorenzo Guardiola y Sáez wrote in 1785, "is to do justice in his kingdom."[1] The legitimacy ascribed to the legal system as a mediator of social conflict was crucial, and colonial subjects defined themselves and found identity largely in juridical terms through special jurisdictions, privileges, and restrictions. The legal system served as a constant venue of negotiation between distinct groups and individuals who comprised this hierarchical society.

Derecho indiano, in its fullest sense, encompassed all law that held sway in the New World, and it stemmed from a variety of sources. These diverse sources can be categorized into two major groupings—one of peninsular provenance, the other of New World origin. In this first group, extremely important in the first century of colonization, was legislation that rested upon the Castilian normative system as established in the *Ordenamiento de Alcalá* (1348) and reaffirmed in the *Leyes de Toro* (1505), *Nueva Recopilación de Castilla* (1567), and *Novísima Recopilación de Castilla* (1805). This juridical ordering gave preeminence to legislation issued by the crown, and it had general application throughout the realm. Beneath royal laws were the local *fueros,* or municipal charters—especially the *Fuero Real,* which many cities enjoyed—to which judges were to resort if no specific royal law applied. On the third tier, applicable only in the absence of royal law or municipal *fuero,* stood *Las Siete Partidas,* a thirteenth-century text attributed to Alfonso X of Castile that sustained the juridical notions of Roman and canon law. Through this legitimization of the *Partidas,* certain aspects of European *ius commune*—especially procedural elements—became fixed in Castilian law.[2]

Because the Indies belonged to the crown of Castile, the Castilian normative system applied to the New World. Initially, *all* Castilian law had automatic force in the Indies. A major turning point in the creation of a discrete body of *derecho indiano* occurred in 1614 when, in recognition of New World distinctiveness, Philip III determined that only laws formulated specifically for the Indies would have force.[3] The appearance of the *Recopilación de Indias* (1681) signaled the consolidation of a particular juridical ordering, for this text took precedence in the normative system of the colonies.

In contrast to laws that emanated from the peninsula were laws of New World origin, what some have termed *derecho indiano criollo.*[4] Royal officials and institutions—viceroys, *audiencias,* governors, *corregidores,* and *alcaldes mayores*—issued much of this legislation, but settlers also had a hand in shaping this ultramarine dimension of *derecho indiano.* Especially prominent was the activity of municipal *cabildos* in regulating local urban affairs. Indigenous law, too, carried weight in supplemental capacity, as long as it did not conflict with royal legislation or European notions of religion.[5] As the colonial period unfolded, and as settlers and royal administrators established a legal order to fit their world, the number of laws specific to the Indies grew impressively. By the eighteenth century, *derecho indiano* had acquired a character distinct from that of Castilian law. These two groups of written laws—Castilian and local in their origins—served as the foundation for *derecho indiano.* But there was more to *derecho indiano* than mere legislation.

Despite its fundamental role in shaping and defining society, Spanish colonial law has remained something of a mystery to modern scholars. Perhaps because of the great chronological and ideological distance between us and the *antiguo régimen,* modern historians often have joined with nineteenth-century patriots and

RECOPILACION
DE LEYES DE LOS REYNOS
DE LAS INDIAS.
MANDADAS IMPRIMIR, Y PVBLICAR
POR LA MAGESTAD CATOLICA DEL REY
DON CARLOS II.
NVESTRO SEÑOR.
VA DIVIDIDA EN QVATRO TOMOS,
con el Indice general, y al principio de cada Tomo el Indice
efpecial de los titulos, que contiene.

TOMO PRIMERO.

En Madrid: POR IVLIAN DE PAREDES, Año de 1681.

Figure 1. Although a fundamental text, the *Recopilación de Indias* was only one of the many sources of *Derecho Indiano*, or Spanish colonial law.

foreign observers in denouncing the colonial legal system. Judicial administration still is often depicted as ponderous, tyrannical, arbitrary, and corrupt.[6] Clearly, many scholars have failed to appreciate the essential qualities of *derecho indiano*. A more careful scrutiny of the historical record reveals an intricate legal system that proved to be adaptable to the peculiar needs of the diverse regions of empire. Local modification of Hispanic law—*derecho vulgar*—was an important feature of this flexibility and constituted a legitimate expression of local self-governance.

No doubt, the misguided view of Spanish colonial law—and the consequent failure to recognize *derecho vulgar*—stems not only from cultural distance, but also, for English-speakers, from language problems. In truth, there is no exact English equivalent for the Castilian word *derecho*, though the word *justice* might come close.[7] Roman law, which greatly influenced Spanish law of the early modern period, made a clear distinction between *ius*—that which is just—and *lex*—a duly promulgated norm, usually written. So, too, did the various Iberian legal systems (though the vernacular *derecho* came to replace *ius*).[8] Heirs to Castilian institutions, jurists in the New World approached the task of making and interpreting law in much the same way as their peninsular counterparts.[9] The *letrado* community certainly distinguished between *ley* and *derecho*. So, too, did the general population. One rarely argued that the *ley* was on his or her side; instead a litigant approached the court seeking one's justice, or "su derecho."[10] Jurists and community alike conceived of Spanish colonial law in this wider sense. People expected their proper "*derecho*," and magistrates endeavored "to give to each his own."

In general terms colonial magistrates were to exercise their experience, knowledge, and prudence in meting out justice.[11] More specifically, they drew from a system that sought justice somewhere in the convergence of written law, *doctrina* (the opinions of jurists), custom, and *equidad* (a communally defined sense of fairness).[12] Under the rubric of written law one must include not only true *leyes reales* (technically only the Castilian Cortes could initiate these), but also other written statutes that had the effective force of royal law—*pragmáticas, mandamientos de gobierno, provisiones, cédulas, órdenes, cartas, sobrecartas*, and so forth.[13] *Doctrina* encompassed the written opinions of both national and international jurists who commented not only on Roman and canon law, but also on royal law.[14] Local usage and long-standing practice also carried the weight of authority under the Hispanic system. This respect for local particularism, even when *contra legem,* has been perhaps the most overlooked dimension of the Spanish colonial legal system.[15] Finally, judicial decisions were to be equitable solutions that not only satisfied the aggrieved party, but that also considered the well-being and harmony of the community. In a stratified eighteenth-century colonial society, ideas about equity might well differ from ours. Yet a clearly identifiable ray of distributive justice served as a guiding light for colonial magistrates "to give to each his own."[16] Keeping these various elements of *derecho* in mind, magistrates were to consider the merits of each distinct case and make a decision accordingly.[17]

Because of this casuistic approach, the precise formula for meting out justice might change, if ever so slightly, with every case. The colonial magistrate, whether a learned *oidor* or a local *alcalde,* exercised a great deal of personal discretion in the judicial process, especially in pronouncing sentence. Known as *arbitrio judicial,* or judicial will, this feature of the system figures as the key to the flexibility of Spanish colonial legal administration. The ambiguity of judicial authority perhaps bothers modern jurists and scholars more than their colonial counterparts, who understood the purpose of *arbitrio judicial.*

Largely misinterpreted as mere whimsy or capriciousness, *arbitrio judicial* allowed Spanish law to be much more than the mechanical application of judicial prescriptions.[18] Through this device, law became a living, organic entity that the local population— citizens and administrators alike—might mold to meet situations peculiar to the region. This mechanism, as well as others, empowered Spanish subjects to modify legislation that they deemed to be unreasonable, unjust, or harmful to the community.[19] Locals often played a significant role in shaping the legal culture of a particular region.

Given the range of possibilities, upon which elements of *derecho* did colonial magistrates rely? Certainly, the *oidor* who sat on one of the thirteen late-eighteenth-century *audiencias* had a much richer repertoire—textually and intellectually—than did a magistrate at the local level. Highly trained professionals invoked the authority of all pertinent sources of *derecho indiano*—law, *doctrina,* custom, and *equidad*—and drew from the sources that seemed to best fit a

particular case.[20] It should be noted that we can never be sure of the
exact judicial reasoning in the verdict, because the Castilian and, by
extension, colonial legal systems forbade magistrates from issuing
a written explanation (*sentencia fundada*) of their decision.[21] From all
evidence, however, these learned judges remained faithful to traditional modes of procedure and maintained their prerogative of
arbitrio judicial even in the climate of enlightened despotism and
increasing regal control in the late eighteenth and early nineteenth
centuries.[22] In a sense they refused to become mere judicial bureaucrats who applied the written law, and insisted instead on remaining true judges who dispensed justice.

While magistrates in the busy centers of empire had a full arsenal
of textual and institutional resources at their disposal, those on the
peripheries did not. Economies that could not support centers of
learning, great libraries, and multitudes of judicial functionaries
simply did without. In fact, *most* provinces of New Spain made do
without a fully staffed judiciary.[23] Honed to the essentials, judicial
administration in these extensive marginal areas nevertheless
squared unmistakably with the Spanish legal tradition. And in
these peripheral zones we can perhaps better appreciate the tremendous strength and flexibility of the Hispanic legal culture.

Streamlined and simplified, nearly all phases of the judicial process in northern New Spain lay in the hands of local magistrates,
the most important of whom was the provincial governor. For the
most part, frontier governors were proven military figures—a
prime attribute in a region on chronic military alert. Able and ed-
ucated they may have been, but no evidence suggests that the
governors of New Mexico or Texas had any formal instruction in
law, nor, in contrast to other areas, did they enjoy ready access to
a legal adviser (*asesor letrado*).[24] Neither did other local magistrates
(*alcaldes mayores* or *alcaldes ordinarios*), who were drawn from the
civilian population.

Not surprisingly, magistrates in northern New Spain—and, for
that matter, in many other parts of the empire—approached legal
administration with less sophistication than their learned urban
counterparts.[25] The scholarly erudition and elegant Latin employed
by practitioners of the *mos italicus* surely were lost on many a frontier magistrate. *Doctrina* played a lesser role in local judicial affairs,
but it was not entirely absent.

Some have argued or insinuated that frontier magistrates operated virtually oblivious of basic legal texts and their respective contents.[26] This simply is not so. Many texts that circulated in the northern borderlands can be classified as legal commentary or *doctrina*. Habsburg-era titles such as *Política Indiana* by Juan de Solórzano Pereira, *Curia Philippica* by Juan de Hevia Bolaños, *Instrucción Política y Práctica Judicial* by Alonso de Villadiego, standard fare in any colonial judicial library, also found their way to northern New Spain. So, too, did the works of later, more practical-minded jurists, who shied away from using Latin and who focused more on royal law than on Roman and canon law.[27] One such work, *Instrucción de Escribanos* by Joseph Juan y Colom, turned up in both New Mexico and Texas in the late eighteenth and early nineteenth centuries.[28] While admittedly sparse, documentary evidence demonstrates the existence and use of these texts in northern New Spain. More striking still, litigants invoked on occasion the authority of the *doctores* in their arguments.[29] Contrary to the conventional view of universal judicial ignorance, then, some frontier magistrates did, indeed, consider *doctrina* in their judgments.

Written law, however, figured more prominently than doctrine in the construction of *derecho indiano*. Nearly every territorial jurisdiction of the Spanish empire had at its disposal the fundamental compilations of laws and ordinances—the *Recopilación de Indias, Nueva Recopilación de Castilla, Novísima Recopilación, Ordenanzas de Intendentes*, and so forth. Northern New Spain was no exception.[30] Contemporary court proceedings include frequent allusions to "these laws of the Indies," to "the royal laws," or less frequently, to a specific piece of legislation.[31] This evidence suggests not only that magistrates (and litigants) were aware of these basic juridical texts, but also that they consulted them. One must keep in mind, also, the never-ending stream of *cédulas*, orders, and decrees sent to all jurisdictions of New Spain. Since public proclamation of new legislation was one of his functions, the *alcalde* certainly would be well informed on many affairs, including judicial matters. Similarly, local magistrates were familiar with the various *bandos de buen gobierno*, issued periodically by either the *cabildo* or the provincial governor. The accessibility and authority of written law ensured that colonial magistrates considered it when making their judicial decisions. Assertions that these officials were unaware of written laws are ill-founded.

While *doctrina* and law constituted important bases for the legal tradition elaborated in northern New Spain, custom and *equidad* loom as perhaps the most critical elements of *derecho indiano* and surely served as the wellspring of *derecho vulgar*. As noted earlier, custom was the vehicle by which local entities throughout the empire might modify or reshape generalized judicial practice. And although the conventional view is that of an absolutist imperial Spain, the crown never gained complete control. Indeed, a surprising degree of self-government existed at local levels during the *antiguo régimen*.

Custom—reasonable and just activity that over time acquires legal sanction—found expression in various ways. One obvious and important form of judicial custom resulted from time-honored local practice or usage.[32] Here, not only the elites but also the lesser lights of colonial society had a hand in shaping the law. While imperial administrators and the "better sorts" of colonists may have been guardians of the dominant culture, the constant negotiation between various strata created, even in the formal setting of the law, what might be termed the consensual hegemony of Spanish rule.[33] In New Mexico, for example, the Pueblo Indians learned to play the legal game in admirable fashion. Their continual activity in the courtroom led to the incorporation of certain customary rights into the legal culture of the province. The so-called "Pueblo league" is the prime example.

For years scholars and jurists have debated the substantive basis of this guarantee to the Pueblos of New Mexico of one league from a central point—often the village church—in each of the cardinal directions, a measurement not common to all of New Spain. In central Mexico, the territorial norm for Indian pueblos was six hundred *varas;* Indian villages in most of Nueva Galicia received one-half league in each direction.[34] Why and when indigenous villages in New Mexico were first granted a full league remains hazy. It is clear, however, that by the early eighteenth century, colonial society in New Mexico recognized the legitimacy of these territorial boundaries. While Spanish conceptions of municipal boundaries may have laid the foundations for this measurement, it was the repeated Pueblo insistence that Spaniards live up to the "rules of the game" that helped inscribe this territorial dimension as the norm in New Mexico.[35] In 1704, for example, two Hispanic settlers petitioned for farmland along the Rio Grande near San Felipe Pueblo. Significantly, the petitioners argued that the land in question lay outside the Pueblo league and thus should be available for settlement.[36] During the decade of the 1780s, the natives of both Santa Clara and San Ildefonso pueblos found themselves in litigation with encroaching Hispanic *vecinos*. The successful legal strategy of the natives rested on pushing Spanish authorities to reaffirm the guarantee of a full league.[37] Like indigenous subjects elsewhere in the Spanish colonial world, then, the Pueblos used the legal system as a venue for negotiation, and thereby helped in some way to establish the legal norms of the colony.[38]

Another significant, though more subtle, form of judicial custom lay in the way that frontier magistrates acquired and passed on their judicial expertise. In an area where formal education of any kind did not exist, transmission of judicial knowledge occurred in an informal manner.[39] Magistrates learned by doing. Having gained an elementary education in the home, the sons of the frontier literati began their juridical formation in early adulthood in a most practical way. Felipe Tafoya, for example, served in various official capacities in New Mexico and gained considerable experience in legal affairs, serving in later years as both a magistrate and a self-styled legal representative (*procurador*).[40] Tafoya and his cohort of local public servants formed the backbone of provincial administration, and they proved to be an indispensable source for staffing the king's judiciary.

These provincially trained magistrates had in their repertoires the accumulated judicial expertise and practice of previous generations. The authority of legal instruments such as wills and testaments depended on strict compliance to prescribed formulas. And, when dealing with this *derecho privado*, frontier magistrates took care to retain the solemnity of language and form that such documents required. The sphere of *derecho público*, however, proved to be much more fluid. In the vast peripheries of New Spain, the crown permitted local magistrates to resort to simplified criminal and civil procedure, relying mainly on "known truth and good faith kept."[41] The so-called *juicio sumario*, which dispensed with the "solemnities of the law," thus became the usual procedural form in much of New Spain.[42] In turn, the cumulative judicial "style" of a local magistracy—always tempered, of course, by crown administrators—became the established method of dispensing justice.

Just as custom formed a crucial ingredient in the legal culture of New Spain, so too did the notion of *equidad* for the common good.

Because of the non-adversarial nature of the legal system, the primary aim of the judiciary was to provide justice, not to determine courtroom winners and losers. In a corporatist world where unbridled individualism was not a virtue, the ideal of community well-being took precedence over personal gain. Magistrates consistently exercised their *arbitrio judicial* to push for compromise and harmony between contending parties—solutions that, implicitly, conformed to community expectations of fairness.

Consider the case of Antonio de Cárdenas, a New Mexican who had worked for Juan Luján from 1728 to 1732 at a salary of six pesos a month. When the latter died, Cárdenas sought to collect an unspecified amount in back pay from the heirs of Luján. Unsuccessful in this endeavor, he turned to the provincial governor, Gervasio Cruzat y Góngora, as "padre de pobres" to rectify the situation. The judicial decision of Cruzat y Góngora is noteworthy. After reviewing the paperwork, the governor observed that nowhere in the *expediente* was there a contract stipulating the terms of employment. By *law*, the plaintiff had no case. Nevertheless, Governor Cruzat y Góngora ordered the heirs to pay Cárdenas. Although not stated explicitly, *equidad* surely played a major role in this decision.[43]

Did magistrates in New Spain's far north fully appreciate the role of *equidad* in the construction of *derecho indiano*? Apparently, some did. In deciding a case that involved "indecorous language," for example, Governor Joaquín Codallos y Rabal observed that the defendant had used "none of the five [words] deemed to be gravely offensive in law." Codallos nevertheless specifically invoked *equidad* ("ussando de equidad") and condemned the man to pay court costs of ten pesos.[44]

Aptly illustrating the emphasis on community harmony is an incident that occurred at Chama, New Mexico, in 1745. Neighbors who also happened to be relatives, Juan Antonio Salazar and Manuel Valerio, had come to a disagreement over that most precious of resources—water. After considering the matter, the provincial governor ordered his lieutenant to urge the two men to meet publicly to settle their dispute. Both would have a right to the water. Lawsuits such as this, reasoned the magistrate, were not only costly but they created "other pernicious consequences, which between relatives and neighbors are scandalous." For the sake of community harmony, the governor urged the two to pardon one another and to reach an amicable agreement that neither would break "in deed or in word, now or forever." And so they did. The litigants "embraced one another, and they agreed on the disputed matter in most admirable fashion."[45]

A magistrate's concern for community harmony might be found not only in urging conciliation at various stages of a legal dispute, but also at the time of pronouncing sentence. The *arbitrio judicial* exercised by local officials at this critical juncture often reflected the values of the Hispanic community. Offenders who disrupted community tranquillity and who overstepped the bounds of acceptable behavior might find themselves excluded from the group. In Texas, New Mexico, and throughout the Hispanic world, crimes such as adultery or fornication often resulted in banishment.[46] In San Antonio, for example, Juan José Vergara—twenty-five years of age, unmarried, "español"—and María Carbajal had carried on an illicit relationship for years. Although unmarried, the union had produced "one or two" children and had continued despite official warnings. As custodian of public morality, Alcalde Ordinario José de la Santa took it upon himself to proceed judicially against the wayward couple. After determining that this "scandal" harmed the community, Alcalde Santa sentenced Vergara to be banished for two years from within forty leagues of the *villa*. The woman received not the "punishment she deserve[d]," but only a warning because, as the *alcalde* noted, her husband was about to return to San Antonio after a twelve-year absence. In the future the woman was to "live in appropriate seclusion and modesty" and to maintain a good reputation.[47] A forced reconciliation with a seemingly negligent husband may appear odd to twentieth-century sensibilities, but it fit the patriarchal ideal of proper order in the family that eighteenth-century *tejanos* shared with the Hispanic world.

Considerable evidence indicates that colonial subjects not only expected authorities to take appropriate action to squelch improper behavior, but also that community members themselves often became direct agents of the system by requesting specific punishments or judicial solutions. The participation of Pueblo groups has been indicated above, and other examples abound. In 1781, for instance, the brothers and uncles of Ana María Trinidad Games appeared before Governor Domingo Cabello requesting that he impede the imminent marriage of the woman to a mission Indian. Although the woman was a "*mulata*," the men believed that a union with Urbano Ynojosa would reflect poorly on the entire family. The plaintiffs must have recognized the likelihood that Cabello would maintain the existing social barriers that hindered racial intermarriage. Indeed, Cabello seemed to display sympathy for the potential horror and injury to one's prestige that such a social mismatch would yield. Before a judicial decision, however, the Games-Hernández clan dropped the suit when Ynojosa declared formally that he wished to marry an Indian woman from the mission rather than Ana María Trinidad Games. In this particular case, the visions of patriarchy and monarchy coincided, and the system upheld the prescribed social order.[48]

To maintain harmony, the law had to provide not only for elites but also for subordinate members of society. They, too, held certain expectations of the legal system. Seeking redress for their grievances, for example, two *genízara* servants complained in 1763 to New Mexico Governor Tomás Vélez Cachupín of mistreatment. The judicial investigation revealed that their Spanish masters had not only neglected to provide properly for the two women but had also failed to instruct them in the Christian faith. Furthermore, one of the servants had been raped while in the fields tending sheep, a task deemed unsuitable for women. In his decision, the governor at once ameliorated the plight of the servants and reminded the "betters" of the responsibilities that accompanied their station. He removed the two servants from under the care of their negligent masters and placed the women in homes "where they might be instructed in the Christian doctrine and customs, and be fed and clothed through household chores appropriate to their sex."[49]

For Antonia Lusgardia Hernández, an unmarried "free *mulata*," Texas Governor Manuel de Sandoval embodied the judicial ideal of "protection of the poor," and in 1735 she appealed to him for the return of her young son, Ignacio. Eight or nine years previously, explained Hernández, she had entered the household of Miguel Núñez Morillo as a servant. She had left, however, because of her master's mistreatment and negligence in clothing her properly, taking with her two infants—"one that I brought into the house of said don Miguel, the other that I gave birth to in his house." Now, she claimed, Núñez and his wife, doña Josefa Flores, had taken the younger child from her "for no other reason" than because he had been born at the house and because the wife had seen to his baptism. Hernández noted also that Ignacio was "the only man I have, who I expect to provide for me as time goes by." When questioned by the governor, Núñez responded that Ignacio had returned of his own accord to the household. Nevertheless the couple was willing to return the lad to his mother and serve as his godparents. Satisfied with the outcome, the governor closed the case.[50]

In the preceding examples, and in a striking number of other cases, provincial magistrates used their judicial discretion to find solutions that met the expectations and upheld the contemporary values of the community. Implicit in this construction, of course, are ideals that reflect an eighteenth-century Hispanic view of society, which at times contrasts sharply with late-twentieth-century values of individualism and self-realization.

Distant in time and imbued with a different ideological perspective, some aspects of the Spanish colonial legal system may well seem curious to the modern observer. But the system had a logic of its own, and it appears to have met the needs of the time and to have functioned reasonably well. Rather than revealing malfeasance, capriciousness, or ignorance, the record indicates that magistrates in northern New Spain usually drew from the appropriate sources of *derecho indiano*. If they relied less on *doctrina* and law than their counterparts in the metropolis, they still acted squarely within the Hispanic legal tradition and relied on what they perhaps knew best—custom and *equidad*—in trying "to give to each his own."

The mechanism of *arbitrio judicial* allowed magistrates to respond to community needs and sensibilities, and it provided a way for colonial society to help define the judicial norms of a given area. In a sense, law and *doctrina* afforded a strong and durable framework for generalized judicial administration in the empire, while local custom and *equidad* proved to be the fabric from which colonial society elaborated distinctive regional variations. This vulgarization process—an interplay of royal will and popular sensibilities—was fundamental to the colonial legal system. Rather than a corruption of justice, however, it often served as a legitimate expression of popular values. As perhaps the most important institutional venue for cultural negotiation, the legal system afforded nearly all strata of colonial society at least some voice in the process. The vitality of *derecho vulgar* underscores the flexibility of Spanish colonial law and forces us to reconsider the common perception that the legal system was inherently corrupt and irrelevant to the mass of society.

PART TWO

The Agents of Royal Justice

❖ ❖ 3 ❖ ❖

A Distant Judicial Elite

A network of institutions and officials throughout Spanish America provided access to royal justice for subjects in the New World. The upper levels of the judicial structure featured a full array of well-trained personnel to dispense the king's justice, yet a palpable decrease in quantity and quality characterized the judiciary on the extensive peripheries of the empire. For many in the Indies, the legal expertise found in the urban centers lay beyond reach.

Like other institutional structures, the colonial judiciary closely paralleled that of Castile. This is only to be expected since from the initial stages of colonization the crown had made a concerted effort to mold the legal foundations of the Indies to peninsular models. This tendency toward normalization found repeated and early expression, notably in generalized royal decrees of 1530, 1571, and 1680. Philip II's Ordinances of 1571 for the Council of the Indies illuminate the crown's desire for conformity, while recognizing at the same time the need for flexibility in colonial administration.

> Because the Kingdoms of Castile and the Indies are of one crown, the laws and order of government of one and the other should be as similar and in agreement as they can be. In the laws and statutes that they might order for those states, [the ministers] of our Council should attempt to reduce the form and manner of governance to the style and order by which the Kingdoms of Castile and León are governed, inasmuch as the diversity and differences of lands and nations permit.[1]

Although laws specific to the Indies—fashioned both in Spain and in the colonies—continued to grow in numbers, Castilian practice always remained the inspiration for their implementation.

The *rey justiciero*

The Spanish monarchy administered its realms largely through its judiciary. At the apex of what might well be termed the "judicial state" of the *antiguo régimen* stood the monarch, whose prime function, according to the medieval *Siete Partidas*, was to "govern and maintain the empire in justice."[2] The king, above all else, was a judge—an impartial and divinely ordained arbiter for all, who towered above base partisan interests. Indeed, a prominent seventeenth-century jurist, Juan de Solórzano Pereira, opined that "there would be nothing more pleasing [to the king] than to lose [a lawsuit] in which he was not justified."[3] Although rooted in the medieval ideology of *ius commune*, this idea held strong appeal throughout the early modern period.[4] However, as royal power grew during the late Middle Ages and the crown's jurisdiction extended, the possibility of a personal administration of justice diminished. The consequence was a rise in the number of officials whom the crown invested with judicial authority and who acted in its name.[5]

This idealization of the judicial figure of the king was especially prominent in the Indies where, free of seigneurial and ecclesiastical domains, the crown's jurisdiction emerged preeminent. While physically distant, the monarch stood as the symbol of equity, and Spanish colonial subjects of all sorts invoked the political abstraction of the impartial and benevolent *rey justiciero* when demanding justice. "Viva el rey, y muera el mal gobierno" (Long live the king, and death to bad government)—a cry that punctuated many a colonial disturbance—embodies this vision of the monarch.[6] The colonial world thus legitimized the pretensions of the crown, respected its authority in judicial matters, and normally sought out the various royal officials who dispensed justice in its name.

The Council of the Indies

In keeping with the conciliar system of government, devised under Ferdinand and Isabel and elaborated in their particular manner by the Habsburgs and Bourbons, the colonial world—America and the Philippines—fell under the jurisdiction of the Royal and Supreme Council of the Indies.[7] Initially, the Council of Castile administered the Indies directly, but by a *cédula* of 1 August 1524, Charles V established the Council of the Indies as a distinct entity to deal with the affairs of the rapidly expanding New World holdings. Like other councils of state, the Council of the Indies exercised a variety of administrative, financial, and judicial functions until 1714 when Philip V created the Secretary of State for the Indies, which assumed all but the judicial responsibilities of the council.[8] As a judicial body, the council served as highest court of appeals for civil litigation emanating from the colonial *audiencias,* and for both civil and criminal cases originating in the Casa de Contratación, an institution that regulated colonial trade. Jurists of considerable stature often served on the Council of the Indies. Indeed, some of its members—Gregorio López, perhaps best known for his gloss of the 1555 edition of *Las Siete Partidas*; Juan de Solórzano Pereira, author of *Política Indiana* (1647); and Antonio Rodríguez de León Pinelo, whose efforts culminated in the *Recopilación de Indias* (1681)—figure among the elite in the history of Spanish law.[9] The juridical character of the Council of the Indies was unmistakable.

Because all colonial legislation from Spain passed through it, this body shaped almost every dimension of colonial administration.[10] In this general sense, its actions affected the daily lives of all colonists, including those in Texas and New Mexico. In a stricter sense, however, the legal concerns of subjects on the northern frontier almost never reached the council during the colonial period. Only a few cases from these regions found their way to this body, and none of these had begun in a provincial tribunal. One case involved the dispute between Governor Diego de Vargas and the cabildo of Santa Fe at the turn of the eighteenth century.[11] Another dealt with the alleged contraband activities of Texas governor Jacinto Barrios Jáuregui, which came to the attention of the council only because of a jurisdictional dispute.[12]

Judicial matters of the periphery remained distant from this highest court largely for economic reasons. Only civil cases involving amounts of ten thousand pesos or more could be appealed to the council from regional *audiencias*.[13] Those sums seldom existed in New Mexico or Texas. Moreover, litigation itself was expensive. The ability to retain adequate legal aid at successive jurisdictional levels simply lay beyond the means of most colonists in the far north. The *cabildo* members who litigated against Vargas, for example, paid not only attorneys' and administrative fees, but they also carried the additional burden of supporting one of their members who had traveled to Mexico City. Anticipating continued litigation on the peninsula, they retained the services of Luis Jerónimo Pastor to represent them "before the King, and in his Supreme Council of the Indies."[14] Only the generous support of Vargas's archrival and nemesis, Governor Pedro Rodríguez Cubero, had allowed the *cabildo* to pursue the case in Mexico City. Sentenced by the *audiencia* to pay court costs, the *cabildo* members faced financial ruin. Judicial recourse to the Council of the Indies demanded wealth, something not easily attained in the far north. Practically inaccessible, then, the Supreme and Royal Council of the Indies played a negligible role in the active judicial life of the region.

The *Audiencia*

More accessible, and thus a more likely tribunal of highest appeal for New Mexico and Texas, was the *audiencia*. Although inspired by their peninsular counterparts, American *audiencias* differed significantly. They were not only judicial bodies, but also wielded administrative and executive powers.[15] The two superior tribunals available to subjects in northern New Spain—the Audiencia of Mexico and the Audiencia of Guadalajara—differed somewhat in composition and function.[16] Hub of the viceroyalty and residence of the viceroy, Mexico City's primacy found expression through its *audiencia*. Not only did the Audiencia of Mexico boast more judges and ancillary personnel, these officials also tended to be more experienced than those of Guadalajara. And, acting as an advisory council to the viceroy (who served as president ex-officio), the Audiencia of Mexico dealt with more administrative matters than did the Audiencia of Guadalajara. In judicial matters, however, the attributes of both tribunals were identical.[17]

According to the *Recopilación de Indias*, the Audiencia of Mexico was to consist of a president (the viceroy), eight *oidores*, four criminal judges (*alcaldes del crimen*), one civil prosecutor (*fiscal de lo civil*), one criminal prosecutor (*fiscal de lo criminal*), one high sheriff (*alguacil mayor*), one lieutenant chancellor (*teniente de gran chanciller*), and "the rest of the necessary ministers and officials." By way of comparison, the Audiencia of Guadalajara included a president, four *oidores* (who also served as *alcaldes del crimen*), one *fiscal*, one

RECOPILACION
SUMARIA
DE TODOS
LOS AUTOS ACORDADOS
DE LA REAL AUDIENCIA
Y SALA DEL CRIMEN
DE ESTA NUEVA ESPAÑA,

Y PROVIDENCIAS DE SU SUPERIOR GOBIERNO;
de varias Reales Cédulas y Ordenes que despues de pu-
blicada la Recopilacion de Indias han podido recogerse
asi de las dirigidas á la misma Audiencia ó Gobierno, como de algunas otras que por sus notables decisiones
convendrá no ignorar:

POR EL DOCTOR

*DON EUSEBIO BENTURA BELEÑA, DEL CONSEJO DE
S. M. Oydor de la misma Real Audiencia, Consultor del Santo Oficio
de la Inquisicion, Juez Protector de la Villa y Santuario de Nrâ. Srâ.
de Guadalupe, Asesor de la Renta de Correos, del Juzgado General
de Naturales, y del Real Tribunal del Importante Cuerpo de
Mineria.*

TOMO PRIMERO.

CON LICENCIA:
Impresa en México por Don Felipe de Zúñiga y Ontiveros, calle del
Espíritu Santo, año de 1787.

Figure 2. Title page of Dr. Eusebio Ventura Beleña's *Recopilación Sumaria*
(1787), a compilation of laws and decrees for New Spain. Unlike the
urban centers, the sparsely populated far north lacked individuals who
possessed this sort of judicial expertise.

alguacil mayor, and one *teniente de gran chanciller.*[18] The numbers of functionaries increased over time in both *audiencias,* but the essential responsibilities remained the same.[19] At this level of legal administration all the elements of the Spanish colonial judicial machinery came into play.

Like those who served in the Council of the Indies, the officials of the colonial *audiencias* tended to be men with considerable professional training. The careers of eminent jurists such as Juan de Solórzano Pereira, Antonio Rodríguez de León Pinelo, Francisco Ramiro de Valenzuela, or Eusebio Ventura Beleña—all of whom served in American *audiencias*—are exceptional, of course, but they nonetheless demonstrate the caliber of those who occupied the highest rungs of the judicial ladder in the Indies. Guillermo Margadant, a leading Mexican legal scholar, typifies the consensus among scholars that the legacy of *audiencia* judges is generally "quite respectable."[20] Like the *audiencia* members, others associated with the tribunal also had adequate professional training. Both a university degree and an examination before the *audiencia,* for example, were requisites for any lawyer wishing to practice in that tribunal.[21] Offices of lesser importance and prestige—*relatores, escribanos,* and so forth—also were occupied by competent professionals.[22] In general, the quality control of the colonial *letrado* community was adequate.

In this brief sketch of the *audiencia,* a picture emerges of an institution staffed with able functionaries. If problems existed in the administration of justice, they usually stemmed from the inevitable venality and corruption or from the sheer volume of legal matters with which the *audiencia* had to deal. Richard Kagan has shown that Spanish society in the sixteenth century was a litigious one, and the demand for royal justice strained the capacity of the court.[23] No comparable study has quantified litigation in the *audiencias* of New Spain, but the docket numbers are impressive. To dispense justice, *oidores* were required to hear cases at the *casas reales* for at least three hours every morning, except Sundays and holidays, and to return in the afternoons to render decisions.[24] Other personnel, too, complied with attendance regulations that specified hours for *audiencia* business.[25] The legislated model of the *audiencia* represents the ideal of royal justice—an institution with all the necessary judicial machinery in place, staffed with adequately trained officials.

Regional *audiencias* functioned as courts of first instance for criminal and civil cases originating within the five-league radius of the city in which the *audiencia* sat. Other instances of original jurisdiction included "cases in which the interests of the crown or its officials were directly involved."[26] The institutional stature of the *audiencia* was not sufficient, however, to dissuade the various city *cabildos* from exerting their own rights, and from time to time throughout the colonial period jurisdictional disputes flared up between *audiencia* and *cabildo*.

More important for this study is the *audiencia*'s role as a court of appeal for cases emanating from lesser tribunals within its jurisdiction. Throughout the period of Spanish rule, New Mexico fell under the jurisdiction of the Audiencia of Guadalajara. The Audiencia of Mexico had authority over the judicial affairs of Texas until 1779 when, during the administrative reorganization of the northern frontier, the Audiencia of Guadalajara became the court of appeal for that province as well.[27] Because of economic and geographic obstacles, only a few cases found their way from New Spain's northern frontier to the *audiencias*. Since Spanish colonial law prohibited appeals in serious criminal offenses, no cases of this nature actually went to the *audiencias* on appeal.[28] On occasion, officials in the north sent criminal proceedings to the appropriate *audiencia* or to the nearest legal expert for an opinion before pronouncing or executing a sentence, but this step did not constitute part of the formal appeals process. The *asesor letrado*—a crown attorney, usually the *fiscal de lo criminal*, or some other qualified lawyer (*abogado del tribunal*)—gave his opinion (*dictamen*) concerning a particular case, and then returned it to the provincial magistrate.[29] Local magistrates usually followed the advice they received, but not always.[30] The strictly assessorial nature of this procedure is shown in the fact that the provincial governor retained jurisdiction in these cases. It also reveals the respect that the crown held for the principle of local administration of justice.

In contrast to criminal procedure, litigants in civil cases could appeal to the *audiencia*, though it is impossible to know how frequently this was done. It appears, however, that of the several hundred civil cases initiated in New Mexico and Texas, only a handful went beyond the confines of provincial jurisdiction. The infrequency of appeals in civil cases was due, presumably, to economic circumstances. Few could afford the expense of long-distance litigation.[31]

An official list of cases handled by the *relatores* of the Audiencia of Guadalajara in 1816 may not be atypical of tendencies throughout the colonial era.[32] Of 605 entries in this notebook, only 49 originated in the northern provinces. Sixteen cases came from Durango; six from Zacatecas; four from Sombrerete; three from Nombre de Dios; two each from Sonora, Fresnillo, Real del Oro, Chihuahua, and Tepic; and one apiece from Bachiniva, Parral, Sinaloa, Presidio del Norte, Indé, Real del Rosario, Guanasevi, Jerez, Mapimí, and the office of the Comandancia General de las Provincias Internas.[33] Clearly, the far north generated little legal business for the *audiencia*. Furthermore, judging from the records, the Audiencia of Guadalajara tended overwhelmingly to local affairs despite being the appellate court for the vast north. Contemporaries dissatisfied with the *audiencia*'s inaccessibility to those on the vast periphery had a legitimate complaint.

The *Comandancia General*

In 1776 the northern provinces of New Spain—Texas, Coahuila, Nueva Vizcaya, New Mexico, and Sonora—became a semi-autonomous military, political, and administrative unit known as the Comandancia General de las Provincias Internas.[34] A product of Enlightenment rationalization in government, the *comandancia general* was an attempt to provide solutions for problems unique to the northern frontier. As the name suggests, most of the functions of the commandant general of the Provincias Internas were military. Indeed, the major reason for creating this entity was to coordinate military efforts against potential foreign invaders and nomadic or semi-nomadic Indian groups hostile to Spanish settlers. Also important were the commandant's duties relative to the royal treasury.[35] A perusal of the correspondence between provincial governors and the commandant general suggests that military and administrative affairs occupied most of their time and energy. Nevertheless, the *comandancia general* represented another tier of the colonial judiciary in New Spain, one that faced the particular challenges of the far north.

In judicial matters, the commandant general oversaw the administration of the military jurisdiction—the *fuero militar*—which extended to both regular and militia personnel.[36] Although privileged with their own court system, the legal procedure followed by military magistrates, including the commandant general, closely resembled ordinary procedure. Thus this official, and other frontier military appointees, were more or less familiar with the rudiments of legal procedure under ordinary royal jurisdiction.[37]

For the provinces of Texas and New Mexico, the judicial apparatus of the *comandancia general* played an important part in legal administration. Particularly important was the *asesor letrado*. Holding concurrently the title of *auditor de guerra*, this official emerged as the judicial figure with perhaps the greatest clout in the far north. The commandant routinely gave legal force to the *dictamen* of his *asesor* who, therefore, served as de facto judge in many cases involving the military *fuero*.

With respect to ordinary royal judicial administration in New Mexico and Texas, the importance of the *asesor* lay in his role as adviser. Long isolated, the provincial governors now had somewhat easier access to judicial expertise. Faced with a particularly vexing legal problem, the provincial governor might send the case file to the *asesor* for an opinion. Although not legally bound to comply with the *dictamen*, the governor usually respected the juridical expertise of this official and often followed his recommendations.[38]

What juridical training did these representatives of royal justice have? The commandant, being primarily a military officer, had no formal training in law. Despite this deficiency, the various individuals who held this command were capable administrators, several of whom went on to higher office.[39] With considerable military experience, the commandant general of the Provincias Internas certainly would be familiar with procedural norms for military cases, which, as pointed out previously, closely paralleled those of ordinary jurisdiction. In the way of legal literature, he undoubtedly had at his disposal the well-circulated work on military law, *Juzgados Militares de España y sus Indias*, by Félix Colón de Larriátegui. Furthermore, standard military regulations that applied to areas under his jurisdiction touched upon legal matters. The *Real Reglamento Para las Milicias Provinciales de Nueva Vizcaya* (1782), for example, contained a section dealing with internal discipline and judicial procedure.[40] Similarly, the well-known *Reglamento* of 1772, a guideline for frontier military administration until well into the Mexican national period, dealt with the matter of judicial administration.

Moreover, the crown issued a constant stream of orders, decrees, and provisions, some of which touched upon matters of law. An assiduous and competent military professional, which all the commandants general appear to have been, would have had a good grasp of criminal and, perhaps to a lesser degree, civil procedure.

Military responsibilities, however, far outweighed other concerns. Overwhelmed with the interminable campaigning against the formidable *indios bárbaros*, officials in the *comandancia general* relegated judicial matters to a back seat. In 1782 Commandant General Teodoro de Croix notified Governor Juan Bautista de Anza that, except for cases involving the *patronato real*, appeals from the provinces were to go directly to the Audiencia of Guadalajara, "to avoid the harm that might arise from [the litigants] appealing to this Superior Government."[41] Later directives underscored the point in unequivocal fashion. Wrote Viceroy Conde de Gálvez to Commandant General Jacobo Ugarte in 1786,

> So that Your Lordship might dedicate all his attention to war operations, you will as of now have nothing to do whatsoever with contentious affairs of justice, leaving them entirely to the charge of the intendants and governors of the provinces.[42]

Occupied primarily with military affairs, the commandant relied on his *asesor* and other lesser officials to carry out his scaled-down judicial obligations.

Among this active second tier, one begins to see the real workings of the judiciary on the northern frontier. While we have few details of the men who held the position of *asesor* and *auditor de guerra*, we do know that they were *letrados*, which is to say that they had earned a university degree in the field of law. One of the most prominent of these *asesores*, Pedro Galindo Navarro, who held the position for nearly thirty years in the decades spanning the eighteenth and nineteenth centuries, had earned the title of lawyer of the royal councils and was a member of the Colegio de Abogados of Madrid, achievements that indicated his success in passing the bar examination administered by the appropriate *audiencia*.[43] His superior, Commandant General Caballero de Croix, felt that Galindo had

> dispatched a multitude of important business with the care and precision one might desire; he is totally disinterested, a lover of

Justice, and has all the other attributes that I desire to help me carry the considerable weight of this command.[44]

The duties of the *asesor* and *auditor de guerra*, separate but concurrent positions, were remarkably diverse. One senses just how much the high command depended upon this invaluable aide. Reiterating his praise for Galindo Navarro, Croix noted in 1781 that Galindo's expertise had been critical in shoring up militia finances in Nueva Vizcaya, instituting the *alcabala* in Sonora, provisioning adequately the various presidial and mobile companies of the north, and rooting out abuses in the missions, especially with respect to temporalities and treatment of Indians.[45] In recognition of his service, the crown in 1782 increased Galindo's annual salary to three thousand pesos and provided him with an extra two thousand pesos for expenses incurred in his unusually arduous voyage from Cádiz to New Spain.[46] Despite his repeated efforts to advance his career through an appointment to the Audiencia of Mexico, Galindo remained an official of the *comandancia general.*

Residing at Chihuahua in later years, and apparently resigned to his destiny on the frontier, Galindo perhaps lost much of the early zeal he had displayed. According to the commandant general in 1795, Pedro de Nava, Galindo had become well connected locally during the course of his long residence. Nava suggested that, because of Galindo's local influence, he be given his retirement outside the Provincias Internas.[47] The source of Nava's displeasure is unclear, but if Galindo had been guilty of unabashed dishonesty, Nava's denunciation no doubt would have been harsher. One suspects that the *asesor* was simply making the best of his situation on the fringes of empire. At any rate, Pedro Galindo Navarro seems to have been remunerated adequately for his work. On occasion, he apparently received supplemental fees for services performed as *asesor*, as well as additional income from extraneous judicial activities.[48]

Despite the talents of officials assigned to it, the *comandancia general*, like other colonial institutions, suffered from a lack of funding and personnel. Deficient funding, complained Commandant General Teodoro de Croix in 1781, hampered the administration of justice, as well as other business. To cover the expenses of his secretariat—"paper, sealing wax, oilskin for enclosing letters, candles, pens, and necessary trifles"—the commandant began to

apply the revenue derived from judicial fines. A nir.
peso penalty assigned to the Cabildo of Saltillo, for exa.
to this fund. Similarly, the *alcalde* of Parral, Pedro Esteba
saw his fine contributed to the secretariat. Of the total l
the secretariat for the period from 13 April 1778, to the en
nineteen hundred pesos (64.5 percent) came from
fines.[49] No direct evidence suggests that Commandant General
Croix imposed monetary penalties merely to meet expenses, but
the fines clearly represent a significant source of revenue for the
secretaría.

Intendants of larger administrative centers, such as San Luis
Potosí and Guadalajara, aired similar complaints about funding
and requested increased allowances for their secretariats.[50] But
Croix felt even more deprived. He pleaded for "one or two"
amanuenses to help expedite official business, since the *comandancia* had neither the services of a clerk (*escribano de gobierno*) nor a
printing press to facilitate the timely dispatch of decrees and orders.[51] Croix proposed that these expenses be met by taking 2
percent of the *alcabala* revenues from the city of Chihuahua for a
period of five years, supplemented by monthly livery fees that
ordinary citizens paid to the military, and by tapping the *ramo de
retenciones de sueldos* (an income withholding fund) of the military
officers under his command. If these three sources proved insufficient for raising the required one thousand pesos, the remainder
was to be met with judicial fines.[52] Croix's persistence paid off.
The crown consented to the plan and not only authorized the
hiring of a clerk, Francisco Matamoros, with an annual salary of six
hundred pesos but also allowed an extra thousand pesos for general expenses.[53]

Architects of the Comandancia General of the Provincias Internas
envisioned, among other things, an entity that might facilitate judicial administration in the far north and ease the burden of local
magistrates. The obstacles for realizing this dimension of the *comandancia*, however, proved nearly insurmountable. The great distances between settlements, the urgency of chronic Indian warfare,
and imperial fiscal problems limited the judicial role of the *comandancia*. While provincial magistrates communicated occasionally
with the commandant or his *asesor*, judicial affairs in Texas and
New Mexico remained largely in local hands.

The Illusory *Audiencia* of the North

In 1805, Governor Joaquín del Real Alencaster declared to the Audiencia of Guadalajara that in New Mexico

> there is no *alcalde* or any other person—nor has there been for years, nor is it probable that there ever will be—with the slightest idea of what legal style is, nor capable of forming a *sumaria* or trial according to law.[54]

The problem, though, went deeper than simply the inconvenience of an ill-formed *sumaria*. At the heart of the matter was the shared belief of many contemporaries that proper judicial administration formed the centerpiece of effective political administration. Indeed, colonial administration rested squarely on bureaucracy invested with judicial powers. And perhaps the most conspicuous symbol of what we might call the judicial state was the *audiencia*. Not surprisingly, then, one proponent, Commandant General Felipe de Neve, proclaimed that the establishment of such a tribunal for the northern provinces constituted

> the most effective means of exterminating the ills and long-standing abuses rooted in the interior of the provinces, which will contribute visibly to improve their constitution, and by which all branches of government might prosper, with considerable increase to the Royal Treasury.[55]

Like others before and after him, Felipe de Neve viewed the *audiencia* as a panacea for the many ills that plagued the northern borderlands of New Spain. Despite these, at times, conspicuous voices of reform, however, a northern *audiencia* never materialized. Obstacles of local, regional, and imperial dimensions proved insuperable. Still, the story of this frustrated attempt to establish a northern tribunal sheds considerable light on the political ideology of the late-colonial Hispanic world and serves to underscore the importance of local legal administration that filled the void.

The impulse to create a separate northern *audiencia* came from two distinct eighteenth-century currents—one evident generally in the empire and one shaped by the peculiar regional circumstances. The first of these currents was the Bourbon effort to restructure institutions and foster economic activity. Having acceded to the throne in 1700, the Bourbons sought to resuscitate a stagnant Spain that had suffered calamitous political and economic decline in the previous century.[56] While French models of statecraft may have served as a point of departure, the Bourbons carried out their reform projects within a decidedly Spanish context.[57] The Indies soon felt the effects of the so-called "Bourbon Reforms."

The cornerstone of the new policy was a thoroughgoing political restructuring for the dual purpose of exercising tighter fiscal control and shoring up imperial defenses in the Indies. Recognizing new social, political, and economic realities—and trying to profit from them—the crown created two new viceroyalties, erected three new *audiencias*, and imposed the intendancy system in the colonial world.[58] In short, no area of the Indies escaped the redrawing of jurisdictional lines.

The provinces of northern New Spain, too, experienced a political restructuring. Here, however, the geographical landscape—physical and cultural—forced the crown to adopt a unique solution—the establishment of the Comandancia General de las Provincias Internas. Perhaps most imposing was the sheer vastness of northern New Spain, which served to isolate these pockets of settlement from the colonial heartland, as well as one from another. Indeed, many bureaucrats shared the view of don Diego de Vargas, governor and recolonizer of New Mexico, who once lamented that his post was "at the ends of the earth and remote beyond compare."[59] Although the crown sought ways to ameliorate this severe isolation through such plans as improved mail service, the north always lay precariously distant from the rest of the viceroyalty.[60]

The distance and distinctiveness of the northern provinces prompted a variety of plans—some inchoate, some well-laid—to facilitate access to a competent magistracy. These various schemes fell into two distinct phases. The first, which might be termed the "reformist" stage, squares with the many plans for territorial readjustment during the mid eighteenth century. In 1751, "captain of cuirassiers" (*capitán de coraceros*) Fernando Sánchez Salvador proposed to the Council of the Indies a rather grandiose project that called for the creation of a new viceroyalty headquartered at San Juan de Sonora, or perhaps some other site in the province of Chihuahua.[61] Naturally, a new viceroyalty would have included a separate *audiencia*. While the council paid special attention to the military aspects of the project, it did not take action. The idea of creating a separate political entity for the northern frontier—with its corresponding *audiencia*—surfaced again in 1760. A quite detailed anonymous report recommended that Durango serve as capital for a new viceroyalty, the territorial limits of which would essentially replicate the current boundaries of the Audiencia de Guadalajara. This tribunal, in turn, would move to the viceregal capital of Durango.[62] While these early proposals never won the support of the crown, the issue of a competent judiciary—as embodied in the *audiencia*—remained a concern.

The creation in 1776 of the Comandancia General de las Provincias Internas seemed a propitious moment for a split with former jurisdictions, in judicial as well as administrative matters. The first commandant general, Teodoro de Croix, found himself under considerable pressure to realize the strategic objectives of his command, and he occupied himself primarily with military matters. But, despite his military orientation and training, Croix articulated the practical aims and goals of the new territorial unit in the context of traditional Spanish political thought. For him, as for his contemporaries, better judicial administration held the promise of an efficient command. To this end, Croix suggested in 1778 a variety of reforms, including the establishment of an independent "half"-*audiencia* at Arizpe, the Sonoran capital of the *comandancia*.[63] This proposal failed to gain royal approval, probably because of the organizational and financial vicissitudes of the newly created *comandancia* and because of the dire economic straits of the empire in general. Nevertheless, Croix's successors resuscitated the idea on a number of occasions over the next decade.[64]

Like his predecessor, Commandant General Felipe de Neve placed almost mystical trust in the inherent beneficial attributes of an *audiencia*. Such a tribunal, explained Neve,

> will be able to watch carefully the conduct of the judges; curb and punish their excesses; reform or revoke those portions of their sentences that might be unjust; facilitate appeals and other recourses that the laws grant to subjects to remedy the harm that they might experience in inferior courts; fashion and arrange with practical understanding the schedules of fees that ecclesiastical and royal tribunals might collect; give instructions that delinquents of all types be pursued, tried, and punished; have jails built for their custody and security; provide funds for their maintenance while their cases are being tried and decided; apportion

destinations to which to send them as punishment for their crimes; [and] disencumber the Real Audiencia of Guadalajara of the business pertaining to all the provinces under my command, which currently occupies much of its attention.[65]

It is significant that a non-jurist expressed such a hopeful, if unrealistic, vision of the *audiencia*. To be sure, jurists traditionally had shaped the ideology that underscored the juridical basis of the monarchy. And, according to this ideation, the aim of the government was to establish a regime that, as Ricardo Zorraquín has phrased it, "might assure the supreme authority of justice."[66] Yet even non-jurists seem to have clung to the tenets of the judicial state. Perhaps both groups found inspiration in the idea of the *audiencia* because it was emblematic of good government.

To finance this seemingly indispensable judicial body— "surely the measure of greatest utility and common benefit for its inhabitants"—Neve proposed to utilize the revenue generated from the sale of *aguardiente mescal*, hitherto applied to public works. Sensitive to the penury of the crown, Neve suggested that the sale of mescal through a government monopoly (*estanco*), which had only operated in Sonora, be extended throughout the Provincias Internas. The estimated annual revenue of fifty thousand pesos would easily cover the costs of the tribunal and would not burden the royal treasury.[67] The crown acknowledged Neve's enthusiasm, as well as his plan, and approved by Royal Order of 16 March 1785, the establishment of an *audiencia*.

Yet when Jacobo Ugarte y Loyola assumed the *comandancia general* late in 1785, no steps had been taken to erect the tribunal. Instead, a reorganization of the Provincias Internas occupied most of the attention of top administrators.[68] Despite other pressing matters, Ugarte y Loyola revived the project for a northern tribunal as a means of securing "the benefits that result from the administration of strict, methodical, and swift justice."[69] Ugarte suggested that, because of the social and economic makeup of the region, the *audiencia* should replicate the one recently established at Caracas.[70] Extremely important for the proposed *audiencia*, believed Ugarte, was that the regent

possess practical, sound, and extensive knowledge of his district, the natural character and respective rights of its inhabitants, the general and particular forms of its governance, and the class of business that ordinarily or extraordinarily is dealt with. For with this understanding, he will enlighten more quickly the rest of the ministers who comprise the *acuerdo* and, of course, obtain a just, wise, and equitable tribunal.[71]

Ugarte noted that long-time *asesor* of the *comandancia general*, Pedro Galindo Navarro, possessed the requisite qualities to head the new body.[72]

As of December 1787, however, no action had been taken, and Ugarte y Loyola once again appealed to authorities to establish an *audiencia*.[73] This time, politics in Madrid and Mexico City dashed the hopes for a northern *audiencia*. A new monarch, Charles IV who became king on 14 December 1788, and a new vision of the role of the *comandancia* ended this proposal. Without the support of the powerful Gálvez faction, and stymied by the new viceroy, Manuel Antonio Flórez, the project floundered and was laid to rest.[74]

Spain faced difficult years in the two decades spanning the eighteenth and nineteenth centuries. Political turmoil in Europe, especially France, and constant international military confrontations dampened the Bourbon reform spirit and drew the empire into costly and compromising alliances. A weakened Spain witnessed the Napoleonic intervention, the appearance of self-styled governing juntas, and the sparks of American insurgency. All augured ill for the *antiguo régimen*.

The second phase—the "constitutional" phase—emerged in an atmosphere of crisis for the Spanish state, a turning point that marked a new era in the political life of the Hispanic world. Amid the political turbulence and changing ideologies of the early nineteenth century, a northern *audiencia* still had its adherents. In contrast to previous plans, the new blueprints placed the idea of a superior tribunal within a constitutional context. Nevertheless, as did their predecessors, a new generation saw in the *audiencia* the quintessence of harmonious administration. Pedro Bautista Pino, New Mexico's delegate to the Cortes of Cádiz, urged the assembly to establish a northern *audiencia* in order to ease the burden of frontiersmen who sought justice at a superior level.[75] One of two delegates from the distant Provincias Internas, Pedro Pino arrived at Cádiz late and was not seated until August 1812, after much of the work of the Cortes had been accomplished.[76] In his *Exposición Sucinta y Sencilla de la Provincia de Nuevo México*, published at Cádiz in

1812, Pino put forth four main points to alleviate the deplorable conditions in New Mexico. Two proposals dealt with ecclesiastical affairs—the establishment of a bishopric and a seminary, both approved by the Cortes but never instituted—and one treated military matters.[77] The fourth point called for the establishment of an *audiencia* at Chihuahua for the four Provincias Internas of the West.[78] Pino reiterated some of the difficulties of judicial administration in the distant northern province of New Mexico.

> The entire province is divided into eight *alcaldías*, served by its citizens without salary, and subject to a political and military governor who resides at the capital of Santa Fe, without *asesor* or *escribano*, because there is neither in the entire province. He has as his assistants two lieutenants and two ensigns. In the decisions of this governor in civil and criminal matters there is no appeal other than the Audiencia of Guadalajara, about 500 leagues distant.[79]

For all his efforts, Pino failed to effect any real changes in judicial administration in New Mexico, and the only lasting consequence of his long and expensive journey was a literary one. New Mexicans still recite the "dicho" that aptly sums up this failed endeavor.

> *Don Pedro Pino fué,*
> *Don Pedro Pino vino.*
> (Don Pedro Pino went,
> Don Pedro Pino returned.)[80]

In the waning years of Spanish rule, others would propose with equal futility similar proposals for an *audiencia* for the western interior provinces.[81] Pino's was perhaps the last best chance for this region.[82]

While Pino's plea for a western *audiencia* fell on deaf ears, the efforts of Miguel Ramos Arizpe, an influential liberal from the eastern province of Coahuila, proved more fruitful. Ramos Arizpe had arrived at Cádiz in March 1811, maneuvered adroitly, and emerged as a leading spokesman for the American position.[83] Less provincial in tone than Pino's *Exposición*, the *Memoria* of Miguel Ramos Arizpe embodies the spirit of early-nineteenth-century liberal constitutionalism.

Ramos cast a wider net, urging political and economic reform not only for the good of his *patria chica*, but also "for the general welfare of all the nation."[84] Ramos's report reduced the unhappy state of the far north to two essential weaknesses—the lack of representative local, or "internal" government and, not surprisingly, the absence of a superior tribunal of appeals. Institutional changes in these two areas, Ramos argued, would lead to economic prosperity which, in turn, would help the empire thwart the aggressive advance of the United States of America.[85]

Miguel Ramos Arizpe's diagnosis of the problems inherent in the current judicial system echoed those of previous observers.

> Contributing to the almost complete collapse of the administration of justice [is] the fact that the provinces are located at distances ranging from two hundred to seven hundred leagues from the superior government and the royal courts of Mexico, Guadalajara, and Chihuahua. . . . The majority of the political chiefs and magistrates, who are military men or of dispositions conformable to the will of the military officer who appointed them, do not have anyone to advise them how to carry on the judicial proceedings with the prudence that judicial affairs require. The courts to which one can appeal are located at a great distance outside the provinces. This makes recourse to them even by citizens of moderate wealth impossible.[86]

Ramos emphasized that the four provinces for which he spoke lay "separated by nature from New Spain, New Galicia, and the western [interior] provinces," and that such a natural division had already found political expression in the separation of the eastern and western components of the Provincias Internas.[87]

To rectify the ills inherent in such a diffuse bureaucracy, Ramos proposed the erection of a "Superior Court of Appeals," situated in Saltillo, "composed of three judges and a prosecutor, all [*letrados*], and named by the king in conference with the [Council] of State," who would pay heed to the "written recommendations of the Superior Executive Council of these provinces."[88]

Unlike his predecessors, but true to his liberal leanings, Ramos Arizpe envisioned a strict separation of powers in the new governmental arrangement—the Superior Executive Council (an elective body for internal government) and the Superior Court of Appeals were to "exercise separately the administrative and judicial powers."[89] Like those before him, however, the learned *coahuilteco* placed high hopes in the effectiveness of the new tribunal.

The Superior Court of Appeals, not being concerned with the affairs of government and being located in the interior of those vast provinces, will give swift attention to the administration of justice. The wicked will restrain themselves on being confronted by a body that with impartiality and wisdom imposes on them prompt punishment. The good will wipe away their tears on seeing within their land a court that guarantees to them liberty and security of their personal property, and all will dedicate themselves peacefully to their respective occupations, from which will come the general well-being of the state.[90]

Miguel Ramos Arizpe argued persuasively. The Cortes adopted his plan for a northern *audiencia*—as well as a number of his other proposals—and incorporated it into the "Reglamento de las Audiencias y Juzgados de primera instancia" of 9 October 1812.[91]

Political instability in the empire, however, sealed the fate of the proposed *audiencia*. Fernando VII returned to power in 1814, and in a decree of 4 May 1814, he annulled in sweeping fashion the legislation enacted by the Cortes.[92] Revoked in the process was the so-called *ley de tribunales* and, perhaps inadvertently, the project for an *audiencia* at Saltillo. When Fernando's annulment decree of 4 May reached New Spain, Viceroy Félix María Calleja believed that it applied also to the enabling act for the *audiencia* and, thus, ceased implementation of the project.[93] On the other hand, Calleja's successor, Juan Ruiz de Apodaca, and the Consejo de Estado both saw as imperative the establishment of an intendancy (with *audiencia*) at Saltillo. Despite the recommendation, the crown opted in May 1819 to defer action on the matter.[94]

Dissatisfaction with Fernando VII's reactionary policies produced a liberal backlash in 1820, which forced the monarch to recognize the constitutional regime. Thus, rather serendipitously, the fabled northern *audiencia* found new life. Implicit in the new political order was the Intendancy of Saltillo, and the crown considered how best to establish the attendant *audiencia*.[95] In the process of resuscitation, however, the proposed tribunal had more than doubled its personnel. It was now to consist of one regent, nine ministers, and two *fiscales* to serve the Provincias Internas of the East—Coahuila, Nuevo León, Nuevo Santander, and Texas.[96] The dream of a northern *audiencia* seemed to be becoming a reality—indeed, the Consejo de Estado had compiled a list of candidates for the various *audiencia* positions. Predictably, there appears to have been no shortage of candidates—mostly *peninsulares*—with qualifications to match the prestige of the positions available.[97] Just as predictably, political events once again intervened.

In the wake of the newly rekindled movement toward Mexican independence, the Consejo de Estado decided on 21 September 1821, to delay implementation of the *audiencia*—"because of the doubt as to whether it would be convenient to do so, given the latest incidents in New Spain"—and to await further royal instructions on the issue.[98] If they ever arrived, those instructions held little consequence—Mexican independence (by the Treaty of Córdoba, 24 August 1821) made irrelevant the establishment of a royal Spanish *audiencia* for northern New Spain. Thus came to an end Spain's political rule in Mexico. Due to a combination of economic malaise, bureaucratic red tape, professional jealousy, and political instability, the long-desired tribunal for the frontier of northern New Spain failed to materialize.

As mentioned earlier, no compelling reason exists to support the contention that an audiencia at Arizpe, Chihuahua, Saltillo, or elsewhere in the north—vast, impoverished, and besieged—could have countered the obstacles of distance, expense, and danger involved in the appeals process. Also enlightening is the fate of subsequent attempts at high-level judicial reform in the north. Following independence, the national Mexican government issued decrees of 20 May and 5 September 1826, that established a system of regional tribunals. As a result, Parral (Chihuahua) became the district seat for the states of Durango, Chihuahua, and the territory of New Mexico, while Linares (Tamaulipas) served the states of Tamaulipas, Nuevo León, and Coahuila-Texas.[99] A full study of the impact of this restructuring remains to be done, but inhabitants of areas such as New Mexico and Texas—for a variety of reasons—appear to have been no more prone to judicial appeal under the new system than before. Nor did the judicial correctness that many supposed might filter down to the local level ever occur. Indeed, because of economic and political necessity, the borderlands judiciary continued to function as under the colonial regime.[100] Socioeconomic and geographic realities weighed heavily and, in practical terms, the mere implementation of an *audiencia* probably would not have altered the status quo in the far north.

The notion that an *audiencia* would create a climate in which "all branches [of government] prosper, with considerable increase to the Royal Treasury" was perhaps excessively optimistic.[101] Yet those who joined the chorus of voices favoring such an institution were by no means naive. All recognized the great difficulties in administering such a far-flung and lightly populated region. An *audiencia* could hardly have induced economic prosperity and social tranquillity. The notion died hard, however. Cynics might see personal aggrandizement, jealousy, greed, and other all-too-human qualities as important impulses that drove the various plans for northern *audiencias*. In part, they would be right.

Yet the repeated invocation of the almost mystical, panacea qualities of an *audiencia* can perhaps be best explained as an expression of shared assumptions about the nature of governance. Despite the enormous political and ideological changes during the last half-century of Spanish rule, many administrators and intellectuals still considered the judicial system as the prime agent for effective administration. While attracted to the seductive possibilities of the budding administrative state, these men at the same time were wed to time-honored notions of statecraft. Even the most innovative and utilitarian proposals sometimes wore the ill-fitting rhetoric of tradition. For the Hispanic world at the end of the colonial era, the *audiencia* was more than just a well-staffed court of appeals. As an ideal, the *audiencia* embodied an entire system of beliefs—it was the essence of good government. Perhaps for this reason, so many expected so much from the ill-starred *audiencia*.

In a way, the fate of the proposed northern *audiencia* aptly characterizes a major feature of the colonial judiciary. Despite the façade of centralization, the empire failed to incorporate the peripheries in a meaningful way into its judicial superstructure. In part, financial constraints at all levels of government determined the impracticability of a real meshing of the provincial and appellate judiciaries. But certainly the long tradition of juridical localism, as well as the socioeconomic circumstances of the sparsely settled frontier, further conspired against the creation of a northern *audiencia*. For those who lived on the extensive peripheries of empire, the well-trained judicial elite of the administrative hubs remained distant.

❖ ❖ 4 ❖ ❖

The Local Judiciary

Colonial subjects in the far north of New Spain had relatively little contact with the well-staffed superstructure of the judicial state. But that did not mean that justice itself was distant—a variety of officials in the borderlands carried the king's *vara de justicia* and dispensed justice in his name. Lacking formal training in law, these men nevertheless acquired rudimentary juridical knowledge through observation and practice, and they relied heavily upon generally shared assumptions of fairness and equity in arriving at their decisions. At the same time, each brought his particular talents, wisdom, and sensibilities to the judicial process, thus leaving a personal stamp on legal administration in his jurisdiction. Preeminent in the colonial judiciary of New Mexico and Texas was the provincial governor, who often served as nexus for crown and community.

The Governor

The office of the governor was a New World innovation, for while the title had existed on the peninsula, the functional capacities of Old and New World counterparts differed.[1] Invested with military, administrative, and judicial authority, the office of governor exemplified the accumulation of powers typical of the political ideation of the *antiguo régimen*. Much more than a magistrate, the governor in fact oversaw the full range of civil government within his jurisdiction and wielded tremendous power.

The reasons for the designation of governor—in distinction to *alcalde mayor*, which held for most of New Spain—are not entirely clear. From the earliest settlement of New Mexico in the late sixteenth century, Adelantado Juan de Oñate held the titles of governor and captain general.[2] Oñate's departure from the province signaled a shift from a proprietary to a crown colony, but subsequent royal appointees continued to carry the titles of governor and captain general, distinct offices that conferred both civil and military responsibilities on the same person. The situation in Texas was nearly identical. The first individual who carried the title of governor was Martín de Alarcón (1717–19), and his successors also held this rank.[3]

The unusual designation of governor probably stems from contemporary notions regarding the structure of government. The principal territorial divisions in the Indies were *provincias mayores* and *provincias menores*. The former had as their nuclei the various regional *audiencias* and were composed of a variable number of subdivisions known in New Spain as *alcaldías mayores* and in Peru as *corregimientos*. So similar were the functions of governor, *alcalde mayor*, and *corregidor* that most contemporaries, as well as later historians, failed to differentiate between them.[4] *Provincias menores*, on the other hand, normally lay on the peripheries of the *audiencia* and were administered by a governor endowed with considerable independence in military and political affairs. The great distances between the *provincias menores* and the imperial centers justified this increased autonomy.[5] In contrast, an *alcaldía mayor* was subject to the direct political supervision of the viceroy or the *presidente-gobernador* of a regional *audiencia*. While a governorship still fell within the judicial network of the *audiencia*, the political powers of the *presidente-gobernador* were confined to the district in which the *audiencia* sat and did not impinge upon a governor.[6]

Not only did a governor enjoy greater autonomy than did an *alcalde mayor*, but also the distinction and prestige of a governorship surpassed that of an *alcaldía mayor*. The aspirations of Diego de Vargas—reconqueror, recolonizer, and twice governor of New Mexico (served from 1691–97; 1703–04)—aptly reflect the manner in which a career bureaucrat might perceive the scale of appointments. Vargas arrived in New Spain in 1673 and soon received the title of *alcalde mayor* of Teutila, located in the modern state of Oaxaca, Mexico. Ever aspiring to positions of greater responsibility, prestige, and remuneration, Vargas won for himself in 1679 an appointment as *alcalde mayor* of Tlalpujahua in Michoacán. Vargas's efforts at advancement culminated in his appointment in 1688 as governor and captain general of the province of New Mexico. At the time of his death in 1704, Vargas was in the midst of pursuing an appointment to a *presidencia-gobernación*, that is, the governorship of a province that housed an *audiencia*.[7] Vargas's goals no doubt mirror the relative standing of the various offices. While they may have been similar in function, a governorship usually represented a higher rung on the bureaucratic ladder than an *alcaldía mayor*.

During the Bourbon period, there were few institutions to counterbalance the tremendous power held by the governor in New Mexico. The cabildo (municipal corporation) of Santa Fe operated only during the first quarter century after the recolonization of the province by Diego de Vargas. From the late 1710s until the turn of the century, when the *ayuntamiento* system was established, the governor had virtually free reign in administering justice in New Mexico. In Texas, the cabildo of San Antonio operated continuously from its creation by Canary Island immigrants in 1731 and may have served to brake somewhat the unlimited authority of the provincial governor. A vehicle for local expression, the *cabildo* frequently protested what they felt were illegal or unfair actions of various governors. Still, the needs of the frontier were such that, like elsewhere in the Provincias Internas, military responsibilities took precedence.

Many governors in the northern provinces were experienced campaigners of Indian wars, and under the *comandancia general* the military dimension of the office assumed even greater prominence than before.[8] Faced with increasing pressure from diverse groups of mounted Indian warriors—Apaches, Comanches, Utes, Navajos, and others—the governors of New Mexico and Texas in the eighteenth and nineteenth centuries dedicated most of their efforts to military affairs. The bulk of the correspondence of the governors reflects their preoccupation with campaign preparations, troop movements, Indian depredations, and stolen livestock.[9] A presidial garrison, augmented by local militia and Indian auxiliaries, comprised the forces at the governor's disposal. In addition to his military obligations, the governor also had administrative duties, such as overseeing fiscal matters, legalizing land grants to local settlers, registering livestock brands, and generally maintaining the wellbeing of the province.[10]

The credentials of Justo Boneo y Morales, governor of Texas from

1743 to 1744, are typical of the men who served as governors in New Spain's far north. Knight of the Order of Santiago, Captain of Grenadiers of the Regiment of the Infantry of Cantabria, Boneo had risen from the rank of *cadete* to his current position in a military career that spanned some thirty-two years.[11] Governor Manuel Salcedo (1808–13) likewise was steeped in military tradition. Son of a prominent military figure, Salcedo enrolled at age seven in the Royal Academy at Ocaña, province of Toledo, and later attended the Royal Seminary of Nobles in Madrid until the age of seventeen. After a stint as an infantry lieutenant in the Canary Islands, he accompanied his father to Spanish Louisiana in 1801 and served as an aide in administering that province.[12]

In New Mexico the situation was much the same. Although many considered New Mexico to be *"pobre y retirado,"* the crown did not appoint novices to the position of governor.[13] All were experienced officers who might be trusted with an important, albeit poor and distant, frontier region. Perhaps slightly extraordinary, but exemplary nonetheless, was Juan Bautista de Anza, the only *criollo* to receive a regular appointment to the governorship of post-Pueblo Revolt New Mexico. Born on the fighting frontier of Sonora into a military family, Anza quickly scaled the promotional ladder of the colonial military and gained respect as an able campaigner of Indian wars. While governor of New Mexico he achieved perhaps the pinnacle of his fame when he defeated the renowned Comanche chief Cuerno Verde and effected a truce that lasted some thirty years.[14] The one conspicuous exception to the tendency of naming a military officer to fill the post of governor is, of course, Diego de Vargas. A government functionary with no apparent formal military training, Vargas exemplifies the transitional age in which he lived. Imbued with the old values and views of the Habsburg empire, he was the last of his kind to serve under the new Bourbon regime.[15]

Because of the dominant position of the provincial governor in both Texas and New Mexico, the preponderance of civil and criminal cases passed before him at some point in the proceedings. Hispanic settlers, as well as subject Indians, frequently brought their cases directly to the governor, perhaps in an effort to avoid the intervention of the local *alcalde mayor* or *alcalde ordinario.* The governor's prominence in the administration of justice was considerable compared to the more populous metropolitan areas of the colonial world, which featured a variety of officials who adjudicated matters of *justicia ordinaria*.

In his capacity as preeminent judicial representative of the crown at the provincial level, the governor was to "hear all with kindness."[16] He attempted to do so in three distinct areas of judicial competency. First, as *capitán general* (under the *comandancia general* he became *comandante de armas*) he adjudicated cases of a military nature under the special jurisdiction known as the *fuero militar*.[17] Second, in his role as *mandatario político*, he oversaw cases relative to government finances—*causas de gobierno* (later known as *contencioso-administrativo*). Finally, as *justicia mayor* of his jurisdiction, the governor heard and adjudicated civil suits and criminal cases in both first and second instance.[18] The *fuero militar*, of course, was a privileged jurisdiction reserved for the military. Elsewhere, this judicial privilege began to encroach upon royal jurisdiction, but such was not the case in either New Mexico or Texas.[19] The non-*letrado* governors of these two provinces may simply have failed to distinguish clearly between jurisdictions, perhaps because legal procedure under the *fuero militar* resembled ordinary procedure.

In the centers of empire, the seemingly insurmountable problems of the royal treasury occupied a great deal of time and energy in the second area of judicial competence—*causas de gobierno*. In Mexico City, for example, the viceroy presided over the Junta de Hacienda, which dealt with a variety of matters relative to the royal fisc. Similarly, the commandant general of the Provincias Internas dedicated considerable effort to resolving financial difficulties.[20] In New Mexico matters of royal finances were decidedly less complex. The relative poverty and isolation of the province failed to generate much judicial activity in the area of *causas de gobierno*.

Because of geographic and economic circumstances, Texas generated somewhat more adjudication of fiscal matters that might be classified as *contencioso-administrativo*. The livestock trade, especially, gave rise to a number of such cases. Most troublesome to the crown was local evasion of a royal tax of four silver reales on all unbranded stray cattle—*mesteños*—which occasioned some judicial activity on the part of the governor.[21] Because of local opposition, the *fondo de mesteñas* never provided the revenue that officials had envisioned.

Another hallmark of the Texas economy was illicit trade between Spaniards and foreign merchants. Unlike New Mexico, Texas's frontier was a vibrant international boundary. The proximity of French and Anglo-American traders and the difficulty and expense of obtaining goods from the heartland of New Spain created a setting ripe for contraband. Sporadically throughout the colonial period, Spain sanctioned an economic *fait accompli* and allowed Louisiana merchants to supply its eastern frontier post at Nacogdoches.[22] Whether sanctioned or not, Spanish subjects found the goods offered in the East to be sufficiently attractive, and in the last half-century of Spanish rule, smuggling in Texas became a major problem for provincial governors and administrative superiors alike.[23]

In the third area of competency—as *justicia mayor*—the provincial governor touched the lives of most frontier subjects. In New Mexico, the governor's role as judicial arbiter proved especially salient because of the absence of a *cabildo* during much of the eighteenth century.[24] In its absence, the governor and his assistants alone administered royal justice. Despite their prominence at the local level of justice, provincial governors can be classified as *justicias* or *jueces legos* who lacked formal training in law, in contradistinction to *jueces de letras* or *jueces togados* who had fulfilled the studies and examinations required of lawyers and judges of high tribunals.[25]

Before the eighteenth century, governors throughout much of Spanish America administered justice personally, without the aid of legal advisers, except in particularly difficult cases. This situation changed during the early years of Bourbon rule, as appointees with legal training began to fill positions of lieutenant governor. The *asesor letrado* became a fixture in most territorial jurisdictions and assumed the judicial responsibilities of the governor, who in nearly all cases simply rubber-stamped the legal opinion of his adviser.[26] Provincial governors in the far north, however, had no readily accessible judicial expert to whom to turn.

In the sphere of ordinary royal jurisdiction the governor adjudicated a variety of civil and criminal cases, but special mention should be made of his authority to serve as judge of first instance for cases involving Indians within the entire jurisdiction of the provincial capital.[27] In the climate of cultural accommodation that began after the reconquest, a highly personal relationship developed between the Pueblo Indians of New Mexico and the Spanish governor. Pueblos frequently circumvented the authority of their local *alcaldes mayores* and brought their cases directly to the governor. The degree of this personalized relationship may have been unique to New Mexico, but certainly Spain sought to cultivate throughout the Indies the notion of the crown as legitimate arbiter for all.[28]

In adjudicating cases involving Indians, the governors of New Mexico often assigned the *alcaldes mayores* of Santa Fe to carry out the initial stages of the judicial process (the *sumaria*), but normally the governors pronounced sentence. In New Mexico, governors routinely handled judicial affairs relative to Indians, regardless of whether the cases began in the jurisdiction of Santa Fe. It was incumbent upon the governor to provide adequate legal counsel for Indians, usually in the form of *defensores* or *curadores*.[29]

In judicial matters, the duties of the provincial governor appear to be somewhat ill-defined. This haziness, however, is characteristic of the Spanish colonial regime. A formula used in the appointment of Tomás Vélez Cachupín to the governorship of New Mexico is standard. It states only that he should observe customary practices "in full, just as your predecessors were to have done, with no difference whatsoever."[30] This apparent lack of definition was common practice in naming other officials of high rank throughout the empire as well.[31] But perhaps the lack of a clear-cut "job description" creates confusion only for the modern scholar unfamiliar with contemporary practice. Alfonso García Gallo may have been close to the mark when he pointed out that those who filled colonial positions normally knew the obligations, perquisites, and limitations of the various offices. They had no need to explain that which was clear to all.[32] The *Recopilación de Indias* (5.2.7) reiterates this rather vague directive to the governor:

> You will do justice to all, with no exceptions; and you will adhere to and comply with all the matters of good governance and laws of the kingdom, the *cédulas* and provisions of His Majesty, and those that are made and given, and might be made and given, for the proper order of the Indies.

With respect to the legal preparation of provincial officials, the crown required all those who held the title of governor to stay abreast of, and obey, current legislation.[33] This general sort of instruction to high royal appointments persisted throughout the colonial period. Article 68 of the *Ordenanza General de Intendentes de Indias* of 1802 was typical.

The Intendants, as well as their *asesores,* will have at hand and make a particular study of all the Laws of the Indies, which prescribe the most learned and adaptable rules for the administration of justice and good governance of the people of those, my Dominions. And they will also examine with particular attention the [laws] established for these Kingdoms [Spain], to which they should conform in the absence of laws for the Indies, as long as neither are contrary to that which is discussed in this Instruction.[34]

Even before the late-eighteenth-century compilations of military orders, governors were obliged to uphold all pertinent laws. A mid-century *instrucción* directed to all *corregidores* and *alcaldes mayores* bound for the Indies made this point quite clear.

You will keep and execute, precisely and exactly, all the orders, *cédulas,* compilations of laws, and all that which is ordered and might be ordered for the proper governance of this office, the good treatment of the Indians, and the better administration of justice. Thus, you must hear all lawsuits and cases—both civil and criminal—that might occur in your jurisdiction, which you can and must hear, and order all things that your predecessors might have ordered and provided. And also you will receive all judicial inquiries and information in the cases and things permitted by law that you believe might be conducive to my royal service, good governance, and the administration of justice.[35]

Similarly, those who held the office of provincial governor after the reform movement began would have had access to the *Instrucción para formar una linea o cordón de quince presidios sobre las Fronteras de las Provincias Internas de este Reino de Nueva España, y Nuevo Reglamento.*[36] Governors in Nueva Vizcaya, for example, had at their disposal a handbook for governing and administering the provincial militia.[37] Title 6, Article 9 of this *reglamento* required all militia officers to possess a copy of this handbook as well as a copy of the *Real declaración de la Ordenanza de Milicias Provinciales de España de 30 Mayo del año de 1767,* so that they might "comply precisely with the former, and instruct themselves in that which is applicable in the latter for the discipline and rule of the provincial troops." Title 8, Article 16 of this important document required military officers to employ in military courts the same procedure used in courts of ordinary jurisdiction.[38]

Besides these general admonitions, the *Recopilación de Indias* specified that all positions of government were to have at their disposal a copy of that text.[39] Evidently, the crown required governors to have this fundamental legal compilation in hand before they took office. On the eve of his departure from Spain, Gaspar Domingo de Mendoza—governor-elect of New Mexico—complained to the Council of the Indies that family obligations had left him without the financial means to "meet the costs of the books of the new *Recopilación*, which he is required to take for instruction in his employment." In a reply dated 7 May 1737, the Council of the Indies relieved Mendoza of the obligation of taking the books before he embarked, but stipulated that he acquire them at the *audiencia* in Mexico City before continuing to his post.[40] Whether all governors of Texas and New Mexico possessed a copy of the *Recopilación de Indias* is open to question, but the fact that the crown required them to own it suggests the level at which governors were expected to perform.

Didactic legal literature was certainly no rare commodity in the larger centers of the colonial world where bibliophiles were well supplied with the latest titles. In his study of colonial juridical literature, Javier Malagón Barceló compiled a list of 422 such books that were available to buyers in seventeenth-century New Spain.[41] The inventory demonstrates a rather rich and varied selection of legal tomes. Many of the books, obviously for specialists, are written in Latin, but a sizeable portion are works aimed for a less-specialized readership, written in Castilian, and targeted for other functionaries such as governors, *alcaldes*, and *escribanos*.

Frontier libraries also included legal works. An example from Chihuahua helps shed some light on the dissemination of legal literature on the far northern frontier. At the time of his death in 1778, Padre Custodio Fr. Juan de Dios Fernández de la Cueva had in his library at the mission of San Gerónimo in Chihuahua a total of thirty-two books. As might be expected, most were of a religious nature—sermons, instructional manuals, and inspirational tracts. Somewhat more surprisingly, he owned two juridical works—a four-volume copy of the *Recopilación de Indias* and one copy of Fr. Juan de Paz's *Resoluciones, y Consultas Teológicas, Jurídicas Regulares, y Morales*.[42] The appearance of the *Recopilación de Indias* indicates that this important legal text was not impossible to come by on the frontier.

Like their counterparts elsewhere, provincial governors in New

Mexico seem to have had available many of the standard legal texts of the day. Evidence is sparse in this respect, but the following list, drawn primarily from Inquisition records and the Vargas inventory, demonstrates that early New Mexico governors had access to, and consulted, the standard legal works. In the form of codices are the *Nueva Recopilación de Castilla* (1567) and Justinian's *Corpus Juris Civilis*. Among the instructional and didactic works are *Curia Philipica* (1603) by Juan de Hevia Bolaños, *Instrucción Política y Práctica Judicial . . . para los Gobernadores y Corregidores y otros Jueces Ordinarios* (1609) by Alonso de Villadiego, *Política Indiana* (1648) by Juan de Solórzano Pereira, *Práctica Civil y Criminal* (1566) by Gabriel de Monterroso y Alvarado, and *Tratado de Escrituras y Contratos Públicos* (1620) by Antonio de Argüello. In the way of moral philosophy pertinent to civil government we find Fr. Juan Márquez's *El Gobernador Christiano* (1612) and the widely circulated *Idea de un Príncipe Cristiano Representada en Cien Empresas* (1640) by Diego Saavedra Fajardo.[43] While the dates of the first editions of these works are quite early, most of the books enjoyed numerous reprintings, and they were standard fare well into the eighteenth century.[44] Joseph W. McKnight's study of legal texts on the northern frontier demonstrates that the governors of Texas also had at their disposal many of the same texts. Governor Manuel Muñoz's library, for example, included the *Curia Philipica*, and several works of more recent vintage such as Félix Colón y Larriátegui's *Juzgados Militares de España y Sus Indias*, Josef Febrero's six-volume *Librería de Escribanos e Instrucción Jurídica Theórico Práctica de Principiantes* (1786), and Joseph Juan y Colom's *Instrucción de Escribanos en Orden a lo Judicial* (1787).[45]

In addition to these legal handbooks and compilations, provincial governors also received from their superiors the latest royal dispatches, including pertinent legislation. Texas and New Mexico were no exceptions in this respect. These communiqués usually contained information of a general nature—decrees pardoning criminals, procedural innovations, and reminders of previous decrees and directives. Occasionally they were directed specifically to these two provinces. In 1760, for example, Governor Francisco Marín del Valle sent notification that he had received a royal dispatch regarding "the manner in which to name Interim *Corregidores* and *Alcaldes Mayores*." He further stated that he had placed the dispatch in the "archive of this government under [his] care."[46]

INSTRUCCION JURIDICA
DE ESCRIBANOS,
ABOGADOS
Y JUECES ORDINARIOS DE JUZGADOS
inferiores:

DIVIDIDA EN TRES LIBROS,

CUYAS ESPECIES EXPLICA LA TABLA Ó INDICE DE ELLA:

FUNDADA EN LOS DERECHOS CANÓNICO
y Real , para descargo de ambos Fueros.

ESCRITA

Por Don Joseph Juan y Colom , Bachillér en Sagrados Cánones
y Escribano de los Reynos de S. M. natural
de Valencia y su Ciudad de S. Felipe.

UNDECIMA IMPRESION.

TOMO SEGUNDO.

CON PRIVILEGIO.
En Madrid: En la Imprenta de la Viuda è Hijo de Marin.
Año de 1795.

A costa de la Real Compañia de Impresores y Libreros del Reyno.

Figure 3. This practical handbook for magistrates and *escribanos,* written by Joseph Juan y Colom and first published in 1736, apparently circulated in the far northern provinces of New Spain.

Besides the practice of sending royal dispatches relative to recent decrees, the above example reveals the colonial practice of placing such documentation in the local government archives, normally housed at the provincial capital in the *casas reales* (government buildings).[47] The archives contained all manner of official documentation of both local and outside origin—royal dispatches, *cédulas*, local civil and criminal cases, land grant records, property conveyances, and wills. Officials in New Mexico and Texas routinely followed colonial practice and, in stepping down from office, dutifully surrendered these records to their successors.[48] In Texas, the *cabildo* maintained a similar archive as required by royal legislation.[49] Having at his disposal both local government archives and pertinent legal texts, the governor would have had access not only to legislation pertaining to the Indies in a general sense, but also to local ordinances and customs, which he was to uphold and recognize.

Impartiality and disinterestedness are two desirable qualities in any judge. To nurture such qualities, the crown discouraged the entrenchment of its appointees into local society. Regulations against marriage to locals, for example, or against nepotism are just two of the ways in which the crown sought to curb overly cozy relations.[50] Special dispensations afforded a way to circumvent these prohibitions, however, and in areas where colonial life was good to the upper echelons, royal officials often found a comfortable position among the criollo elite.[51]

Because colonial documents generally ignore the personal affairs of colonial administrators, we know little of the families of the men who served as governors of New Mexico and Texas. Still, some general observations can be made. In the Bourbon period, the governors of Texas and New Mexico showed little inclination to marry into local families. In all probability, like don Diego de Vargas, they viewed their assignment on the frontier as a stepping stone in their careers of government service. Few of these men established close relations with the people under their jurisdiction. Among those governors who were married at the time of their appointments, most showed a disinclination to bring their families to the far north. Similarly, apart from the normal entourage that evidently accompanied every governor (but of which little is known), there is scant evidence that the governors of New Mexico and Texas filled local positions with relatives. Only during the regime of Governor Juan

Domingo Bustamante y Tagle (1722–31), who appointed his nephew or younger brother (the relationship is unclear) as lieutenant governor, do immediate family members appear as part of the local political regime.[52]

Family ties, then, played a minimal part in the direct administration of these frontier governors. Royal wishes against such local familiarity were fulfilled, probably not because of the laws themselves, but because of the social and economic circumstances of the periphery. With the frequent turnover in governors, the settlers had recourse to relatively disinterested justice at the highest provincial level.[53] Or, if the settlers found a particular governor to be ill-tempered and irrational, they might wait and hope for greater impartiality from a new governor.

Historians of colonial administration have paid considerable attention to the issue of sale of public office in Spanish America.[54] The general consensus is that the *venta de oficios* proved to be a shallow and ineffective solution for deeper fiscal problems and that the long-term effects proved detrimental to the crown's interests. Technically, offices that carried with them judicial responsibility were at no time saleable (*oficios vendibles*), but for all practical purposes, the custom affected even those positions. Under the legal fiction of the *beneficio* or *servicio*, an aspiring office seeker bypassed legal prohibitions and paid a fee to the crown for his title. As some Spanish legal historians have pointed out, contemporaries made an important distinction between the outright *venta de oficio*, which allowed the title holder to resell the office, and the *beneficio*, which did not.[55] The crown thus retained greater control over the office in question.

All the regularly appointed governors of New Mexico from 1700 to 1719 paid for their titles by way of donation.[56] After this date, probably because of Bourbon fiscal reform, New Mexico's governorship ceased to be a purchasable commodity.[57] In contrast, the governorship of Texas seems never to have been sold, although Tomás Cantelmi attempted to purchase the title in 1745. The crown returned his money when it was determined that the office was not for sale.[58] In sum, the officials who held the title of governor in both New Mexico and Texas were salaried officials who, except for the first two decades of the century, owed their titles not to purchase but to merit. By not having to pay the *servicio*, these individuals may have been less prone to make their appointments "pay" by taking advantage of the local populace or by skewing justice for self-serving purposes. This fact, coupled with limited family ties to frontier society, perhaps accounts for the relative disinterestedness of the provincial governors of Texas and New Mexico as agents of judicial administration.

Alcaldes Mayores and Alcaldes Ordinarios

'A host of lesser judicial officials operated under the provincial governor and clearly represented local interests. Sons of frontier society, steeped in its cultural milieu, they formed the backbone of the legal structure in the far north. Not one alcalde mayor or alcalde ordinario of New Mexico or Texas had any formal legal training and often their execution of legal matters failed to comply precisely with juridical norms. Yet their notions of justice and appreciation for the basic precepts of Spanish law allowed them to carry out something of the crown's vision for judicial administration and the maintenance of social harmony, and they participated willingly in the legal system.

Communities in the Indies quite often had a variety of local magistrates, including the alcalde ordinario, alcalde provincial (or de la Hermandad), alcalde de barrio, and juez de aguas.[59] In the far north, two officials of this sort played a significant role during the colonial period—the alcalde ordinario in Texas, and the alcalde mayor in New Mexico. With the establishment of the constitutional form of government in the second decade of the nineteenth century, alcaldes constitucionales appeared sporadically and exercised essentially the same judicial functions.

Subordinate to the governor, the alcalde mayor was the judicial official with whom frontiersmen in New Mexico had the most consistent dealings.[60] These officials should in no way be confused with their namesakes elsewhere in Spanish America. Normally, the alcalde mayor was a crown appointee, roughly the equivalent of the corregidor and governor.[61] The alcaldes mayores of New Mexico were appointees not directly of the crown, but of the provincial governor who had the authority to name as alcaldes mayores those persons whom he deemed most suitable and to replace those who failed to carry out their duties.[62] In turn, the alcaldes mayores appointed their own tenientes and assigned them to the principal settlements of their jurisdiction. Evidently, the appointments of alcaldes mayores and their *tenientes* did not require the approval of any superior body or official.[63] Those familiar with colonial Latin American history will do well to regard the New Mexico *alcaldes mayores* as *tenientes de alcaldes mayores* (although assistants of the *alcaldes mayores* in New Mexico also bore the title of *tenientes*). The office of *alcalde mayor* in New Mexico persisted after the Ordenanzas de Intendencias abolished them elsewhere in New Spain in 1786 because New Mexico fell outside of the intendancy system and, perhaps, because the local variation was not a true *alcaldía mayor*.

Invested with the accumulation of powers typical of the *antiguo régimen*, the *alcalde mayor* oversaw a diversity of affairs. Indeed, his full title—*alcalde mayor y capitán a guerra*—was more than honorific, and, as with the governor, indicates two distinct spheres of responsibilities. Except for the jurisdiction of Santa Fe, which had regular army units, the *alcalde mayor* headed the militia within his jurisdiction, and he directed the bulk of his military efforts toward campaigns against the *indios bárbaros*.[64] Besides military functions, the *alcalde mayor* also had administrative and police duties. In judicial matters, the *alcalde mayor* functioned—like the governor—as a *justicia* who had both judicial and executive powers, especially in enforcing the ordinances of "good government," and thus was more than a mere judge. On a lesser scale and in a reduced jurisdiction, then, the responsibilities of the *alcalde mayor y capitán a guerra* mirrored those of the *gobernador político y militar*.

For most of the eighteenth and nineteenth centuries the province of New Mexico consisted of eight *alcaldías mayores*, the territorial jurisdictions of the respective *alcaldes mayores*. No clear explanation has emerged to account for this specific number, although apparently it took root in the seventeenth century and became fixed in the administrative structure following Spanish recolonization of New Mexico in the 1690s.[65] Perhaps considerations of geography, as well as demography, account for the distances between seats of one *alcaldía* and another. To better facilitate royal justice (and to better administer a given area) the *alcalde* could be reached in at least a day's journey. An examination of the well-known 1779 map of Bernardo Miera y Pacheco reveals this tendency in shaping the administrative units of colonial New Mexico and underscores the importance of close supervision in Spain's approach to colonial rule. If the accessibility of magistrates was laudable, however, the formal expertise of these officials was less so.

The problem of inadequate instruction, or unfamiliarity with the law, did not confine itself to the northern borderlands of New Spain. Indeed, it was a common phenomenon throughout the empire. In the Indies, the peripheries commonly suffered a lack of legal personnel who, as Governor Fernando Chacón put it, could "properly pursue a criminal case."[66] In many respects the local magistrates in the far north faced the same obstacles as their peninsular counterparts. Writing in 1757, Valencian jurist José Berní y Catalá lamented,

> The confusion that some *alcaldes ordinarios* suffer has caused me pity, for despite their zeal, they know not what to do when administering the staff [of justice] that is conferred upon them for one year, . . . And since the *alcalde* and subjects usually are farmers, they fashion justice in their own manner, which hardly anyone can understand.[67]

More evidence of how local magistrates shaped local justice throughout the empire comes from another eighteenth-century *práctico*, Vicente Vizcaíno Pérez—"[they] had no more instruction than that of custom, of seeing how their predecessors had acted." Ignorant of the exact obligations of office, local *alcaldes*

> were directed by the *escribano* or some other who in the small villages tend to have the reputation of being intelligent, only because they are bolder or less coarse than the others. They did not know how to make any ruling whatsoever, though perhaps they have a doggedness to sustain their whims.[68]

Many writers—contemporary and modern—have shown more than a little contempt for the qualities of the *alcaldes mayores* of New Mexico. Particularly harsh were the clergy, most of whom appear to have had an axe to grind with civil officials. Bishop Pedro Tamarón y Romeral of Durango, for example, noted in his visitation of 1760 that the position of *alcalde mayor* was "a career aspired to by useless or ruined men." Similarly, Fray Juan Agustín Morfi spoke of these officials as being "unfortunates without education or breeding, mostly half-breeds with an occasional Spaniard."[69] Complaints of the *alcaldes'* abusive treatment of Indians were especially prominent.[70] Some late-colonial civil authorities likewise criticized the deficient qualities of the *alcaldes mayores*, though on technical grounds. Governor Joaquín del Real Alencaster—a contentious and disagreeable figure in his own right—wrote to the Audiencia of Guadalajara in 1806 that the *alcaldes mayores* of New Mexico were "absolutely lacking in [legal] principles and . . . are incapable of acting efficiently or according to the law."[71] Modern scholars have taken the cue.[72]

Yet one might question the accuracy of these contemporary assessments of the abilities and scruples of the *alcaldes mayores* in New Mexico. The second half of the eighteenth century was a period of general reform in the Spanish empire. In the contemporary spirit of reform, government officials emphasized deficiencies and trouble spots in colonial administration. The well-documented journey to the Indies of Jorge Juan y Santacilia and Antonio de Ulloa from 1735 to 1746 is only one example of Bourbon efforts to investigate and eradicate imperial corruption.[73] Closer to home, the military inspections of Pedro de Rivera (1724–28) and the Marqués de Rubí (1766–68) also embodied this same mood of reform. Despite their distance from the political center, New Mexico and Texas were not immune from close scrutiny. Furthermore, much of the criticism came not from civil officials but from the clergy, whose prestige and influence was under constant and systematic regalist attack during in the eighteenth century.[74] Rivalry and jealousy ring loud in their accusations. An added dimension of this controversy in New Mexico, as Richard Greenleaf has noted, lay in the squabble between the Franciscans and the secular clergy, who charged that the former had failed to do their spiritual jobs. Thus, Franciscan accusations against the *alcaldes mayores* seem designed to exculpate their own failure and cast the blame elsewhere.[75]

A closer look at the *alcaldes mayores* helps dispel some of the notoriety. Almost without exception, those who filled the position of *alcalde mayor* in New Mexico were prominent members of their communities, a tendency that squared with the juridical ideal of appointing the "better sorts" of society to the magistracy.[76] Morfi's list of villains among *alcaldes* reads like a *Who's Who* of colonial New Mexico—Clemente Gutiérrez, Francisco Trébol Navarro, Baltasar Baca, Pedro Pino, Manuel Vigil, Cristóbal Vigil, and José Miguel de la Peña.[77] Some of these individuals were indeed involved in questionable activities. But contrary to implication, they did not owe their wealth and status solely to their positions as *alcaldes mayores*. Instead they were entrusted with office precisely because of their abilities and social standing. Trébol Navarro, according to military sources, served admirably in a number of official endeavors—as an Indian campaigner, leader of the annual trade caravan to Chihuahua, interim governor of the province—and Commandant General Caballero de Croix praised him for his "integrity and honor."[78] Similarly, those who served as *alcaldes mayores* of Santa Fe performed competently in the relatively simple society in which they operated.

Consider the figure of Juan González Bas, *alcalde mayor* of the Albuquerque jurisdiction from 1712 to 1743. Born in pre–Revolt New Mexico, González Bas was among the contingent who returned to recolonize the province in 1692. Typifying the "half-breed" of Morfi's complaint, the Albuquerque *alcalde* was not pure Spanish, as his neighbor and nemesis Fernando Durán y Chaves reminded him in 1712, though the epithet "perro indio griego" that don Fernando had hurled at him was perhaps excessive.[79] González Bas did not deny the racial slur, and instead cited a lack of respect for royal authority in bringing charges against Durán y Chaves. Don Fernando's disapproval notwithstanding, González Bas figured prominently in local colonial society. Not only did he enjoy the position of *alcalde mayor* of Albuquerque, but he also was a member of the prestigious *cofradía* of La Conquistadora. Apparently others recognized his good standing also, for his children married well.[80]

Men of lesser ability occasionally held *alcaldías* in the outlying jurisdictions, but the *alcaldes mayores* of Santa Fe, the provincial capital, were men of distinguishable talent. A good example is Carlos Fernández. Born in 1700 at Villalcampo, province of Zamora, Spain, Fernández found his destiny in colonial New Mexico, marrying a Taos woman sometime before 1744. At Taos he became *alcalde mayor y capitán a guerra* under Governor Joaquín Codallos y Rabal. In 1757 he was named *teniente* of the presidial garrison of Santa Fe and later served as *alcalde mayor* of Santa Cruz de la Cañada from 1762 to 1763. In 1778 Fernández became *alcalde mayor* of Santa Fe.[81] Clearly, those who served as *alcalde mayor*, particularly in Santa Fe, were not the "unfortunates" that some have described.

But what training and preparation did these men have to adequately discharge their duties as *justicias*? When compared to the centers of empire, where functionaries of the legal system proliferated, the formal legal training of New Mexico officials was deficient. I have found not one instance of a civil official in New Mexico who studied law in a formal sense. Still, the legal culture in the northern borderlands surely must have possessed a deeper strength. Levels of wisdom and common sense no doubt varied among New Mexico's magistrates, but they were community leaders who had a vested interest in the well-being of the province, and who had shown an ability to make something of themselves. In this sense, their selection as *alcaldes* who commanded the respect and admiration of their neighbors represents a tacit recognition by the crown of local interest and input at the provincial level. Although outsiders denounced their ignorance, every *alcalde mayor* could read and write. The penmanship of these officials may have varied from poor to magnificent, but all were literate. Just how these individuals acquired their training in legal procedure remains unclear, although sifting the evidence reveals some clues.

As has been noted, the governors of the province had at their disposal a variety of legal texts. Particularly for Santa Fe, there is no reason to believe that a solicitous *alcalde* might not have used those same texts in deciding legal matters. General allusions by several *alcaldes* to "estas leyes de Indias," or "las leyes reales," or an occasional citation of a specific law indicate familiarity with such standard texts as the *Recopilación de Indias* or the *Nueva Recopilación*.[82] Moreover, as noted earlier, high-level officials routinely sent new decrees northward to the frontier. Since one of his duties was to publicize incoming legislation within his jurisdiction, the *alcalde* was surely abreast of the current laws and decrees.[83] Furthermore, the *alcalde* also would have been familiar with the various local *bandos de buen gobierno*, issued periodically by the governor.

Probably the most common method of transferring legal knowledge, however, must have been accomplished in an almost folkways method. Learning by doing was clearly a major ingredient in the preparation of these instruments of the royal judiciary. In fact, not only did New Mexico lack the institutions for imparting legal knowledge, but also there was a consistent lack of any kind of formal educational facility. That some native New Mexicans were literate attests to the strength of the family setting in passing on the rudiments of education.[84]

The person of Felipe Tafoya offers a marvelous example of this hands-on transmission of the Hispanic legal culture. Born in early-eighteenth-century New Mexico, Tafoya enjoyed the advantages that a good home education might provide in northern New Spain. Beginning in the 1730s, he appeared as a witness in attendance (*testigo de asistencia*) in a number of civil and criminal proceedings. As the years passed, he continued his legal apprenticeship as a notary (*notario*) in the ecclesiastical court of the province, assumed positions of responsibility in local government, and bolstered his social position as member of a prestigious religious confraternity.

The crown recognized his talents and achievements, and in the 1760s appointed him *alcalde mayor y capitán a guerra* of Santa Fe. There at the provincial capital, Tafoya also served as a self-styled legal representative (*procurador*) in a number of court cases, and Indians and Hispanics alike availed themselves of his expertise.[85] Such esteem on the part of the crown and the local population demonstrates, if not the brilliance, at least the competence of this man, sufficient to satisfy the requirements of judicial practice in colonial New Mexico. True to form, Tafoya's stepson, Felipe Sandoval, would go through the same informal learning process and become the provincial *protector de indios*, a crown-appointed official who represented Indians in formal litigation.[86] Through years of experience in provincial government and service in a variety of capacities, and through the informal transmission of legal knowledge, the literate elements of the region helped elaborate the judicial style that held sway in New Mexico.

No conclusive evidence has surfaced regarding the purchase of *alcaldías mayores* in New Mexico, but a few outsiders felt that this indeed was the case. Writing in 1760, Fray Juan Sanz de Lezaún declared that the office of *alcalde* went to "he who gives the most mules and sheep; this is so well known that not even the little children are unaware of it. What justice can these [men] give?"[87] If the *alcaldes mayores* bought their posts, they did so illegally, for no official record exists of their sale. In other areas of the northern frontier "contributions" for holding *tenencias* (the equivalent of an *alcaldía* in New Mexico) had been standard practice. According to a report that Governor Felipe Barri submitted in 1777, he received annual *beneficios* for various *alcaldías* and *tenencias* in Nueva Vizcaya, the amounts of which ranged from one hundred pesos for minor posts such as San Andrés de la Sierra or Cuencamé to seven hundred pesos for important jurisdictions like Parras and Saltillo.[88] In New Mexico purchases of such visibility were unknown.

While the *alcaldías mayores* appear not to have been purchasable, occasionally aspirants solicited the office. One instance of this occurred in 1774 when Eusebio Durán y Chaves sought the *alcaldía* between Santa Fe and Albuquerque that consisted of the Indian villages of Sandia, San Felipe, Santo Domingo, and Cochiti. Documents confirm that Durán y Chaves—member of a prominent New Mexico family—in fact completed the long trip to Spain where, as family tradition would have it, he secured a personal audience with King Charles III.[89] In his petition to the crown, don Eusebio recounted his alleged accomplishments, as well as those of his father and grandfather, in the pacification and ongoing Indian wars of the province. In recognition of his service, the supplicant asked that he be granted for life the *alcaldía* of "the four conquered pueblos" of Sandia, San Felipe, Santo Domingo, and Cochiti. For his sons, Juan Blas and Juan Miguel, the father requested lifetime *alcaldías* for the villages of Jemez, Zia, and Santa Ana, and Laguna, Acoma, and Zuni, respectively.[90]

Impressed with the claim of "twenty-six years in campaigns of conquests of Indians," the crown directed the viceroy of New Spain to find for Durán y Chaves a position appropriate to his merits, an apparent approval of the petition.[91] Don Eusebio returned to New Spain, penniless, but with the crown's financial support of over 350 pesos for his journey from Veracruz to Albuquerque. More to the point, Durán y Chaves arrived in New Mexico with a letter that instructed the governor to place him in a suitable office.[92] So far, things had gone well for the aspiring *alcalde mayor*. Back home, however, his luck ran out. "At present all the *alcaldías mayores* of this province," wrote Governor Pedro Fermín de Mendinueta, "are continually besieged by [Indian] enemies, and therefore [the *alcaldías*] demand subjects of sufficient action and valor to maintain and defend their respective districts and villages." Mendinueta made it clear that don Eusebio absolutely lacked these vital qualities. Furthermore, the governor noted, local informants had described Durán y Chaves as "a continual fugitive in this country, because of his debts."[93] As a result of his poor local reputation and the governor's opposition, Eusebio Durán y Chaves never served as an *alcalde mayor* in New Mexico.

Eusebio Durán y Chaves's ambition to secure an *alcaldía* makes a romantic episode, but the paucity of such petitions indicates that this practice was not widespread. In the two extant examples from the nineteenth century, both petitioners were denied their request for office.[94] As Governor Joaquín del Real Alencaster replied tersely to one such request, "those who should serve as *alcaldes* are sought by him who appoints them."[95] Clearly, the choice was still up to the provincial governor.

Unlike their immediate superiors, the *alcaldes mayores* did not receive a salary. In judicial matters, they operated on the fee system, which, under the circumstances, proved to be a suitable alternative to a fixed salary. Like nearly every magistrate in the Spanish empire, the *alcaldes* were to collect their fees according to officially approved schedules known as *aranceles*.[96] It cannot be said for certain whether royal officials in New Mexico adhered closely to these *aranceles*. Apparently, provincial officials received occasional notification reminding them of judicial fee schedules.[97] Shortly after the recolonization of New Mexico, at least, adherence to some sort of *arancel* (revealed in the assessment of court costs—the *tasación*) is evident.[98] Yet, if at times they followed a schedule, in other instances the governor seems to have assigned fees at his discretion.[99]

A prime example of the *arancel* is found in a case brought by Isabel Medina against her husband, Bartolo (or Bartolomé) Garduño, for criminal assault. In carrying out the preliminary investigation, Alcalde Mayor Francisco Guerrero prepared the following list of fees that had been collected.

Adjustment of the legal costs of the proceedings according to the judicial *arancel*.

For the claim and complaint of the woman . . . 1 peso
For the declaration of the same . . . . 2 pesos
For that of the defendant . . . . 1 peso 4   reales
For the ratification of his wife . . . . 1 peso
For the confession of the defendant . . . . 2 pesos
For the *careo* between the two . . . . 2 pesos
For the declaration of Aliri . . . . 1 peso
For that of the Indian woman . . . . 1 peso
For the ratification of Aliri . . . . 1 peso
For the declaration of the Gutiérrez woman . . 1 peso
For the ratification of the same . . . . 1 peso
For the declaration of Unanue . . . . 1 peso
For the decree of remission . . . . 2 pesos
For twelve sheets of paper . . . . 0 pesos 7 reales

————————————
18 pesos 3 r.s[100]

The fee system proved to be particularly well suited to the sparsely settled peripheries of empire. Unlike more populated areas, where the numbers of fee-collecting functionaries seemed endless and resource-draining, the northern borderlands (and most of New Spain) differed markedly. Here, lacking the full array of functionaries, only a handful of officials collected fees for legal services, surely a blessing in such a poor region. Furthermore, by employing the fee system instead of a system of salaried officials, crown and locals alike avoided the expense of maintaining full-time officials for the part-time administration of justice.

The income derived from judicial fees, particularly in the outlying areas, was insufficient to support an *alcalde* and his family. The *alcalde* of Jemez, for example, complained in 1808 that his relatively sparse jurisdiction rendered "absolutely nothing in the way of judicial fees, not even six pesos a year."[101] On the other hand, except perhaps in Santa Fe, judicial business was not abundant enough to warrant a full-time salaried official. Therefore, the *alcaldes mayores* of New Mexico, who tended to be men of substance—often the leading landowners, stockraisers, or merchants—did not abandon these endeavors when they assumed their judicial offices. They did not depend upon judicial fees alone to maintain themselves and their families.

While the fee system may not have provided adequate remuneration for an *alcalde mayor* in New Mexico, he often managed to supplement his income from other government sources. As a *capitán a guerra*, a concurrent position, the *alcalde* probably received some amount from the crown for his military duties. In the diary of his 1729 inspection of the province, for instance, Brigadier Pedro de Rivera noted that "the *alcaldes mayores* that are appointed [in New Mexico] enjoyed the privilege of '*reformados*' by virtue of the salary with which the king maintained them."[102] And, he added sardonically, the locals "enjoyed the salaries of presidial troops, with titles of *alcaldes mayores, alféreces reales,* adjutants, field captains, and '*reformados,*' while serving no purpose."[103] The practice of bestowing *alcaldías* upon persons holding military titles continued even after the considerable reforms of the late eighteenth century. Carlos Fernández, a peninsular who served as *alcalde mayor* of Santa Cruz from 1762 to 1763, held at the same time the title of *teniente* of the garrison at Santa Fe. During the late 1780s, he became *alcalde mayor* of Santa Fe, while at the same time he received the title of *primer soldado distinguido* of the presidial company at the capital.[104]

In spite of the scanty emoluments, the position no doubt carried considerable prestige and clout among the local population. Surely some abused their office for economic advantage, but probably not to the extent pictured by church officials. Significantly, many of the complaints aired by non-clerics appear in legal proceedings against corrupt or negligent *alcaldes*. The provincial governor often punished a wayward *alcalde* in some way, ranging from a written reprimand to deprivation of office.[105] Despite occasional abuses, most *alcaldes mayores* seem to have carried out their duties in a rational and equitable fashion. Instead of the prevailing image of corruption and bizarre legal procedure that has been proffered as the norm, a different picture emerges.

Alcaldes mayores do not appear to have occupied their posts for life, as some have claimed.[106] Entrenchment in office was the exception and took place usually in areas of marginal Spanish settlement such as the alcaldía of Laguna. Other jurisdictions, especially the capital, saw a regular turnover of personnel.[107] Similarly, the administration of justice was not as arbitrary and capricious as convention dictates. True, the range of expertise varied greatly, and many of the procedural formalities were wanting, but the written record shows that *alcaldes* normally dispensed justice according to basic precepts of Spanish law. The *alcalde mayor* in New Mexico may have sprung from a simple society, but he was often a perceptive and astute observer of human behavior. Indeed, some of the extant criminal investigations demonstrate considerable skill in uncovering the pertinent evidence in order to render a just decision.

Assisting the *alcaldes mayores* were their lieutenants. Generally speaking, the responsibilities of the *tenientes de alcalde mayor* were fewer than those of their immediate superiors. Their principal duty was to ensure that harmonious relationships prevailed within the community. They intervened in verbal disputes, served legal instruments of the court such as writs and warrants, and helped the *alcalde mayor* in the general discharge of his duties, whether judicial, police, or military.[108] Appointees of the *alcaldes mayores*, the *tenientes* normally resided in the largest settlement within a subdivision of the *alcaldía*, but they may have exercised authority not only in their subdivision but throughout the entire *alcaldía* as well.[109]

In general the level of competence of the *teniente* was inferior to that of the *alcalde mayor*. At least one *teniente*, Diego Romero of Taos, could not sign his name, though this appears to be quite exceptional.[110] On the other hand, several individuals who later achieved prominence in provincial affairs began their public careers as *tenientes de alcaldes mayores*. Inconsistent—rather than uniformly incompetent—perhaps best characterizes the abilities of the *tenientes de alcaldes mayores* as a group.

Unlike the *alcalde mayor*, the *alcalde ordinario* was not a crown appointee, though he, too, administered royal justice. Instead, this official came from the ranks of the municipal corporation, or *cabildo*. Because of this appointment, the *alcalde ordinario* represented perhaps a somewhat greater degree of local interest than the *alcalde mayor*. As a judicial figure, the *alcalde ordinario* played a more prominent role in the history of colonial Texas than in New Mexico.

To more fully appreciate the source of the *alcalde*'s authority, some mention should be made of the structure, composition, and powers of the *cabildo*.[111] Firmly rooted in medieval peninsular practice, the *cabildo* quickly became a feature of municipal life in the colonies. The most vigorous periods of *cabildo* activity in New Spain were the sixteenth century and, later, the period just before Mexican independence. In much of New Spain, routine sale of *cabildo* offices, greater crown control, and relative local inertia characterized these middle years. Still, some *cabildos* remained vibrant focal points that represented local interest. Such was the case in San Antonio, where those who sat on the council exerted considerable influence on community affairs.

The somewhat curious and frequently mistranslated formula "cabildo, justicia, y regimiento" aptly conveys the diverse attributes of this local institution.[112] *Cabildo*, derived from the Latin *capitulum*, refers to its preeminence in the municipality; *justicia* denotes its authority in judicial matters; and *regimiento*, from *regir*, indicates its ruling powers within the municipality.[113] These powers included the right to partition municipal lands, fix prices of basic commodities, maintain public tranquillity, and make and enforce local ordinances of public order, or "good government." This important local source of *derecho indiano* gave legitimate expression to the peculiarities and customs of each municipality within the larger political and legal framework. In a very real sense the *regidores* and their judicial agents, the *alcaldes ordinarios*, created much of the legislation that affected the daily lives of the local population.[114] In its capacity to pass local ordinances of "good government," the activity of the *cabildo* represented an important autochthonous source of *derecho indiano*.[115]

The number of *cabildo* officials varied relative to the size and importance of the municipality. In the eighteenth century, viceregal capitals such as Lima or Mexico City had as many as twelve *regidores* and two *alcaldes ordinarios*. Smaller municipalities had only six.[116] All officeholders of the *cabildo* had to be *vecinos* of the municipality, which according to the Ordinances of 1573, was "understood to be the son or daughter of the settler of a new town or his relatives within or without the fourth degree, who have distinct and separate houses and families."[117] Like many in New Spain, New Mexicans and Texans used loosely the term *vecino* to mean nearly any resident of a particular locale.[118]

The *cabildos* that existed in New Mexico and Texas can best be described as anomalies. In the case of New Mexico, the municipal corporation ceased to exist by the end of the second decade of the eighteenth century and only reappeared in the next century as a result of political changes common in the empire. In addition to its brief existence in post–Revolt New Mexico, the Santa Fe cabildo differed from more vibrant corporations in other ways. Conspicuously absent was any significant activity in vital concerns such as granting lands, awarding contracts for provisioning basic foodstuffs, and elaborating town ordinances.[119] Perhaps because of the Santa Fe cabildo's vituperative disagreements with a succession of provincial governors, the crown allowed it to pass out of existence.[120] After its demise, the *alcalde mayor* assumed the judicial and police powers of the *cabildo*. Although the office of *alcalde ordinario* (traditionally associated with the *cabildo*) reappeared in 1803, there is no hard evidence that a municipal council also was resuscitated from its century-long slumber. The political changes wrought by the Cortes of Cádiz signaled the return of municipal government in New Mexico in 1814, when not only Santa Fe, but also Albuquerque, Belen, Bernalillo, El Paso, and Santa Cruz de la Cañada created their respective *ayuntamientos*.[121] In adhering to the Constitution of 1812, the *ayuntamientos* assumed responsibility for many local affairs, including the administration of justice. This resurgence was short-lived, however, because of Fernando VII's nullification of the constitutional system following his return to the throne in 1814.

In contrast to New Mexico, the *cabildo* in Texas played a continuous and prominent role in the history of municipal rule, from its formation on 1 August 1731, to Mexican independence in 1821 and beyond.[122] The municipal corporation in San Antonio, for example, played an active part in the crucial distribution of land and water within its jurisdiction. A radius of five leagues typified the territorial extent of municipal jurisdiction, but the establishment of San Fernando in the immediate vicinity of pre-existing civil and mission communities led to several bitter disputes over the extent of the *cabildo*'s authority. While the presence of a presidio and several missions perhaps served to curb its authority, the *cabildo* figured as a vibrant force in the San Antonio community.

The *cabildo* in Texas also assumed a more active role than its New Mexico counterpart in shaping and enforcing local ordinances of public order and in providing justice.[123] The makeup, too, differed. The first officeholders were part of a wave of Canary Islanders who emigrated to various parts of the Americas, including Texas, in the eighteenth century. Insisting upon their newly gained privileges as *hidalgos* (a rank of lower nobility), the *isleños* successfully monopolized several *cabildos* in the New World, including the one at San Antonio.[124] Despite having mingled with others in the community and assuming a *tejano* identity by the end of the eighteenth century, descendants of Canary Islanders maintained a prominent position in all aspects of San Antonio life, including the *cabildo*.[125]

If the story of San Antonio's *cabildo* is well documented, little is known of the workings of the *cabildo* in Santa Fe. It probably functioned in similar fashion to its seventeenth-century counterpart.[126] Like the individuals who comprised it, the cabildo of Santa Fe survived the Pueblo Revolt of 1680 and resumed its activity in exile at El Paso del Norte. What the composition of the *cabildo* was when it returned to Santa Fe with Diego de Vargas in the 1690s is unclear, but in 1716 the following individuals held office: *alcalde ordinario de primer voto*, Juan García de las Rivas; *alcalde ordinario de segundo voto*, Juan de Archibeque (a nationalized Frenchman); *procurador*, Francisco Casados; *escribano*, Juan Manuel Chirinos.[127] From all indications, this corporation had fewer functionaries than the *Recopilación de Indias* allowed for a *villa* of its importance.[128]

Better documentation exists for the establishment and initial elections of functionaries of the San Antonio *cabildo*. The first *cabildo* of San Fernando, comprised entirely of *isleños*, had a legal right to establish this municipal corporation by virtue of their contract for colonization. As allowed by royal law, it consisted of six *regidores*, two of whom also served as *alcaldes ordinarios*, one *escribano de consejo y público*, one *mayordomo*, and one *alguacil mayor*.[129] Not surprisingly, the *cabildo* at San Antonio was pared to the essentials and did not boast the diversity and numbers of functionaries associated with *cabildos* in the larger colonial cities.

The officials directly responsible for the administration of justice were the two *alcaldes ordinarios* of the *cabildo*. Elsewhere, the *cabildo* appointed individuals who were not already members, but in New Mexico and in Texas the *alcaldes ordinarios* came from within the ranks of the municipal corporation itself. The *cabildo* selected both judicial officials, probably not by secret ballot but by general consensus of the *regidores*.[130] The proceedings from the Santa Fe *cabildo* elections of 1 January 1713, shed some light on the election process. Assembled at the *ayuntamiento* building, "the *cabildo, justicia*, and *regimiento*" offered as candidates—due to their "many merits"— General Juan Páez Hurtado for *alcalde de primer voto* and Captain Juan García Jurado for *alcalde de segundo voto*. The corporation then implored Governor Juan Ignacio Flores Mogollón, "as its president, to be kind enough to confirm this new election so that they might receive the staffs [of justice] and take the accustomed oath and begin their duties."[131] Elections of *alcaldes* in San Antonio are similar.[132]

These documents reveal several significant points concerning the nature of these frontier *cabildos*. First, consensus rather than secret ballot seems to have been the key determinant in the selection process. Second, the potential veto power of the provincial governor, as president of the *cabildo*, is quite apparent. Indeed, the governors of Texas intervened in several *cabildo* elections in the late eighteenth century.[133]

Like the *alcaldes mayores*, the *alcaldes ordinarios* were men of stature within the community, but they, too, lacked any formal legal training. In 1716, for example, the two elected *alcaldes* of Santa Fe were probably unusually qualified, given the setting. Both Juan Páez Hurtado and Juan García de las Rivas possessed considerable experience in the administration of frontier government. Páez Hurtado, for example, played a key role in the reconquest and recolonization of New Mexico following the Pueblo Revolt. Serving in a variety of offices—*sargento mayor, alcalde mayor*, lieutenant governor, interim governor—Páez Hurtado represents as well as anyone the second tier of colonial officials who, in large measure, ensured the administrative continuity from one gubernatorial regime to the next. Here was an individual cognizant of the formalities required of government documents. The case of Juan García de las Rivas is similar. Although not as prominent as Páez, García nevertheless was fully acquainted with notarial procedure, which implied some degree of legal knowledge, having served in a variety of official capacities.[134] Other turn-of-the-century *alcaldes ordinarios* in New Mexico had similar backgrounds. Those who carried the *vara de justicia* as *alcaldes ordinarios* in early-eighteenth-century New Mexico knew well the rudiments of the Spanish legal system.

The situation differed somewhat in Texas. If the qualifications of the first two *alcaldes ordinarios* of San Fernando are any indication, Texas suffered more than New Mexico from unfamiliarity with legal procedure. Little is known of the personal circumstances of the *isleños* before they arrived in the New World. It seems clear, however, that they came from the lower strata of Canary Island society and were natives of the island of Lanzarote, the poorest of the archipelago. It is doubtful that they left their homes because life had been good. Juan Leal Goraz, *alcalde ordinario de primer voto* and patriarch of the immigrant *isleños,* could sign his name, but *alcalde de segundo voto*, Salvador Rodríguez, could not.[135] His illiteracy reveals a notable lack of preparation for office, one that violated royal law.[136]

As a matter of policy the crown intended for the members of the municipal *cabildo* to be of the upper classes. This was undoubtedly the case in the large centers of New Spain, as Reinhard Liehr has shown for Puebla, and it was true of the *cabildo* members of Texas as well.[137] Their positions as leading *vecinos*, however, stemmed from their having been granted titles of *hidalguía* upon immigration, rather than from having accrued a noticeable economic advantage. Especially before the last quarter of the eighteenth century, the economy of Texas was simply insufficient for any group to acquire great wealth. In contrast to Mexico City, where wealth meant access to the elite, *isleño* ancestry was often crucial in gaining a share of the scarce resources and, thus, achieving prominence in colonial Texas.[138] The "upper classes" of the northern borderlands shared with their neighbors the economic rigors of frontier life in a way unknown to the elites of the great cities.

While juridical preparation of the *alcaldes ordinarios* appears to have been better in New Mexico than in Texas, neither province boasted local officials who could be considered well-educated by colonial standards. Since none had any formal instruction, these men learned through "hands-on" practice. Like their counterparts, the *alcaldes mayores*, they learned by doing. Initially, the *alcaldes ordinarios* of Texas were at a distinct disadvantage in this respect. Not only had they no formal training, but they also lacked practical experience in government administration. Indeed, the first members of the San Fernando *cabildo* all listed their occupations as farmers. Over time, and as their seemingly endless litigations continued, the *alcaldes* of the *cabildos* no doubt acquired some degree of expertise in proper procedural techniques.

Besides practical experience, the *alcaldes ordinarios* of Texas and New Mexico had access to written legislation of various types. For example, a copy of the *Recopilación de Indias* existed from at least mid-century at the *casas reales*, as stipulated in that compilation.[139] Depending on their relationship with a particular governor, they may have had at their disposal this and other legal works of a didactic nature described above. A far more important source of legal knowledge, however, must have been the numerous dispatches of pertinent laws and decrees that found their way to the far north. Routinely, many of these documents were made known to the inhabitants of the province. Similarly, *bandos* issued by the provincial governor constituted yet another source for informal legal education.

As established in the *Recopilación de Indias*, *alcaldes ordinarios* served as judges of first instance for all civil and criminal cases in their jurisdictions except those involving Indians, which were the domain of the provincial governor.[140] Both New Mexico and Texas adhered to prescription in this respect.[141] Appeals of the *alcalde*'s decisions went to the provincial governor and, as noted earlier, from there to either of the two *audiencias*.[142] In areas where there existed no *alcalde de la Hermandad* (essentially, a rural police force with judicial powers), the *alcaldes ordinarios* were to assume their judicial authority.[143] The Santa Hermandad never existed in these two northern provinces, but neither did the *alcaldes ordinarios* assume their functions.[144] In New Mexico, it was the *alcalde mayor* who investigated and heard cases involving crimes committed in the rural areas of his jurisdiction and, in Texas, the governor or his subordinates did so.

In addition to the more or less permanent magistrates, the provinces of New Mexico and Texas also relied on individuals appointed for specific cases. Known variously as *juez comisionado, juez delegado*, or *juez receptor*, these temporary appointees of the governor acted when one of the ordinary magistrates was incapable of doing so. A *juez comisionado* might be named by a governor, if he were busy with other duties, to rectify an ill-formed indictment (*sumaria*), or less frequently, because a magistrate of a particular jurisdiction was involved as a party in the legal proceedings.[145]

In the first half of the eighteenth century, those designated as *juez comisionado* tended to be either *alcaldes ordinarios* or *mayores* who merely acted on appointment outside of their normal territorial jurisdictions. Less frequently, the lieutenant governor served as a delegate magistrate.[146] Because of the growing prestige of the professional army in the latter years of Spanish rule, however, military officers often served as *jueces comisionados* during this period.[147]

Whatever the circumstances of the *juez comisionado*'s appointment, the governor required a competent official. Significantly, in these instances, the delegate judge often was the *alcalde mayor* of Santa Fe, an official who normally had considerable experience with legal procedure and one who usually worked closely with the governor. In either case, be it an outside *justicia* or a competent military officer, the abilities of the *juez comisionado* probably compared slightly favorably with his regularly appointed counterpart.

Local settlers, then, figured prominently in the makeup of the provincial magistracy, and they partook actively in the administration of justice. Their appreciation for the distinct social and economic settings of their particular regions made them valuable assets to the crown.

Legal Professionals

Unlike the great administrative centers and a few scattered outlying provinces, New Mexico and Texas featured no true professional class that made a living solely from practicing law.[148] Nevertheless, a few individuals in these provinces attained a rudimentary expertise in legal matters from which they drew some sort of income. Their frequent appearance in the colonial documents suggests that locals called with regularity upon their skills to aid them in legal matters.

As an informal *escribano* skilled at drawing up legal documents, Pedro José Tejada plied his trade in San Antonio during the 1770s and 1780s. In January 1778, for example, he complained to the governor that the *cabildo* of San Antonio had failed to remunerate him for writing a petition on their behalf, a sum of seven pesos, one real. The *cabildo* eventually paid up, but only after Commandant General Croix ordered them to do so.[149] This squabble did not produce a long-lasting enmity, for in 1783 Tejada again acted in the service of the *cabildo,* this time as an *escribano* for the court of *regidor* and *alcalde de primer voto,* Fernando de Beramendi.[150] A number of private parties, too, sought Tejada's expertise in articulating their legal concerns. In a dispute over an inheritance, for example, Pedro José Tejada wrote a petition "at the request of" Antonia Rosalía de Armas, who believed she had gotten less than her fair share.[151]

Another figure who evidently offered his expertise to others in San Antonio was a retired militia captain and former lieutenant governor of East Texas, Antonio Gil Ybarbo. This individual owned several important and useful legal texts, including the practical legal manuals acquired from Governor Manuel Muñoz's estate, Pedro Melgarejo's *Compendio de los Contratos Públicos* (1652), *Praxis Ecclesiasticae et Saecularis* (1609) by Gonzalo Suárez de Paz, and a copy of the *Recopilación de Indias.* Locals availed themselves of Gil Ybarbo's knowledge of the law and sought his assistance in drawing up legal documents.[152]

New Mexico, too, had its legal "professionals." Early in his career, Felipe Tafoya served as a *notario nombrado* in the ecclesiastical court of Vicario Santiago de Roybal.[153] As early as 1749, and on numerous occasions thereafter, Felipe Tafoya appears in court documents as *"procurador,"* a designation that suggests he acted on behalf of others in legal proceedings.[154] In 1767, for example, he served as the *procurador* for the settlers of Sabinal in their legal tiff with their neighbors at Belen, and in 1763 he represented the natives of San Ildefonso Pueblo in their conflict with Hispanic *vecinos* over land.[155]

Others besides Tafoya also boasted the title of *procurador,* further evidence that a cadre of frontier settlers derived some income from legal activities. For example, Ramón García Jurado, who styled himself *"procurador* of this *villa* of Albuquerque," represented José Mariano Yturrieta (acting on behalf of his sister, Eduarda Yturrieta) in a dispute over the payment of a dowry.[156] Another active figure in the Río Abajo area at mid-century was Isidro Sánchez of Fuenclara, who seems to have been adequately versed in legal formulae. Sánchez aided the *alcalde mayor* of Albuquerque, José Baca, who in 1744 referred to him as "my *escribano.*"[157] Hoping to capitalize on his legal expertise, Sánchez also solicited business from among his neighbors, much to the annoyance of Governor Joaquín Codallos y Rabal. The governor judged the entrepreneur to be "a scheming, restless man," who fomented litigation among "a few poor *vecinos*, . . . writing and cooperating in their petitions for the earnings that they bring." So that the "poor might not suffer any setbacks in their meager incomes," Codallos y Rabal ordered Isidro Sánchez to cease this activity, under pain of a fifty-peso fine and fifteen days in stocks for the first infraction, and banishment from New Mexico for the second offense.[158] The stern warning aside, Sánchez seems to have continued to service his clientele, though without signing his name on any documents.[159]

Another font of judicial knowledge in New Mexico was the ecclesiastical court of the province. Felipe Tafoya, it has been noted, served as notary of that court in the mid eighteenth century. In the early nineteenth century, others also served as "*notario público*" for the ecclesiastical court, apparently in conjunction with their positions as *cantor* in local churches. Some, like José de la Peña from Mexico City and Antonio Estanislao Ruiz, were outsiders. These men evidently were not involved with any civil jurisdiction, but their participation in legal affairs underscores the vitality of a local legal culture that received constant infusions from the larger Hispanic world.[160]

A review of the local structure of the Spanish colonial judiciary in New Mexico and Texas perhaps best reveals the nature of the legal culture in northern New Spain. In these peripheral areas of empire, there were no hosts of trained functionaries who seemed to plague the larger cities. This lack of legal machinery underscores a problem in the colonial regime—the crown simply could not staff in all geographic areas the full array of officials that some jurists might have desired. Given the relative poverty of these two regions, however, the fee system, which supported the colonial judiciary, worked well. Residents paid only for the judiciary when they needed it.

Too much has been made of the corruption of local *alcaldes* in New Mexico and Texas. To be sure, some of these agents of the royal judiciary behaved improperly on occasion, but generally they were respectable elements of a rude frontier society who were literate and, as we shall see, acted responsibly. Legal training, woefully inadequate on the frontier, was at best a "hands-on" experience with little or no supervision from experts. None of the magistrates who served in colonial Texas and New Mexico—governors, *alcaldes mayores, alcaldes ordinarios*, and their assistants—were well-trained *jueces de letras* or *jueces togados*; rather, they were *justicias* or *jueces legos* who lacked formal instruction in law. The informality and great variety in the legal training of the judiciary in the vast peripheries must certainly be one of the hallmarks of the Spanish colonial system. Yet, while legal expertise may have been desirable, it was not absolutely indispensable. With all its faults, the local magistracy served crown and community as mediators of social conflict.

PART THREE

Judicial Procedure

❖ ❖ 5 ❖ ❖

The *Sumaria*

In 1787, an exasperated Commandant General Jacobo Ugarte y Loyola enumerated the many difficulties of local judicial administration
in the far north of New Spain.

> The lack of training of subordinate judges, of *letrados* to advise
> them, of *escribanos* to form judicial proceedings, of jails to secure
> delinquents, of funds to provide for their maintenance while their
> cases are being heard, and the cost of shackles, paper, post, and
> other necessities were not obstacles easy to overcome. These are
> the same that continue to exist and stand in the way not only of
> proper administration of justice, but also the execution of any
> political order that one might contemplate.[1]

Top-level administrators frequently voiced their dissatisfaction
with the judicial system in the northern borderlands. Formally
trained *letrados* who served as *asesores* or *fiscales* of the *audiencias*
pointed out in their *dictámenes* the ways in which provincial functionaries erred in technical aspects of legal procedure. At times this
criticism bordered on officiousness, though more serious faults—
inadequate defense or insufficient proof to sustain a guilty verdict—also came to light.[2] Yet, for all its deficiencies, the system
functioned reasonably well, and it provided the means for Spanish
subjects in the far north to settle differences in an organized and
rational way.

Presented in the next two chapters is a composite of the procedural elements normally found in criminal and civil cases adjudicated in New Mexico and Texas—the *sumaria*, the *juicio plenario*,
and the *sentencia*. Not all steps appear in every case, nor was the
prescribed order of procedure adhered to strictly in most cases.
Furthermore, differences in the abilities, education, and wisdom of

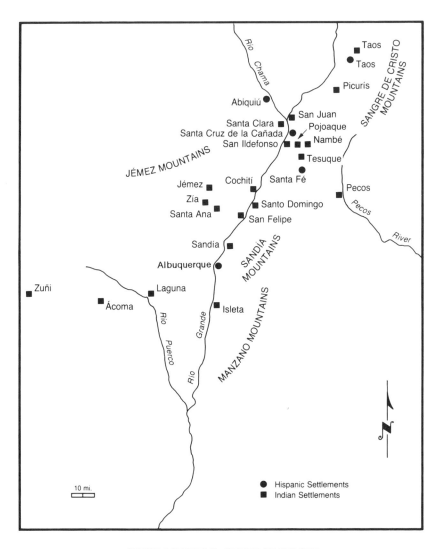

NEW MEXICO SETTLEMENTS
IN THE LATE COLONIAL PERIOD

numerous magistrates, as well as variations in specific local circumstances, perhaps accentuate the wide range of judicial styles found in the historical record. Although apparently symptomatic of maladministration, this diversity of procedural form characterized the Spanish legal culture under the *antiguo régimen.*

While variety characterizes its actual implementation, the prescribed elements of legal procedure remained substantially the same throughout the colonial period. Castilian legal procedure rested upon the foundations of the thirteenth-century *Siete Partidas* of Alfonso X and had been elaborated by a juridical community steeped in the *ius commune* tradition, the product of both Roman and canon law. Transplanted to the New World, the procedural rules in the Indies as applied in the high tribunals conformed to those found on the peninsula.[3] Even with the dynastic change in the eighteenth century, little altered. Indeed, the Bourbon regime had a greater effect upon legal practice in Spain itself, where, as a result of the Philip V's *Decretos de Nueva Planta,* some regional distinctiveness succumbed to an imposed Castilian uniformity in judicial administration.[4] As part of the patrimony of Castile, the Indies adhered where possible to Castilian models; thus, judicial administration in the New World suffered no great upheaval with the advent of the Bourbon regime.

From its medieval beginnings, Castilian penal law had experienced two important changes by the mid sixteenth century. The first of these was the shift from accusative to inquisitive modes of procedure. Under accusative procedure (found in the *Siete Partidas* and in English law) an aggrieved party denounced a specific criminal activity and brought charges against the alleged perpetrator, who, in turn, responded immediately to the accusation.[5] The magistrate acted as an impartial judge in the proceedings, having no particular stake in the outcome of the trial. During the fifteenth and sixteenth centuries, the accusative form gave way to another method. The steady growth of royal authority in the administration of justice and in policing the realm brought a greater degree of government activism to criminal prosecution.

The crown now encouraged its magistrates not only to judge cases but also to look after the public well-being. As monitors of the community, the judiciary investigated and prosecuted any illegal activity within their jurisdictions.[6] Maintenance of public order— rather than simple adjudication—became a prime function of the

L A S   S I E T E

PARTIDAS DEL SABIO REY

don Alonfo el nono , nueuamente Glofadas por el Licenciado Gregorio Lopez del Confejo Real de
Indias de fu Mageftad.

Impreffo en Salamanca Por Andrea de Portonaris, Impreffor de fu Mageftad.

Año. M. D. L. V.

Con priuilegio Imperial.

¶ Efta taffado el pliego a cinco marauedis ,

Figure 4. Title page of *Las Siete Partidas*, glossed by romanist Gregorio López, who served on the Council of the Indies. Steeped in the *ius commune* tradition, the *Siete Partidas* provided the foundations for judicial procedure under Spanish law.

local magistracy, a political innovation that altered the nature of criminal procedure. Instead of an impartial judge, the magistrate emerged as an active participant in the prevention and prosecution of crime. In short, he became the accusing party, the court investigator, and the judge.

The effect of royal activism upon criminal judicial procedure carried with it enormous consequences. As outlined in the *Siete Partidas*, criminal procedure consisted only of the *plenario* and the *sentencia*, but by the mid sixteenth century, criminal procedure commonly featured a preliminary third phase—the *sumaria*. So important did this investigative phase become that it eventually overshadowed other portions of the procedural routine. Indeed, the *sumaria* imbued criminal procedure with decidedly inquisitorial attributes.[7] The *inquisitio* placed the accused at a distinct disadvantage because he or she was not informed of the charges, nor was it possible to respond to them until after this initial phase. Thus, the *sumaria* loomed large in criminal procedure because of the weight accorded to it in subsequent portions of the trial.

A second important innovation in criminal procedure was that of simplification. While the addition of the *sumaria* had greatly changed the nature of judicial proceedings, the remaining two phases—the *plenario* and the *sentencia*—still followed the rather long, drawn-out *proceso ordinario* found in the *Partidas*. In reaction to the sluggishness of the *proceso ordinario*, judicial figures elaborated swifter, simplified forms of procedure during the early modern period. Especially important were the magistrates of the king's court (*alcaldes de casa y corte*) who took the lead in this development. With tacit approval of the crown, the so-called *estilo judicial* of the royal tribunals became recognized as a legitimate mode of procedure. The crown favored this procedural streamlining, not only because it proved expeditious, but also because it reenforced the power of the state, usually at the expense of the defendant. By the eighteenth century, this new *estilo* of the tribunals had overshadowed the older *proceso ordinario* as the favored—and, of course, legitimate—procedural method as practiced in the higher tribunals (the *chancillerías* and *salas de casa y corte*) of Castile.[8]

Simplification appeared not only in the *estilo* of the high tribunals, but more important, also in the forms of the *juicio extraordinario* or *juicio sumario*. Drawing inspiration from the papal dictum "Saepe contingit" of Clement V (1306), which sought to regularize and simplify canon law procedure, the Cortes of Alcalá of 1348 gave legal sanction to judicial simplification in Castilian tribunals.[9] Legal professionals seem never to have been comfortable with this precept—certainly at odds with the elitism implicit in their profession—which may explain their tendency to carp on judicial administration in the provinces. If not always enthusiastic, however, jurists did agree that the *juicio sumario* dispensed with the long, drawn-out formalities of the *proceso ordinario*. A practical-minded jurist of the early nineteenth century, Juan Sala, summed up the essential qualities of simplified form. "The judge," Sala wrote of the *juicio extraordinario*, "hears [the case] briefly and summarily, rejecting the prolonged solemnities of the law, and attending only to the truth."[10] This definition describes particularly well judicial practice in Texas and New Mexico, where the "solemnities" of the *juicio ordinario* were conspicuously absent. Whether referred to as *juicio sumario* or *juicio extraordinario*, simplified procedure proved to be the most common in the borderlands, where nearly all of the extant cases fell into this category.[11]

The validity of simplification was crucial in legitimizing the legal culture in the peripheral regions of the Spanish empire. As pointed out earlier, much of New Spain, and evidently the rest of the Indies, was woefully understaffed in terms of adequately trained legal personnel. Ordinary legal procedure, both civil and criminal, could indeed be a time-consuming and highly technical affair that required a good measure of expertise to administer. Simplified form, however, alleviated much of the complication and suited well the circumstances of a simple society. While it lacked formal training, the local judiciary might still carry on their duties in a rudimentary, yet lawful manner.

Immanent in Spanish law, the summary proceedings on the northern frontier are not necessarily the judicial oddities that some have perceived. It cannot be overstressed that although frontier legal procedure usually did not conform to most legal texts—which usually described the lengthy *juicio ordinario*—it was nonetheless legally valid. Stricter adherence to ordinary procedure may have been a feature of legal administration under the *comandancia general* in the late colonial period. The dearth of legal records for the period after the creation of the *Provincias Internas* suggests that local officials may have routinely sent these documents to the commandant's *asesor* for his *dictamen*. Yet we have no way of knowing the number of cases forwarded to the commandant general because the papers of the *comandancia general* perished in flames in 1941. No doubt legal opinions at this superior level rested upon considerations of legal doctrine to a greater degree than in the provinces. Presumably, better communication and greater supervision on the part of the commandant general and his *asesor* might have served to impose more standardization in the judicial process at the local level. But the extant documentation simply does not support such assumptions. The *juicio sumario* and *juicio extraordinario* seem to have prevailed at the local level.[12]

While simplification proved the norm in the far north, it still met with criticism from a variety of sources. Throughout the eighteenth and nineteenth centuries, provincial governors complained, somewhat defensively, that they had no one to advise them in legal matters.[13] As career military men, perhaps they felt uncomfortable with their judicial responsibilities. Yet the persistence of summary proceedings, in the northern borderlands as in Spain itself, suggests the acceptability of simplified form.[14] Indeed, in the absence of sufficiently instructed personnel, the best approach may well have been to proceed, as Sala explained, "briefly and summarily, rejecting the prolonged solemnities of the law, and attending only to the truth."

Magistrates sought the juridical "truth" in two types of proceedings—criminal and civil. Contemporaries defined the essential characteristics of civil and criminal jurisdiction differently than today, and they usually based their distinctions upon considerations of public versus private spheres of activity. Writing in the late eighteenth century, Andrés Cornejo defined the *juicio criminal* as

> that which has as its object the ascertainment of all types of crimes, the perpetrators, accomplices, and punishments and . . . the indemnification of the aggrieved, the subject of which our laws treat at length.[15]

And an earlier writer, the enigmatic Juan de Hevia Bolaños, stated,

> One says civil when it deals with something that is [civil], without having a criminal origin; also, despite having proceeded from [a crime], when it deals principally with private utility, in which one applies a fine or penalty to a party. And one says criminal when it deals principally with crime that pertains to public utility

Figure 5. Portrait of jurist Félix Colón de Larriátegui, painted by Francisco de Goya in 1794. Because contemporary military law conformed largely to ordinary civil procedure (*justicia real ordinaria*), some governors of Texas and New Mexico may have followed this author's manual entitled *Juzgados Militares de España y sus Indias.* (© Indianapolis Museum of Art, Gift of Mr. and Mrs. Herman C. Krannert. Reproduced by permission.)

and punishment, from which can occur corporal punishment, banishment, or a fine applied to the fisc.[16]

In other words, actions that adversely affected the common weal were considered to be criminal.

Criminal proceedings might begin by accusation (*acusación* or *querella de parte*), by notification (*denuncia*), or at the magistrate's initiative (*de oficio*).[17] An accusation required the aggrieved or injured party to bring charges before a magistrate.[18] A *denuncia*, on the other hand, was in theory nothing more than notification to authorities by a third party that some crime had been committed, though at times this third party was the aggrieved.[19] Eighteenth-century jurist Antonio Javier Pérez y López explained that the primary difference between an *acusador* and a *denunciante* is that the former "is he who presents before the judge the crime of the delinquent, to take revenge, accusing him and asking that he be condemned in punishment for the [crime]." In distinction, the *denunciante* simply "makes known to the judge the crime of the delinquent, not to take revenge but to warn him, asking not that he be condemned to punishment nor obligating himself to prove it, for by asking [for punishment] and obligating himself [to prove it], he would be an accuser."[20] Freed of the burden of proving the charges, the aggrieved party might enjoy a much safer juridical position by assuming the role of *denunciante*. And in practice the distinct theoretical division between *denunciante* and *acusador* became somewhat blurred.[21] Whether borderlands magistrates were aware of the difference is arguable. As elsewhere in the empire, criminal cases in New Mexico and Texas often began by *denuncia* despite the fact that the *denunciante* had been the victim of a particular crime. The third manner in which a criminal case might be initiated reflected best the activist judiciary of the *antiguo régimen*. When acting *de oficio*, a magistrate exercised his authority to investigate and prosecute any unruly or criminal behavior within his jurisdiction. This maintenance of public tranquillity was a major responsibility of the *justicia*.

All criminal cases, however begun, included the all-important *sumaria*, somewhat akin to the indictment of Anglo-American legal tradition. According to contemporary jurists, the *sumaria* was strictly a fact-finding inquiry, carried out by the magistrate and his assistants simply to clarify the facts surrounding the commission of

a crime.[22] But magistrates usually marshalled evidence to incrimi-
nate the suspected party, and this information formed the basis of
the prosecution's arguments. The weight of this phase was such
that, in one scholar's estimation, "in it the trial was configured and,
one could almost say, decided."[23] Carried out with no participation
from the defendant, the entire process presumed the guilt of a
suspect.

Displaying the police powers of his multifaceted office, the magistrate began the *sumaria* by noting the information upon which he
had begun his investigation. The details in this opening statement—the *cabeza del proceso*—might be provided by the accuser, by
the denouncer, or by the magistrate himself. Typically, the magistrate reported that he had learned of a specific crime and, as a
consequence, that he had begun his investigation. Bear in mind that
the magistrate who carried out the initial investigation often was
the same individual who subsequently served as judge. This is
especially so in the provincial capitals of Santa Fe and San Antonio,
where the *alcalde mayor* or *alcalde ordinario* often oversaw the proceedings from beginning to end. It is difficult to imagine that the
magistrate, tinged with first impressions of a crime and being personally acquainted with most of the inhabitants of his district,
could not already have formed some opinion as to the guilt of the
suspect.

Not only qualitatively, but quantitatively as well, the *sumaria*
comprises the bulk of the criminal court records. In her study of
criminal procedure in Castile, María Paz Alonso Romero estimates
that the *sumaria* comprised approximately two-thirds of the total
criminal proceedings.[24] An examination of criminal trials conducted in the *audiencias* of Guadalajara and Mexico City reveals a
similar tendency, as do the records from New Mexico and Texas.
Because of circumstances on the peripheries, however, the *sumaria*
may have had even more significance than in other areas of the
Spanish empire. Lacking the intellectual formation and the legal
expertise to decide on points of law and legal doctrine, magistrates
in the northern borderlands may well have given more consideration to the "facts" uncovered during the course of the investigative *sumaria*. Surely the legal reasoning of courtroom personae in
subsequent phases of litigation was unsophisticated and leaned
toward a common-sense explanation of events. In the simplified
arena of the frontier colonial courtroom, the *sumaria*—a fact-finding

stage—might influence the subsequent stages of the trial to a greater degree than in a well-staffed tribunal.

If injuries had occurred, the *sumaria* next moved to the *reconocimiento de heridas* or *fé de heridas*, a physical examination of the injured party conducted in judicial form by an individual recognized as a medical expert. According to one eighteenth-century text, the *fé de heridas* consisted of a declaration of the type of wound, the weapon used, and the present state and prognosis of the victim.[25] In Texas and New Mexico, where formally trained physicians were scarce, the court accepted the findings of an individual who practiced medicine in the community, perhaps a *curandero,* a surgeon (*cirujano*), a barber (*barbero*), or in cases of rape, a midwife (*partera*).[26] The graphic documentary descriptions of wounds, filed by either the healer or the magistrate, vividly bring to life the personal agonies of a distant time.

Typical is the report of "maestro de barbero y curandero" Antonio Durán de Armijo of New Mexico, who in 1713 examined the lifeless body of Catalina de Valdés. He noted the many scratches and the three wounds to the woman's head, and he described what he believed to be the mortal blow above her brow: "Inserting the probe, [I found] that the skin was broken, as was the fatty tissue, the meaty membrane, the pericraneum, and the craneum; and the skull was cracked in the form of a half-moon." Initially believed to be an accident, a fuller investigation later ascribed the deed to the victim's husband, Miguel Luján, whose white buckskin moccasins revealed the telltale spots of human blood.[27] A document from colonial San Antonio provides equally explicit detail. In his investigation of a shooting incident, Alcalde Ordinario Alberto López Aguados y Villafuerte recorded that the victim had suffered a gunshot wound

> that entered the right side of his rib cage and emerged four fingers below his navel, through the opening of which emerged a piece of the bullet; and through the opening in his ribs emerged melon seeds, from which I inferred [the wound] to be mortal.[28]

The crown displayed its judicial activism as monitor of public tranquillity in the requirement that a healer notify a local magistrate before attending to a wounded person. Roque Jaramillo of Santa Cruz, for example, reported in 1731 that his son and another man had been involved in a rather bloody fight. Asked if he wished to file a complaint (*querella*), Jaramillo replied negatively, stating that he simply had notified authorities "so that both might be cured."[29] So routine was this practice of notification that even when a person suffered considerable physical harm, local healers were reluctant to cure their patients until royal officials had been notified. The *alcalde mayor* of Santa Fe, Francisco José Bueno de Bohórquez y Corcuera, reported in 1719 that a fourteen-year-old boy lay unconscious, his skull fractured, but that local residents "had not cured him until I had seen him."[30]

Following the *fé de heridas,* the magistrate began the process of questioning the witnesses to the crime. These often included the aggrieved party or those who could corroborate his story, though not the suspect.[31] Typically the magistrate sought such information as the type of crime committed, the location and circumstances under which it was committed, and the identity of the perpetrator.[32] In his study of crime in central and southern Mexico during roughly the same period, William Taylor has noted a fair degree of consistency and detail in the information gathered in this phase of the investigation.[33] In Texas and New Mexico, however, criminal proceedings often lack details such as the time of day and the precise location of the crime, the weapon used, and so forth. Procedural guidelines appear to have been followed a bit more consistently in Texas than in New Mexico, but the *sumarias* nevertheless provide only sketchy detail and the range of information deviates markedly. This inconsistency is perhaps a good indicator of the variation in judicial styles on the northern frontier.

In a later phase of the trial, the *plenario,* the suspect or a representative had the right to block the testimony of certain witnesses if it could be shown that in some way they had an interest in the case. Yet in the *sumaria,* because of its ostensibly fact-finding nature, this safeguard did not exist.[34] Thus, corroborating testimony in the *sumaria* was acceptable from witnesses who at a later stage might be legally disqualified. In this respect, then, the position of the suspect suffered during the investigative stage of the trial. Freed from certain restrictions found in the *plenario,* some magistrates displayed considerable aggressiveness in uncovering the truth, as illustrated by an incident that took place in early-eighteenth-century New Mexico.

Several members of the Romero clan were accused of having stolen and butchered an ox belonging to the Indian governor of

Pojoaque, Lucas Abenbua. After getting nowhere with the initial witnesses, Governor Juan Ignacio Flores Mogollón called before him the daughter of the principal suspect. Only eleven years old, the girl no doubt felt intimidated by the governor's methods of examination. "Tell the truth, or I'll shackle you," threatened Flores. "Tell the truth and do not deny it, for if you do, I'll punish you."[35] The girl—ordinarily an unsuitable witness because of her age and because of the exemption from testifying against one's relative— caved in under such pressure and revealed not only the guilt of her kin, but also described their involvement in three other such incidents.[36] Although a violation of strict procedural rules, Governor Flores Mogollón had nonetheless discovered the "truth," always the objective of the *sumaria.*

Race and class played ambiguous roles in determining one's qualifications as a witness. Stigmatized as social inferiors and as legal minors, indigenous subjects occupied a position which some felt compromised their testimony. The anonymous writer of an eighteenth-century legal dictionary, for example, rejected the view that "Indians say whatever they please because of their cowardice"; nevertheless, he believed that witnesses from "among the Indian nations, however truthful they may be," were not to be valued as highly as others.[37] A jurist of the stature of Juan de Solórzano Pereira posited that it was "best for the Indians" to not lend credence to their testimony, which, "because of their lack of strength and stability of judgment," was prone to falsehood. He also warned that the testimony of six Indians was not worth that of "one proper witness."[38]

These notions, however, seem not to have had much impact on procedure in New Mexico and Texas. On rare occasions, certain Indians were found to be not "capable" of taking the oath, but these seem to be the exception.[39] Undoubtedly more subtle ways existed to discredit one's testimony. The court surely valued the word of a leading citizen or a long-time resident over that of someone from the lower strata or a drifter. Given the intimate connection between race and class in the Spanish colonial world, one might also presume that cultural and racial prejudice played a role in judicial proceedings. Nevertheless, especially in New Mexico, Indians of various tribal backgrounds appear quite frequently as eyewitnesses in criminal proceedings, whether testifying against other Indians or against *españoles.*

The assessment of the abilities of one Indian woman, who testified against her master, was not unusual. When Juez Comisionado Juan Páez Hurtado summoned the Indian servant Isabel before him, he noted that she was "quite fluent in the Castilian language and capable of reason." He therefore administered to her the oath as witness "in due legal form."[40] Such examples abound in court records. Evidently, the judiciary in the borderlands routinely viewed indigenous subjects as qualified witnesses.

In other ways, too, the judiciary of the far north often treated Indians as capable adults, despite their official status as minors. A document dated 1744 reveals the ambiguous legal minority of indigenous subjects under the Spanish regime. When María Calabacita of Santo Domingo Pueblo died intestate, local officials took a detailed inventory of her property, valued at the considerable sum of 1,486 1/2 pesos. After dividing a portion of her estate equally, "according to law," among her four illegitimate children (*hijos naturales*), officials apportioned the remainder to María's father, Francisco Calabacita, whom they also named "*tutor* and *curador* of the aforementioned minors, that he might care for them and administer said goods with all due correctness and integrity."[41] This document calls into question the blanket assumption of Pueblo Indians being juridical minors, since a minor could hardly be appointed as *tutor* or *curador*. And one cannot argue that the father must have been Hispanicized, or at least *ladino*, for he required an interpreter in making his judicial declaration. While Spanish law relegated indigenous subjects to minority status, adult Indians seem to have been recognized as capable and responsible in matters of everyday legal administration.[42]

Like Indians, persons of mixed blood also were frequent witnesses in legal proceedings. In the colonial world the lines between *mestizo* and *español* were blurred, and although a racial hierarchy existed, its construction hinged more upon community perception and one's self-identification than upon simple biology, especially in the socially fluid north.[43] Those who lived in the Hispanic manner and who shared Hispanic cultural values were generally referred to as *español*, despite the fact that few were of pure peninsular heritage. In the end, the nuances of a racially tinged social hierarchy played out in innumerable ways, but there is little evidence that racial categorization figured overtly in determining one's suitability as a witness.

After questioning witnesses and weighing the evidence, normal procedure called for the imprisonment of the accused and the confiscation of his property, the *embargo de bienes*. In earlier times the magistrate might confiscate the goods of both plaintiff and defendant.[44] By the late sixteenth century, however—and until the end of the colonial period—the *embargo de bienes* had been limited to action against the defendant only.[45] In this form the *embargo de bienes* reached New Mexico and Texas. This judicial step occurred infrequently in New Mexico, probably because most suspected criminals—indeed, the population in general—had few possessions, and it was more common early in the eighteenth century than later. Much the same can be said for Texas, where a mere handful of criminal cases feature the *embargo de bienes*. At the conclusion of the trial, the amount owed to the court might then be extracted from the value of the goods that had been confiscated.[46] The purpose of this step was to ensure payment of possible fines and court costs of the defendant.[47] Therefore, confiscation of so little would not likely serve its underlying purpose.

In cases where the *embargo de bienes* occurred, it often lacked the figure so prominent in its execution in other parts of Spanish America, the *fiel ejecutor*. Selected from the ranks of the *cabildo,* this official had the responsibility of watching after all property confiscated in judicial proceedings.[48] His responsibilities outweighed the income derived from his duties, however, and by 1799 the office had been abolished throughout the Indies.[49] When the *embargo de bienes* occurred in New Mexico, the confiscated goods were entrusted not to this municipal official, but simply to an individual of financial solvency and of upstanding character.[50]

Perhaps another reason for the *embargo de bienes* was to deter the flight of a suspected criminal. By gaining control of his worldly possessions, officials could be assured that a suspect of means would stay in the area and appear in court. In regions where the general population had little in the way of material goods, such as New Mexico and Texas, this purpose of the *embargo de bienes* must have been secondary. The infrequency with which it was executed in the borderlands suggests that officials saw no good purpose for it and, like other procedural elements, the *embargo de bienes* was jettisoned on the frontier.

Following the preliminary testimony of the witnesses, and coincidental with the *embargo de bienes,* a magistrate issued an arrest

warrant, or *auto de prisión*. Symptomatic of the procedural confusion common during the *antiguo régimen*, however, the imprisonment of a suspect might occur at various stages of the *sumaria*.[51] In
New Mexico and Texas the *auto de prisión* often occurred simply
upon notification of a crime, though at other times after the preliminary questioning.[52] In fact, it was not unusual for the suspect to
be imprisoned without a formal writ from a competent magistrate.
The combination of executive and judicial functions of the *alcalde*
perhaps explains this occurrence—the "*alcalde*-policeman" simply
anticipated the next step of the "*alcalde*-judge."

Not all delinquents could be easily located, in which case the
military or a more informal "posse" might help to apprehend the
suspect.[53] Consider the drama of the accused kidnapper and apos-
tate Apache, Luis Quintana, who had scaled the walls of the guard-
house in Santa Fe in his attempted escape to freedom. On orders
from the governor, Alcalde Mayor Juan José Lovato advised the
Spanish and Indian communities of the jurisdiction of Santa Cruz
de la Cañada to be on the lookout for the fugitive. Lovato and
"those of [his] retinue" managed to catch up with Quintana, and
"summoning various times the name of the King, Our Lord (May
God Keep Him) and with the [judicial] staff in my hand, I remon-
strated that he stop and lay down his arms." The king's men captured Quintana and imprisoned him once again.[54] Some suspects
never were captured, but the contemporary legal system allowed
for them to be tried and convicted in absentia (*en rebeldía*).[55]

Most large settlements in the Indies normally had jails, but not in
Texas, New Mexico, or other areas of the far north. Instead, the
judiciary made do with a secured room in either the presidio or the
casas reales.[56] From time to time a well-intentioned governor sought
to construct a more conventional jail, but throughout the colonial
period all efforts to this end failed. Texas governor Barón de Ripperdá (1770–78), for example, noted that despite official directives
to build both military quarters (*cuartel*) and jail, San Antonians had
failed to exert even the smallest effort.[57]

While the provincial capitals benefited from the presence of a
military presidio as a place for incarceration, the surrounding areas
had no such facilities.[58] How did a magistrate in an outlying area
carry out the *auto de prisión*? If the crime were serious, say murder
or contraband on a large scale, the magistrate might secure the
suspect with rope or handcuffs and send him—along with the

sumaria—to the Real Cuerpo de Guardia at the capital's presidio.[59] This was more often the case in New Mexico than in Texas, because in Texas there was more than one presidio that might serve as a jail.[60] Administrative centers in New Mexico such as Albuquerque and Santa Cruz, both of which ranked as *villas*, had no jails. The *alcaldes mayores* of those jurisdictions and their subdivisions had to devise other solutions.

A curious account from the jurisdiction of Albuquerque underscores the problems of incarceration in the province. In June 1747, two *genízaros* from Belen had been detected in the act of stealing the goods of Juan del Pino, an itinerant merchant from Mexico City residing in Santa Fe. Advised of the crime, Teniente Alcalde Miguel Lucero apprehended one of the suspects, "el Cuajo," who freely admitted that he had robbed Pino.[61] The merchant requested that legal proceedings be initiated and that the delinquent be imprisoned. To this Lucero replied "that he had no jail in which to secure [the prisoner]; that if [Pino] wished, he would secure him in [Pino's] room until he received an order to imprison him." Lucero did incarcerate the suspect, but used the same room from which "el Cuajo" and his accomplice had stolen the merchandise. In a rather comical denouement, Lucero's immediate superior, Alcalde Mayor José Baca, released "el Cuajo." Having had two full days to ponder the possibilities, he returned to his erstwhile prison and proceeded to clean out the rest of Pino's wares. The frustrated merchant had only his criminal complaint to take to the governor.[62]

One alternative to jailing, and a feature not uncommon in the rest of the Hispanic world, was "house arrest." If the crime were not grave and the suspect posed no real threat to society, the magistrate occasionally required only that the suspect be confined to his or her premises.[63] One early case from San Antonio demonstrates just how lax house arrest might be. In 1735 a tiff developed within the ranks of the newly formed *cabildo*. Juan Leal Goraz jailed three other *cabildo* members for their "disrespect for Royal Justice"—more specifically for their refusal to help clean the community *acequia* and for their failure to keep their livestock away from crops. While under house arrest, however, the three men had virtually come and gone as they pleased. One witness reported that he often had seen one of the defendants take a siesta at the house of the presidial captain.[64] From all evidence, good sturdy jails were not a priority in the borderlands.

The reason for such inattention had much to do with contemporary notions of imprisonment. In theory, incarceration was not for the purpose of punishment, but instead was merely a method of preventing flight and ensuring the defendant's presence throughout the course of the trial. This notion, rooted in the *Siete Partidas*, predominated in juridical thought during the *antiguo régimen*.[65] An elaborate penitentiary system—typical of today—was not only costly but also unnecessary because punishment or rehabilitation was not the aim of incarceration. By the eighteenth century, however, actual practice challenged judicial theory. Although not primarily for punishment, incarceration—and the express threat thereof as a deterrent to crime—had become a standard feature of the justice system. In 1753, for example, Governor Tomás Vélez Cachupín threatened to impose a fine of fifty pesos and three months in jail for violating a local ordinance. A similar decree in 1705, which prohibited the pasturage of animals at the ciénega de Santa Fe, threatened violators with one month in jail.[66] And in 1808 citizens of Santa Fe declared that Governor Joaquín del Real Alencaster had "administered justice with prudent deliberation, punishing certain vices that harmed the general public with days or months of prison."[67] While not a usual form of punishment, jail sentences nevertheless were applied for minor crimes. More commonly, magistrates commuted or reduced the sentence of a convicted criminal who had been incarcerated during the course of the trial. From the provincial level to the *audiencia*, so widespread was this particular practice that one must conclude that most magistrates viewed incarceration as punishment, and not simply as a neutral step in the judicial process.[68]

Following the imprisonment of the suspect came the *auto de confesión*. As elsewhere in the Spanish empire, this was often the first time that a suspect participated directly in the judicial process.[69] But, in contrast to practice in Castile, magistrates in Texas and New Mexico appear to have been less concerned about prying from the suspect an admission of guilt.[70] Indeed, the "confession" of the defendant usually took the form of a denial, or at least, a declaration in which he gave his version of the story.[71] In practice, so close to a simple declaration was this step, that often it was referred to not as a *confesión* but as a *declaración*.[72] And in at least one case the defendant gave both a *declaración* and, later in the trial, a *confesión*.[73]

Curiously, in this respect judicial administration in the far north of New Spain conformed closely to the arguments of legal theorists, many of whom maintained that the *confesión* was equivalent to the *litis contestatio* of civil procedure, in which the defendant had a chance to counter the accusation against him.[74] To be sure, an imprisoned suspect occasionally admitted his guilt, but the usual tenor of a *confesión* in Texas and New Mexico is that of denial of guilt or an explanation of mitigating circumstances.[75]

Authorities in some parts of the eighteenth-century Hispanic world occasionally employed torture at this juncture as a means of eliciting an incriminating statement.[76] (As with other procedural elements, however, this step might occur also during a subsequent stage of a criminal case.) Influenced by the writings of Cesare Beccaria, some Hispanic jurists urged an end to judicial torture. The leading voice for reform was a native of New Spain, Manuel Lardizábal Uribe, who spent much of his adult life in Castile and in 1782 wrote *Discurso sobre las penas contrahidas a las leyes criminales de España para facilitar su reforma*, a tract designed to expose the barbarism and futility of judicial torture. Despite his efforts, torture continued as a legitimate procedural step during the *antiguo régimen*. Perhaps its use was more widespread on the peninsula, but judges in the Indies applied this step only occasionally.[77] Not one example of judicial torture, however, has surfaced from among the hundreds of criminal cases in either New Mexico or Texas. Perhaps because they recognized the gravity of this step and their lack of expertise, frontier magistrates were reluctant to take this drastic measure, though they evidently knew that torture existed as a legitimate component of criminal procedure. After failing to obtain a self-incriminating *confesión* from one defendant, for example, the *alcalde ordinario* of Santa Fe, Juan Páez Hurtado, suggested to the governor that the proceedings be sent southward for the opinion of a legal adviser "so that, according to the merits of [the case], you might pronounce a sentence of torture or whatever might be suitable, and it can be carried out."[78]

The completion of the *confesión* normally signaled the end of the *sumaria*. Although theorists proclaimed its objective nature, the *sumaria* set the tenor for the remainder of the trial. More than a simple and impartial fact-finding investigation, the *sumaria* often proved to be an exercise in marshalling evidence against the suspect. Unable to intervene on his own behalf before his *confesión*, the defendant stood at a disadvantage. Perhaps only the personal attachments between courtroom actors, a strong sense of community, and the magistrate's aim of maintaining harmonious social relations lessened the potential for abuse that such a system invited.

✤ ✤ 6 ✤ ✤

The *Plenario* and the *Sentencia*

In the *juicio plenario,* the contestants offered judicial proofs of their respective positions. Because most legal proceedings in the far north were simplified *juicios sumarios,* and because prescribed formulas lay at the heart of the *plenario,* it perhaps strayed further from the judicial ideal than other phases of the judicial process. One scholar has characterized this phase as being "minutely elaborated, which sought to establish with strict rules the conduct to be followed in each of the innumerable situations that might arise."[1] Try as they might, provincial magistrates simply could not conform in every detail to the requirements of Castilian theorists. With no formal preparation, lacking ready access to trained advisers, and faced with imposing geographic obstacles, provincial magistrates were in no position to implement the niceties of juridical doctrine.

So inconsistent are the proceedings of the *juicio plenario* in New Mexico and Texas that an exact description of the procedural steps is difficult. Indeed, frequently the entire phase failed to materialize in the court record, or did so only in abbreviated or haphazard fashion. Such procedural irregularity in the *plenario* only underscores the importance of the *sumaria* and of summary proceedings in the colonial judicial process. When a discernible *juicio plenario* arose, however, it often contained the elements described below.

If the *sumaria* had been drawn up in an outlying jurisdiction, and if it were a case of sufficient gravity, the local *justicia* remitted the written proceedings to the governor at the provincial capital. Again this is perhaps more typical of New Mexico, where a more centralized administration prevailed. At this time, the accused, and any suspected accomplices, were also frequently sent along with the case file (*expediente*).[2]

With the preparatory steps fulfilled, the haphazard *plenario* often began with the *auto de cargos*, in which the magistrate formally charged the defendant with the specific crime for which he was to be tried.[3] Frequently he appointed a *defensor* or, if the suspect appeared to be a minor, a *curador* for the legal defense of the accused.[4] The magistrate might also name an interpreter to aid an Indian defendant. In contrast to Mexico City, where apparently all Indian defendants received this aid, the appointment of an interpreter was rare in the northern borderlands. Perhaps as a result of close contact with Hispanics, Indians usually were proficient in Castilian.[5]

In the presence of a legal representative, the defendant prepared to ratify his or her *confesión*. During the *ratificación*, an unspecified court functionary (probably the magistrate, the *escribano*, or a *testigo de asistencia*) read the previous statement and then asked if the defendant understood what had been read and if he or she wished to add or withdraw information. Normally, the answer was that the defendant understood and had nothing else to say. Since the *declaración* often denied any wrongdoing, the accused sometimes added information that might better his legal position.

If the charges had been brought by a second party, as in the case of an *acusación* or *querella,* the plaintiff presented another formal statement against the defendant and, often, a suggestion regarding appropriate punishment. The plaintiff might ask, for example, that stolen property be returned, that the cost of medical services be paid, or that an individual be banished.[6] Most frequently, however, the party pressing charges asked only that justice be done and left the punishment to the discretion of the magistrate.

At some point in the *plenario,* both the defendant and the plaintiff might once again call upon witnesses to reaffirm their respective positions, or if the case were being pursued *de oficio,* the magistrate might order the appearance of a new witness. In this stage of the trial, witnesses might be disallowed by virtue of a process known as the *tacha*. A witness might be disqualified for a variety of reasons, including being a "relative, spouse, friend, master, servant, interested party," or known enemy of one of the litigants.[7] Upon closing their declarations, witnesses usually stated that they were not disqualified by law ("no les tocan las generales de la ley"). Despite the haphazard nature of judicial proceedings in the borderlands, locals seem to have known about these disqualifications. For example, the defendant in a case of criminal trespass, Juan

Estevan García de Noriega, disqualified two of the plaintiff's witnesses on the grounds of kinship ties. In making the *tacha*, García de Noriega declared that Antonio Tafoya had

> presented as witnesses Juan de Herrera and Gerónimo Tafoya, who are disqualified by law, inasmuch as Juan de Herrera is his brother-in-law, being married to the illegitimate daughter of Cristóbal Tafoya; and Gerónimo Tafoya is first cousin of Antonio Tafoya, being the son of Juan de Tafoya. Thus, I disqualify them from testifying in and out of court.[8]

In citing the unacceptability of a known enemy, litigants were able not only to invalidate witnesses but also the participation of a particular magistrate.[9]

A key feature of the *plenario* was the defense of the accused. The defendant often spoke on his or her own behalf, though at times he or she had legal representation of some sort. Spaniards of means and Pueblo Indian communities occasionally hired a *procurador*, or the court might appoint legal counsel for the defendant.[10] An Indian defendant, for example, might enjoy the services of a *defensor*, a *curador*, or the *protector de indios*.[11] A representative (usually a *curador*) intervened on behalf of a minor.[12] As mentioned before, the literate sector of frontier society functioned in these various capacities and, although not true "professionals," a number of individuals supplemented their incomes by serving as courtroom representatives or by drawing up legal documents for use by litigants.[13] Unlike jurists in the upper echelons of the system, these local figures appear to have been qualified only by the fact that they were literate and, in the case of *procuradores*, were able to inspire the confidence of their clients. The legal arguments—*alegaciones*—of these representatives were unsophisticated, more often guided by the "facts" surrounding the case and a culturally ingrained sense of right and wrong than by doctrine.[14]

While these legal representatives appear sporadically in contemporary documents, the most important figure by far in the questioning phase was the magistrate himself, as he was in every other step of the judicial process. Once again, the individual skills and wisdom of a particular magistrate loom as crucial variables in the Spanish colonial legal system, for it was he who shaped the questions to be asked of witnesses and defendants.[15] The predetermined set of questions to be asked of all witnesses—the *interrogatorio*—

usually seems reasonable enough, and sometimes shows considerable insight into the nature of human motivation.

Magistrates were not always successful at uncovering the truth during the questioning of witnesses and defendants. Not surprisingly, the *plenario* often brought to light testimonies that differed substantially. In these instances, the magistrate might initiate a most interesting process known as the *careo*, a face-to-face confrontation between parties. Some jurists disapproved of the *careo*—which, in a criminal case, sometimes occurred during the *sumaria*—but magistrates commonly employed this procedure throughout the empire.[16] New Mexico and Texas were no exceptions. Use of the *careo* differed from place to place and from judge to judge. Some, like Alcalde Mayor Francisco Guerrero of Santa Fe, resorted regularly to this step.

The *careo* often turned up some rather ingenuous statements. Take that of Mauricio Trujillo, suspected of theft and the illegal sale of livestock. In a *careo* with Juan Antonio de Avila, to whom he had sold some of the animals, Trujillo admitted to the magistrate that he had lied in his original statement about the numbers involved.

> The defendant answers that what [his adversary] Juan Antonio Avila says is true. And asked why he had denied the truth in his *declaración*, he answers that it is because Avila was not present, and now that he is, [the defendant] confesses that it is true.[17]

Apparently, the actual physical presence of an adversary or of a conflicting witness could make a telling difference in the proceedings, and for this very reason some jurists opposed the process. A quicker, more clever mind could easily take advantage of the situation. Or an adversary of higher social standing might intimidate his inferior. These were real problems. As jurist Joaquín Escriche pointed out, the magistrate who guided the questioning must take care to temper a sharper wit.[18] As for the question of intimidation, no *careo* has surfaced that involved persons from markedly different social classes, perhaps because in the judicial system that undergirded the social hierarchy of the colonial world, the word of the "better sorts" took precedence over that of witnesses from the lower strata and thereby rendered the *careo* superfluous. The *careo* often cleared up a disputed point, but not always. On occasion, the witnesses stuck faithfully to their stories, and the *careo* shed no further light on the dispute.[19]

For a variety of reasons, the records of criminal cases in Texas and New Mexico often end abruptly at various points in the proceedings. Frequently the aggrieved party dropped the charges against the defendant, often ascribing their benevolence to Christian charity or to considerations of family or community well-being.[20] While noble sentiments may have accounted for a good deal of the pardoning process, it is likely that monetary considerations also played a part. Like their peninsular counterparts, litigants in the northern borderlands appear to have been occasionally susceptible to giving their pardons for a price. Perhaps rooted in the medieval custom of *avenencias*, as discussed in the *Siete Partidas*, the practice of settlement by fee had a long tradition in Spanish law, although legislation tended to ignore the general topic of pardons.[21] While the purchase of a pardon does not appear in the judicial record, circumstantial evidence suggests that the practice existed in colonial New Mexico and Texas as it did in other parts of the Spanish empire.[22]

Take the case of Alonso Rael, son of Alonso Rael de Aguilar, a prominent figure in early-eighteenth-century New Mexico. Accused of having murdered Francisco Tamaris, Alonso *el mozo* avoided arrest by taking refuge successively in several different churches. Meanwhile, the wife and son of Tamaris noted in various statements that they were being hounded by creditors of the slain victim. Finally, some seven months after the murder, the younger Tamaris and his mother formally pardoned Rael. Had this pardon been bought? Perhaps so. The burden of debt left by Francisco Tamaris may have tempted his survivors to accept an economic settlement. Although they cited Christian charity as their motive, the economic charity of Alonso Rael, Sr., may have been the deciding factor.[23]

Another suggestive case comes from San Antonio, where in 1774 recently arrived merchant Santiago Villaseñor complained to the governor that he had been robbed of seven hundred pesos, four hundred "in goods and coins" and the remaining amount in "pesos fuertes." The initial investigation focused on a pair of drifters— easy targets in a communally centered environment—but later investigation exposed a local, Pedro Leal, as the likely culprit. When some of the money surfaced, the governor traced it to a late-night gambling session attended by prominent San Antonio personalities. Less than two weeks after the robbery, Villaseñor reported that all his money had turned up on two different occasions and, thus, he wished to "pardon said aggressor" and drop the charges.[24]

Strict rules of legal procedure called for the arguments of the various parties to be sent to the opposition for their contestation. Like so many other portions of the *plenario*, this facet of judicial procedure in the northern borderlands fell far short of the ideal.[25] The *plenario* was always a haphazard phase of frontier judicial administration, and strict adherence with all the rules of procedure was rare. In cases that display some semblance of regularity, however, the chance to answer one's courtroom opponent seems to have been fairly standard in the judicial record.

Unlike the minutely detailed *plenario*, the final major phase of any judicial proceeding—the *sentencia*—was purposefully flexible. The magistrate took the lead—trial by jury did not exist in the Spanish legal system—and used his discretion in punishing criminal activity. The pivotal role of the magistrate in meting out justice underscores important points about the legal culture of the Hispanic world. First, it reflects the sole authority of the crown in dispensing justice, a power acquired at the outset of the early modern period. Second, the usual sentences themselves suggest a social consensus regarding punishment. In other words, the punishment imposed by judicial authorities both conformed to expectations of the participants and satisfied the political will of the state. Because of the legitimate place of judicial discretion in Spanish law—*arbitrio judicial*—and because of community consensus on what constituted a fitting punishment, the *sentencia* figures as the key to the viability of the judicial system in peripheral zones.

One great obstacle to a full understanding of the judicial process under the *antiguo régimen* is the fact that Castilian law did not require, indeed prohibited, an explanation of the legal points on which a magistrate founded his *sentencia*.[26] Even the best-administered cases, which follow in minute detail the scruples of legal formula, lack the so-called *sentencia fundada*. In proceedings involving jurists with considerable training, as found at the *audiencia* level, one gets a good idea of the legal arguments being used in specific cases from the *alegaciones* of lawyers, or from the *dictámenes* of the *fiscal*. Yet, one cannot be certain that a judicial decision rested solely upon these arguments and not upon other considerations. Valuable in this respect are such rare items as Juan Antonio de Torquemada's "Varias Alegaciones Jurídicas…" in which the author, a lawyer who practiced in the Audiencia of Mexico, often comments on whether his courtroom arguments had been successful.[27]

Although some scholars allude to a "judge's explanation of the verdict and sentence," magistrates tended toward brevity in their verdicts.[28] Conforming to Castilian practice on this matter, *oidores* of the *audiencia* did not expound on points of law or doctrinal interpretations thereof.[29] Instead, it was the *fiscal* of the *audiencia*—the crown's prosecuting attorney—who founded his arguments upon specific laws, doctrine, customs, or points of equity; the *oidores* themselves gave no such written explanation.[30] The same holds true for sentences at the provincial level, though local magistrates—especially the governors—appear to be somewhat concerned with justifying their decisions. The usual explanations, however, are not technically sophisticated. Magistrates state tersely, for example, that the sentence is for "the punishment of the culprit and as an example to others," or that the decision conforms "to the laws of these kingdoms." But these are far from *sentencias fundadas.*

Freed of the obligation to found their decisions on any specific legal point, magistrates exercised their judicial discretion—"the power . . . to choose between two or more alternatives, when each of the alternatives is lawful"—in arriving at their sentences.[31] In no other phase of legal procedure is the importance of *arbitrio judicial* so apparent. In the hands of a wise and learned man, *arbitrio judicial* might serve to humanize and make more equitable the cold letter of the law. Indeed, this admonition to the magistrate—to exercise his functions with wisdom and compassion—appeared in fundamental texts and was agreed upon by jurists.[32] But might not the element of *arbitrio judicial* play into the hands of those with hearts and minds less noble? With no need to explain a decision, the potential for abuse is clear. Yet no overwhelming evidence supports this view. While sentences of magistrates in the northern borderlands were not steeped in learned doctrine, they do appear to rely upon common sense and community values or, more precisely, *equidad.* A judge had several options at the time of pronouncing sentence. He might absolve the defendant, impose punishment, or strike something of a compromise between parties.

The practice of absolving, rather than declaring a defendant innocent, is noteworthy. First, it underscores the importance of the *sumaria*, for the presumed guilt of the defendant was implicit in any case that passed beyond this initial stage. Presumption of guilt, of course, is untenable for present-day sensibilities. But the practice of absolution also points to a justice system that recognized real problems that needed remedy. The aim of the magistrate was to find justice and to restore social harmony, not to declare all-out winners and losers. Because of the construction of *derecho indiano,* one could not be found "innocent" merely because of faulty procedural technicalities or because one party had presented the best case. Through judicial absolution, the magistrate and community at once forgave the social sin while they recognized that some misdeed had occurred.

On 30 May 1768, for example, Vicente Amador of San Antonio assaulted José Antonio Villegas who, on orders from the *alcalde ordinario,* was attempting to round up Amador's stray mare, which had caused damage to the fields of other *vecinos* on various occasions. After beating Villegas with a stick, which left an open wound to the head of "three fingers, more or less," Amador muttered, "Tell the *alcalde* that I say he is a *cabrón,*" and then took refuge at Mission San Antonio de Valero. Criminal proceedings began, and the suspect's goods were embargoed, but on 16 August a contrite Amador presented himself to authorities, "repentant of his excesses, expressing himself in all piety and commiseration." Alcalde Ordinario Jacinto Delgado observed that the victim had fully recovered from the wound, and he therefore absolved Amador "of the punishment that corresponds to his crime." But, he warned, "in the future [Amador] must contain such excesses and show due respect for the magistrates, under pain of being punished rigorously" and of having to face these same charges once again.[33]

Another instance of absolution comes from New Mexico, in a case of criminal assault perpetrated by a young Spaniard, Francisco Padilla, against Juan Antonio, a Suma Indian who seems to have been quite acculturated. In mid-June 1737, the two had gotten into an argument over the Spaniard's stray livestock. As tempers flared, Juan Antonio called Padilla a "snot-nosed dog" (*perro mocoso*). Padilla's response was physical—he attacked his adversary with a stick, delivering several blows to the head and allegedly breaking Juan Antonio's arm in the process. Juan Antonio brought a formal complaint (*querella*) before Alcalde Mayor Juan González Bas, who initiated the *sumaria,* imprisoned Padilla, and remitted both the paperwork and prisoner to the governor in Santa Fe. One month later, Juan Antonio had recuperated from the attack, as verified by the *alcalde mayor*, and dropped his complaint against Padilla. At this point, Governor Enrique de Olavide y Michelena rendered his decision. He freed from prison and absolved Francisco Padilla because the suit had been dropped and because the victim ran "no risk to his life or to his health" and had recuperated sufficiently to pursue his livelihood. Yet the governor assigned to Padilla not only the cost for the cure of all injuries, but also the "damages that, by reason of being impaired, Juan Antonio has incurred," including his daily maintenance while unable to work. The young man and his father satisfied the debt—2 pesos for the *curandero*, 45 pesos to Juan Antonio, and 7 pesos 5 reales for judicial costs—to secure his release. Finally, Governor Olavide y Michelena warned Francisco Padilla "to restrain himself in wanting to punish the Indians, not meddle with them, nor look for disputes with anyone, under pain of being punished severely and with all the rigor of the law" should another complaint be brought against him.[34] Judicial absolution, then, rarely was total. In some way, the wrongdoer expiated his guilt.

Far more frequently than absolving the defendant, magistrates imposed punishments of varying degrees. With rare exception, fundamental juridical texts of the *antiguo régimen* are silent on how each type of crime should be punished, nor did Hispanic jurists dwell on the subject. Yet most contemporaries agreed on the purpose of judicial punishment. The prime function of punishment, of course, was to repair the damage done to society and, for some eighteenth-century thinkers, to correct the defect of the guilty party.[35] But another purpose, perhaps more important, also existed—punishment was to serve as a deterrent to others.[36] A seventeenth-century jurist employed a naturalistic metaphor to demonstrate this dual purpose of punishment. "It has the effect of lightning," wrote Gerónimo de Cevallos, "which, striking to punish one, frightens many; and so with one blow, it serves as example and punishment."[37] Magistrates in the far reaches of New Spain shared this understanding of these essential qualities of punishment. When Alcalde Ordinario José de la Santa sentenced an adulterer to banishment from San Antonio in 1782, for example, he acted within the norms of Hispanic legal culture and punished the culprit "as a lesson to him and an example to the rest."[38]

In order to serve both ends of punishment, then, the public as well as the culprit had to be made aware of the sentence. One effective method was public proclamation of the magistrate's sentence. In 1745, Manuel Baca refused to obey a local ordinance that allowed all residents to cut firewood in the thickly wooded *bosque* along the banks of the Rio Grande near Pajarito, just south of Albuquerque. Magistrate Salvador Martínez warned him "one, two, and three times" to comply with the ordinance. Viewing Baca's refusal to obey as a challenge to royal authority, and in direct violation of Governor Joaquín Codallos y Rabal's order, the governor himself issued the final sentence.

> And so that it might serve as a lesson to the defendant and as an example to others, I order that this decree be made known on a feast day, after the celebration of the Sacrament of the Holy Mass, in the most public place of said *villa;* and that it be kept, fulfilled, and executed inviolably, allowing neither pleas nor petitions regarding its content.[39]

Not only was the sentence made public, but it was done in a way that would attract as much attention as possible in the community.

As the preceding case demonstrates, not only public pronouncement, but public humiliation might also play a role in shaping the *sentencia.* Manuel Baca, and those who knew him, would always remember the day that his punishment was pronounced in the "most public place of said *villa.*" Other forms of public humiliation likewise served the dual end of punishment. In San Antonio, for example, Alcalde Ordinario Vicente Amador sentenced cattle thief Francisco Hernández to a rather fitting and humiliating punishment.

> So that he might purge his sin, I ordered and do order by this decree—considering this with the greatest charity and forgiving him as I do forgive him—that he be walked through the accustomed streets with the entrails hanging from his neck, in payment for his crime.

In addition, Hernández was to work for one month on the munitions storeroom that was currently under construction.[40]

As deterrents, public humiliation and shame work best, no doubt, in close-knit communities where peer opinion carries considerable weight. In many respects, colonial New Mexico and Texas were pre-modern environments where nearly "every individual had some sort of social and familial relationship with everyone else" and where local magistrates were "loath to pass a severe sentence upon a defendant who was known in the community and probably on familiar terms with members of the judicial staff itself."[41] In these simpler social settings, then, public shame often proved to be an appropriate form of punishment.

Inextricably linked to humiliation and shame are the ideas of honor and respect—notions held in highest esteem, even on the frontier.[42] The judicial system reflected these values. Consider the case of María de los Dolores Gallego and Andrés Martín against Eusebio Chaves. In a heated quarrel over land and water use, Chaves had assaulted his father-in-law, Martín, causing serious physical injury. After a well-conducted *sumaria* by Teniente de Alcalde Mayor Baltasar Griego, Governor Tomás Vélez Cachupín sentenced Chaves to pay court costs of 15 pesos 6 reales as well as medical expenses incurred in the course of Martín's recuperation. Moreover, the governor also required Eusebio Chaves to kneel and beg forgiveness of his father-in-law in full view of the entire community. In this way the crown reminded society of the proper respect that is due a son to his father, thereby reenforcing patriarchal notions of community and, by extension, social and political hierarchy.[43]

Concern for community harmony can be found in yet another aspect of the sentencing process. Those who upset the social equilibrium and transcended accepted norms of morality faced exclusion. As noted previously, crimes such as adultery or fornication often resulted in banishment. The case of adulterers Juan José Vergara and María Carbajal, who lived in San Antonio, serves to illustrate this point.[44] Similarly, justices in New Mexico sought to maintain or restore community standards of morality with their sentences. In 1744 Juana Martín brought a complaint against her husband, José de Armijo and his alleged mistress, Gertrudis de Segura, with whom he had been carrying on for some fifteen years. In her complaint (*querella*), Juana Martín asked that Gertrudis de Segura be banished; as for her husband, Martín suggested that the judge "impose upon him severe punishment, so that—because of this complaint or in revenge—he might not mistreat me in deed or in word." In the end, the married couple reconciled; and Segura, the "mulata soltera," was exiled to El Paso, "or some other distant place," a sentence later commuted to banishment at Santa Cruz de la Cañada (some twenty-five miles from the capital) for a period of four years.[45]

Carnal relations between persons of the same sex and bestiality also created public scandal by violating accepted standards of behavior, and magistrates took measures to halt such activity. In these matters, provincial judges evidently proceeded with caution, for in the very few cases that exist, they required clear proof of the crime. In New Mexico, for instance, Antonio Yuba of Tesuque Pueblo and Asensio Povia of nearby Nambé, were brought before authorities to face charges of sodomy. Scrupulous in conducting the case, Governor Gervasio Cruzat y Góngora appointed Antonio Ulibarri as *curador* for Povia, who appeared to be a minor, and Juan Manuel Chirinos as *defensor* for Yuba. He also saw fit to provide the two Indians with an interpreter, Francisco Rendón. In their declarations, both suspects denied any intent to commit the *pecado nefando*, or abominable crime, though Asensio Povia, the younger of the two, acknowledged that while the two of them were in a secluded area of the woods, Yuba had grabbed his penis in order to "excite" it. Only one person—the *denunciante*, Manuel Trujillo of Santa Fe—had witnessed the misdeed, however. In arguing for Antonio Yuba, Juan Manuel Chirinos displayed not only the cultural values of his time but also considerable knowledge of Spanish law.

> His innocence is demonstrated through the lack of proof, because in cases of this nature it must be as plain and clear as the light of day, for a man's person is the most noble thing in the world; and, thus, in cases such as these that are doubtful, one must absolve or give only a light punishment, being up to the discretion of the judge ("por ser arbitraria a los señores jueces") to do so, as determined by all the rules of law which deal superabundantly with these matters.

Because of this lack of proof, the governor suspended the case; but to ensure the physical separation of the two men, he exiled them for four months to different parts of the province.[46]

As discussed in the previous chapter, judicial authorities construed incarceration as a form of punishment. While evidence of jailing in Texas and New Mexico exists, the documentary record shows that magistrates seldom resorted to this as the prime form of punishment. Instead, they preferred other methods for deterring undesirable behavior. A common form of punishment was to impose fines. Most of these fines went to cover court costs (*costas procesales*), and they perhaps followed prescribed rates, though whether they did so consistently is arguable—surviving court assessments (*tasaciones*) range from a small amount to forty or more pesos.[47] Less frequently, a magistrate sentenced a criminal to pay for certain damages that had resulted from his criminal activity, most commonly in cases of assault. Typical is the case of José Manuel Trujillo against Antonio and Juan Domingo Valverde, both from the jurisdiction of Santa Cruz de la Cañada. During a fight over the alleged deflowering of Trujillo's daughter, the Valverdes had beaten Trujillo over the head with a stick and a hoe, instruments handily available to farmers. After the *sumaria,* Governor Joaquín Codallos y Rabal punished the Valverdes by imposing a fine of twenty pesos to cover the costs of curing Trujillo's wounds.[48]

Forced labor was another customary punishment. Given the relative lack of specie in New Mexico and Texas, the practice of work punishments, rather than judicial fines, prevailed. In cases of lesser severity, criminals were often assigned to some form of public works project, as in the above-mentioned case of Francisco Hernández at San Antonio. In New Mexico, similar instances of assignment to public works appear. For his criminal assault of Cristóbal Maese, Tomás Méndez was condemned not only to pay the cost of Maese's cure, but also to "make 500 adobes to repair this *villa* of Santa Fe."[49]

Crimes of greater magnitude brought more punishment than making adobes. A frequent sentence for those convicted of particularly heinous crimes, or for habitual offenders, was that of being sent to an *obraje*, especially the mining works in various parts of Nueva Vizcaya. No *obrajes* existed in either New Mexico or Texas during the colonial period, though in the 1780s officials proposed such a plan for New Mexico.[50] While magistrates in other parts of New Spain, and in Spain itself, often sent convicts to the dreaded presidio at San Juan de Ulúa, this does not seem to have been the case for sentences emanating from either New Mexico or Texas.[51] (The presidio on the northern frontier was a distinctive entity, essentially a professional military outpost, that bore little resemblance to the classic presidio-prison found in the rest of the empire.)[52] To be sentenced to an *obraje* in New Spain's far north was apparently a severe measure, and only brutal crimes received such a punishment.

In December 1775, for example, four Indians from the mission of San Bernardo on the lower Rio Grande confessed to the murder of a Spanish settler. Apprehended and tried by Texas governor Barón de Ripperdá, the defendants admitted that all four had robbed and assaulted the victim—one beating him with a rifle barrel, one spearing him with a lance, one shooting him with arrows, and the fourth beating him with a stick. Despite the brutality of the crime, the four men received sentences of only six years at the *obrajes* of either Patos or Bonanza (both in Coahuila). Fray Manuel Pérez pleaded on their behalf, and as a result, Ripperdá commuted the sentences to three years of hard labor.[53]

Perhaps somewhat surprisingly, given the authoritarian nature of the Spanish state, there exist only a few cases of capital punishment in either New Mexico or Texas during the colonial period. Common to all is the particularly brutal, cruel, or treacherous means by which the crimes were committed. Spanish authorities, for example, executed after lengthy consideration a notorious character known as "Quemaculos," (literally, "Butt Burner") an accused rustler, adulterer, and murderer whose unsavory nickname derived from allegedly having burned his wife's genitals with lighted corn husks. Ultimately convicted of robbery, breaking jail, and having killed one man and wounding another in a fight, local authorities sentenced Rafael Gutiérrez to two hundred lashes and six years of presidio. In this case the weight of Gutiérrez's notorious past sealed his fate. For his long-standing deviant behavior—especially damnable was "having killed his wife in the most cruel of manners"—the *oidores* of the Audiencia of Guadalajara concurred with the request of the crown's prosecuting attorney and sentenced "Quemaculos" to die.[54]

To execute a death sentence, a provincial magistrate first had to send the criminal proceedings to some superior authority. And from at least 1765, any judicially imposed corporal punishment also required *audiencia* approval.[55] Documentary evidence indicates that even before this date provincial governors in both New Mexico and Texas routinely sent cases of a grave nature to some sort of legal adviser for an opinion.[56]

The reluctance to impose capital punishment was not unique to the far north of New Spain. Throughout Spanish America, as well as on the peninsula, the death sentence was rare.[57] A report on the affairs of the Audiencia of Guadalajara for 1798 shows that of the 265 persons tried in criminal cases during the year, the tribunal did not issue a single death sentence, although seven were so con-

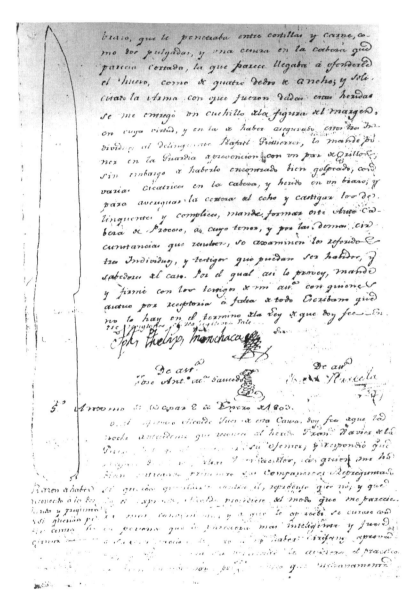

Figure 6. In the margin of the sumaria is the outline of the weapon wielded by the notorious criminal Rafael Gutiérrez, alias *Quemaculos.* (Source: Biblioteca del Estado de Jalisco, Guadalajara, Mexico)

demned in absentia. To the contrary, over half (142 or 53.6 percent) received no judicial punishment at all. If one includes those who eluded authorities, an even greater number escaped castigation. The breakdown of the *audiencia*'s sentencing is as follows:

> 46 sent to [work] prison; 29 condemned in absentia to the same destination; 19 to public works in this city [Guadalajara]; 7 to the gallows in absentia; 3 to [the Hospital of] Belén because of illness; 3 dead; 114 set free; 8 women sentenced to the house of correction of this city; 5 women to the same destination in absentia; 1 who hanged himself; 2 insane, one to Belén in this city, the other to the one in Mexico City; 28 who were not put in prison because it was deemed not appropriate to the merits of their cases; total 265.[58]

This lenitive quality of the sentences is, to many, one of the more surprising features of Spanish colonial justice. Yet, considering the nature of many colonial communities—with their close social and familial relationships—it is understandable.

One of the characteristics of the *antiguo régimen* was the notion of inequality—or perhaps, as Abelardo Levaggi has suggested, "relative equality"—under the law.[59] Indeed, the legal system bolstered the ideal of social hierarchy, granting privileges, exemptions, and special treatment according to one's corporate identity (clergy, military, guilds, universities, Indian communities, and so forth). On the peninsula, lineage, corporate membership, and profession served as indicators of one's social standing and legal status. These were important in the Indies, too, but racial identity was perhaps a greater determinant of one's place in society because it affected so greatly one's possibilities for corporate association. Not surprisingly, the judiciary in Spanish America considered race when determining appropriate punishment.

Such racial distinctions also were made in the far north, but their actual implementation is somewhat ambiguous. In 1768, for example, the governor of New Mexico, Pedro Fermín de Mendinueta declared that for robbery, "if the person is of *color quebrado* [a half-breed] they will receive twenty-five lashes at the pillory; if white they will be tied to the pillory and shamed publicly with the item they stole hanging from their neck."[60] To be sure, those who did suffer the lash were of lower castes. Convicted in 1742 of apostasy and flight, kidnapping, and breaking jail, the *genízaro* Luis Quintana paid for his errors with two hundred lashes in public and four years of labor at the mining works of San Felipe el Real de Chihuahua.[61] On the other hand, Cayetano Pasote, a mixed-blood *lobo*, had a better fate. Pasote was convicted of having assaulted the governor's cashier—wounding him seriously with a knife thrust to the face—and, on another occasion, of having broken into the house of the daughter of a prominent citizen, Felipe Tafoya, with intent to kill the latter. Cayetano Pasote managed to avoid the two hundred lashes of his original sentence because he had spent one and a half years in confinement, a circumstance that Governor Tomás Vélez Cachupín felt was a suitable substitute. (Additionally, the convict was banished downriver to Tomé, just south of Albuquerque, for ten years.)[62] Yet the paucity of instances of corporal punishment—as opposed to the overwhelming evidence of other, non-corporal forms—suggests that magistrates in New Mexico and Texas sought to avoid such dramatic, violent, and perhaps socially disruptive displays of discipline.

Indians also had special status under colonial law, but unlike for persons of mixed blood, theirs was judicially favorable. Despite their very real social and economic subordination, as legal minors indigenous persons were in theory to be treated with mildness when correcting their faults. According to Juan de Solórzano Pereira, "their punishments must be tempered," and a late-eighteenth-century jurist, Juan Gregorio de Zamudio, noted that "all the authors . . . recommend that judges be temperate in cases [involving Indians], that they lessen their punishments, that they behave with the love of true fathers and not with the severity of rigorous judges."[63] Furthermore, as one New Mexico governor pointed out, magistrates were to conform to "royal orders that say that crimes committed against Indians must be punished with greater rigor than those committed against Spaniards."[64] Little evidence supports the view that Indians were truly given lighter sentences, but neither were they punished with greater severity, and occasionally their supposed ignorance played to their advantage. This is perhaps because, especially in New Mexico, Indians comprised a vital and stable element of the colony. And, as members of the larger community, their persistent and daily contact with Hispanic neighbors helped to assure more evenhanded treatment by the judiciary.

In the event of conviction, one might always hope for an *indulto*, or a pardon from the crown. Usually, *indultos* applied generally throughout the empire. Milestones in the personal lives of the royal family—marriages, births, and accessions to the throne—often found expression in an empire-wide *indulto*. A convict languishing in the presidio at San Juan de Ulúa or making adobes in the hot desert sun surely derived special satisfaction from hearing of some such joyous event. Officials announced and effected *indultos* more often in Texas than in New Mexico, but no good reason explains this imbalance. Typical of the general pardons were those that took place in 1781 on the occasion of the "felicitous delivery of the Princess of Austria, Our Lady." The commandant general proclaimed the good news throughout his jurisdiction, and authorities in New Mexico and Texas publicized the corresponding *indulto*.[65] More important for convicts in the far north, like others in New Spain, they apparently secured their releases.[66] José Guadalupe Urrutia, for example, had been sentenced in 1808 to public works in San Antonio when authorities received word of the recently publicized general *indulto*. Urrutia received his freedom, along with a warning to cease his criminal ways.[67]

Provincial officials also invoked *indultos* on their own authority, but apparently only in the pre-*comandancia* era. Félix Martínez in 1716 offered a general pardon to all those who had taken asylum in New Mexico churches in exchange for serving in a military campaign against the Hopi Indians.[68] The practice of issuing local *indultos*, however, seems to have disappeared by the late eighteenth century.

Thus, work punishments, fines, and banishment appear as the most common ways to punish criminal activity in the provinces of Texas and New Mexico. Capital punishment was rare. Fines supported the judicial system; public works helped alleviate the fiscal drain on an already impoverished provincial treasury; and banishment helped maintain harmony within the community.

Similar to criminal cases, the sentences on the northern frontier for what we would call civil cases might best be described as based upon *equidad* and common sense. All but a few civil cases could be classified legally as small claims (*de menor cuantía*), which allowed for the use of the *juicio sumario* and freed magistrates from following strict procedural rules.[69] The inadequate legal training of the *alcaldes* and governors of Texas and New Mexico, then, posed no tremendous setback to the administration of equitable justice in those provinces. Reflecting the magistrates' obligation to uphold the public good and to maintain harmony within the community, the sentences in civil cases often effected some sort of compromise. Often the parties simply reached an out-of-court agreement. With the commonweal in mind, colonial frontier magistrates encouraged compromise, even if arrived at extrajudicially.[70]

In 1770, for example, Fray Juan José de Ynojosa and Pedro Pino became involved in a short-lived legal dispute. Two weeks after the proceedings began, both parties appeared before Governor Pedro Fermín de Mendinueta to request not only that the case be ended but also "that the proceedings in said litigation . . . be burned." Mendinueta consented to this request and noted in a memorandum that, because of the agreement of the two parties, he had ordered the destruction of the legal documents.[71] While perhaps an aberration, Mendinueta's official consent to this documentary destruction underscores the emphasis on conciliation.

Compromise proved to be a guiding principle for provincial magistrates of Texas and New Mexico in rendering equitable decisions. This spirit is especially conspicuous with regard to the adjudication of water rights. In his masterful study, *Water in the Hispanic Southwest*, Michael C. Meyer argues that the doctrine of equity and principle of the common good, while difficult to define precisely, provided magistrates with a juridical flexibility that enabled them to render satisfactory decisions. He concludes that

> compromise and concern for the common good were not merely lofty goals rejected cavalierly in the courts of the Hispanic Southwest. . . . They were fundamental principles brought to bear even in the most complex of water adjudications and even when the status of one of the litigants would have suggested that his opponent stood no chance in the impending case.[72]

Another expert, Daniel Tyler, points out that no user had a paramount right to the water, and magistrates under both the Spanish and Mexican regimes aimed to ensure its equitable and proportional distribution—a notion that Anglo-American courts have found to be problematic. "Water was for everyone," notes Tyler, "and when problems arose due to carelessness, greed, or accidents of nature, local officials attempted resolution in the spirit of compromise. . . . [The magistrate's] job was to keep peace amongst all water users."[73]

An example of this peace-keeping role of the magistrate occurred near Albuquerque in 1732, when a dispute arose between Cristóbal

García and José Montaño. García complained to the local *alcalde mayor* that his neighbor, Montaño, had refused him the right of way for an *acequia* to run through Montaño's property. Alcalde Mayor Juan González Bas summoned the two to "the house of Juan Griego, to hear verbally [García's] petition and, depending upon the declarations of each party, decide in fairness what is most suitable." Whatever verbal solution the *alcalde* had, Montaño did not agree with it, and written proceedings were forwarded to Governor Gervasio Cruzat y Góngora in Santa Fe. There, the two *vecinos* came to an agreement: Montaño acquiesced to having the *acequia* cross his land but insisted upon his right to make use of it. He also promised to help maintain it but only with judicial assurance that he would be reimbursed for any damages that the ditch might cause.[74] In a subsequent disagreement over the placement of another point of diversion—involving García and other neighbors—the judiciary intervened once again in order to effect a compromise in choosing an alternate site for the *saca de agua*.[75] In Texas, too, landholders—even the Canary Islanders—learned to share the precious liquid and looked to judicial authorities to assure appropriate distribution.[76]

The element of *arbitrio judicial* lent itself well to the type of magistrate found on the frontier. Given wide discretion at the moment of pronouncing judgment, and under no obligation to give judicial reasons, provincial officials could rely on conventional wisdom and community norms in administering punishments or effecting compromises. In considering these "common sense" judgments, however, one must emphasize that innate community values and contemporary views of equitable solutions often coincided with established legal precepts. This convergence of community expectations and royal law underscores the crown's role as legitimate arbiter of social discord and indicates the strength of shared values in colonial society. For this and for more practical reasons, appeals were infrequent.

The creation of the Comandancia General of the Provincias Internas might have facilitated the appeals process for colonials on the northern frontier. Indeed, Commandant General Caballero de Croix literally invited New Mexicans to air their complaints before him.[77] But by 1782, all appeals in civil matters, except those relating to the Royal Treasury, were to be directed to the Audiencia of Guadalajara. The perennial problem of distance once again loomed as an obstacle with which to contend.[78] Among the hundreds of criminal cases initiated in New Mexico and Texas, few were appealed. In civil cases, appeals frequently reached higher authorities within the province. A party dissatisfied with the judgment of an *alcalde mayor* in New Mexico, or an *alcalde ordinario* in Texas, might take the case before the provincial governor.[79] Furthermore, it is worth recalling that many differences were adjudicated verbally by a lesser magistrate— perhaps the *alcalde* of the district or his *teniente*.

More common than formal appeals were cases that came before a higher authority because of dissatisfaction with the way in which it was being handled, as illustrated in the case of "el Cuajo."[80] This process of "appeal," of course, did not follow established procedural rules, which provided for such a step after the pronouncement of a judge's sentence.[81] Litigants in the far north appear to have taken it upon themselves to seek other avenues of justice at any point in the proceedings, when they thought it in their interest to do so.

Particularly interesting in this regard are the actions of various Pueblo Indian groups in New Mexico, who, during the course of Spanish dominion, learned to employ the legal system to maintain intact a minimal land base that ensured their survival. Picking and choosing from a variety of officials available under the Spanish system, the Pueblos showed their understanding of litigation and their propensity to use those officials who might best further their interests—be it *alcalde mayor*, his *teniente*, the *protector de indios*, the provincial governor, or on occasion, the commandant general and *oidores* of the *audiencias* to the south.[82]

Illustrative of this point is the case of Taos Pueblo, which in 1730 and 1731 chose to circumvent the authority of the local *alcalde mayor* and instead presented directly to the governor its complaint against various Spaniards for trespass. Similarly, in 1815 the pueblo chose not to make extensive use of the *protector de indios*, who apparently proved to be unsuitable in pursuing its cause.[83] Also pursuing higher authority to resolve government inaction at a lower level, the Pueblo de Cochiti sent in 1816 a delegation of leaders not only to the commandant general at Chihuahua but all the way to the Juzgado General de Indios (General Indian Court) in Mexico City. This particular case made its way eventually to the Audiencia of Guadalajara, which decided in favor of Cochiti.[84]

Like the *sumaria*, the last two phases of the judicial process—the *plenario* and the *sentencia*—displayed remarkable variation in form and content. Perhaps the weakest phase of frontier judicial process, the *plenario* unfolded in haphazard fashion rather than in strict accordance to legal formula. Indeed, many of the court cases from New Mexico and Texas, especially criminal proceedings, fail to include an identifiable *plenario*. In regions that lacked jurists, it is not surprising that this should be the case. Because of the predominance and legitimacy of summary proceedings, however, a meticulously conducted *plenario* was not absolutely necessary for the proper administration of justice.

The *sentencia* also displayed a variety of judicial styles. In this particular phase, the frontier judiciary probably acted in much the same way as their provincial counterparts throughout the empire and sought to resolve disputes in ways amenable to local sensibilities. Using their *arbitrio judicial,* magistrates in Texas and New Mexico relied more upon *equidad* and community values than upon legal doctrine in arriving at their decisions, perhaps because they recognized their lack of expertise. Despite their inexperience and ignorance as jurists, they appear to have met the needs and expectations of the local inhabitants whom they served.

Epilogue

In *The Last Years of Spanish Texas,* Odie Faulk echoed the views of many when he characterized Spanish notions of justice as ranging "from the serious to the ridiculous." Somewhat more pointedly, Stanley Stein and Barbara Stein assert that "to the unprivileged, law was arbitrary and alien, therefore without moral force." And Charles Gibson maintained that "between the individual and the law in Spanish America there was always a certain irrelevance."[1] These assessments betray a twentieth-century reading of the historical record, however, and they deny the legitimacy of a legal system capable of meeting the needs of those whom it served. Evidence demonstrates that colonial subjects of all stations recurred readily to the judiciary to resolve their conflicts. It is unlikely that they would have done so if they, too, had viewed the legal system as "ridiculous," "alien," or "irrelevant."

An examination of the legal system in practice reveals more than the juridical principles of the monarchy. The quotidian implementation of Spanish law demonstrates just how important the judiciary was to the colonial political structure. The legal system provided the fundamental ordering mechanism for colonial society. It gave and reenforced both corporate and personal identity, and it afforded a rational means by which to settle conflict. A study of the judicial system from the bottom demonstrates the strong juridical quality of Spanish colonial rule, which reached even the remote parts of the empire.

The fact that the local population played a considerable, and legitimate, role in shaping the nature of regional legal administration dispels the common assumption of an "absolutist" colonial regime. Although outside appointees were ever present, the crown relied in great part on its New World subjects to staff its judiciary—

especially in areas removed from the administrative centers—and it entrusted them with the important task of maintaining order and harmony in their respective locales. The crown demanded the respect of locals in legal matters, but it also granted to them various mechanisms to lawfully modify its orders and decrees.

The convergence of crown and subject in the administration of justice underscores the consensual hegemony that characterized the Spanish colonial regime. The judicial records provide some of the best evidence of how locals negotiated their social relationships. Colonial subjects respected the figure of the monarch, and, in turn, his judicial agents sought to "give to each his own." In a sense, both the ruler and the ruled ceded some ground to establish a system for resolving conflict and preserving peace. The visions of none, perhaps, were ever fully realized; but there was enough common ground to assure the continuation of Spain's control in the Indies. Not only the elites, but also subordinate members of colonial society participated in the legal system, a participation that was not simply passive. Although stigmatized by their poverty or racial categorization, the lesser of society appealed to the king's judiciary to obtain what they insisted was their just due. Their expectations were met often enough for them to participate on a constant basis throughout the late colonial period. Those of lower status, then, also consented to and thereby legitimized the hegemony of Spanish colonial rule because it assured them some degree of protection and because it was partly of their making.

This study of the local elaboration of Spanish law underscores the importance of *derecho vulgar* in the colonial legal system, a crucial element that many have missed because of their concentration on the major urban areas of the Indies. Yet the New World domains of the Spanish monarchy were vast and varied, and most regions did not conform to the institutional models found in the big cities. Simplified in its administration, this *derecho vulgar* was something that the majority of colonial subjects experienced. Judicial practice in New Mexico and Texas should not be construed as the precise norm for other peripheral regions, each with their distinctive social and geographic settings. Understanding the spirit in which law was administered in these two provinces, however, provides a way of appreciating the flexibility of the colonial legal system and the legitimacy of regional peculiarities.

Notes

Introduction

1. Archivo General de la Nación (hereafter cited as AGN) Escribanos 22, exp. 10. "Año de 1803. Exp.te formado a consecuencia de R.l cédula que previene se informe el número de Abogados que existen en el distrito de esta R.l Audiencia." Antonio Porcel to Real Audiencia de México. Madrid, 22 December 1802.

2. AGN Escribanos 22, exp. 10. Josef Maldonado to [Real Audiencia]. Coatepec Chalco, 11 August 1803. *Recopilación de Leyes de los Reynos de las Indias* (Madrid: Julián de Paredes, 1681; facsimile reprint, Madrid: Cultura Hispánica, 1973), 1.12.1, prohibited the clergy from carrying the titles of alcalde, escribano, or abogado.

3. AGN Escribanos 22, exp. 10. Subdelegado Fernando Benito Martínez del Castillo to Real Audiencia. Real y Minas de Pachuca, 12 August 1803.

4. AGN Escribanos 22, exp. 10. José Barreyro y Quijano to [Real Audiencia]. Acapulco, 19 July 1803.

5. AGN Escribanos 22, exp. 10. Intendente Benito Pérez to [Real Audiencia]. Mérida de Yucatán, 10 August 1803; New Mexico State Archives and Records Center, Santa Fe, New Mexico, Spanish Archives of New Mexico, (hereafter cited as SANM)II:1593, Chacón to Real Audiencia. Santa Fe, 28 March 1802.

6. AGN Escribanos 1, exp. 2. "Plan que manifiesta el número, y clases de Escribanos que hay en los Partidos de cada Provincia de este Reyno." [México, 7 December 1798].

7. Archivo de la Real Audiencia de Guadalajara, Biblioteca Público del Estado de Jalisco (hereafter cited as ARAG), sin catalogar (s/c), n.5, Civil 1809–1819. "Real Cédula para q.e se aumenten en este Distrito el número de veinte y dos Abogados." Aranjuez, 28 February 1807. Durango also reported three crown officials with legal training, including the legal adviser of the Commandant General of the Provincias Internas.

8. Hans W. Baade, "Número de Abogados y Escribanos en la Nueva España, La Provincia de Téxas y La Luisiana," in José Luis Soberanes Fernández, ed., *Memoria del III Congreso de Historia del Derecho Mexicano (1983)* (México: Universidad Nacional Autónoma de México, 1984), pp. 119–28. AGN Escribanos 22, exp. 10. "Año de 1803. Exp.te formado a consecuencia de R.l cédula

que previene se informe el número de Abogados que existen en el distrito de
esta R.l Audiencia."
    9. SANM II:1593, Chacón to Real Audiencia. Santa Fe, 28 March 1802.
    10. Baade, "Número de Abogados."
    11. The prime example of this approach is Alfonso García Gallo; see his
Estudios de Historia del Derecho Indiano (Madrid: Instituto Nacional de Estudios
Jurídicos, 1972), a collection of his work on colonial law, and *Metodología de la
Historia del Derecho Indiano* (Santiago de Chile: Editorial Jurídica de Chile,
1970). Other scholars of this tradition include Rafael Altamira, Ricardo Levene,
Silvio Zavala, Lesley Byrd Simpson, José María Ots Capdequí, and Clarence
Haring.
    12. This is also true in other fields of colonial history, though some notable
recent work has focused on the peripheries to shed light on major themes of
the colonial period. See, for example, Ramón Gutiérrez, *When Jesus Came, the
Corn Mothers Went Away: Marriage, Sexuality, and Power in New Mexico, 1500–
1846* (Stanford: Stanford University Press, 1991); Ida Altman and James Lockhart, eds., *The Provinces of Early Mexico: Variants of Spanish-American Regional
Evolution* (Los Angeles: University of California Press, 1976); Woodrow Borah,
coordinator, *El Gobierno Provincial en la Nueva España, 1570–1787* (México: Universidad Nacional Autónoma de México, 1985).
    13. See, for example, the comments of José Cuello, "Beyond the 'Border-
lands' is the North of Colonial Mexico: A Latin-Americanist Perspective to the
Study of the Mexican North and the United States Southwest," in Kristyna P.
Demaree, ed., *Proceedings of the Pacific Coast Council on Latin American Studies* 9
(San Diego: San Diego State University Press, 1982), pp. 1–24. Even Herbert
Eugene Bolton, "Father of Borderlands History," warned against "mistaking
the tail for the dog." Quoted in David J. Weber, ed., *New Spain's Far Northern
Frontier: Essays on Spain in the American West, 1540–1821* (Albuquerque: Uni-
versity of New Mexico Press, 1979), p. xii.
    14. Prominent has been Myra Ellen Jenkins, who has written numerous
articles and reports dealing with land and water use in New Mexico. Her
articles include "The Baltasar Baca 'Grant': History of an Encroachment," *El
Palacio* 68 (Spring and Summer 1961): 47–64, 87–105; "Spanish Land Grants in
the Tewa Area," *New Mexico Historical Review* 47 (April 1972): 113–34; "Taos
Pueblo and Its Neighbors, 1540–1847," *New Mexico Historical Review* 41 (April
1966): 85–114. Other examples include Betty Eakle Dobkin, *The Spanish Element
in Texas Water Law* (Austin: University of Texas Press, 1959); Michael C. Meyer,
Water in the Hispanic Southwest: A Social and Legal History (Tucson: University
of Arizona Press, 1984); G. Emlen Hall, *Four Leagues of Pecos: A Legal History of
the Pecos Grant, 1800–1933* (Albuquerque: University of New Mexico Press,
1984).
    15. See N. M. Farriss, *Crown and Clergy in Colonial Mexico, 1759–1821: The
Crisis of Ecclesiastical Privilege* (London: The Athlone Press, 1968); Teófanes
Egido, "El Regalismo y las Relaciones Iglesia-Estado en el Siglo XVIII," in
Historia de la Iglesia en España (Madrid: Editorial Católica, 1979); Alberto de la
Hera, "La Legislación del Siglo XVIII sobre el Patronato Indiano," *Anuario de
Historia del Derecho Español* 40 (1970): 287–311. Tomás de Aquino García y

García, *El Derecho de Asilo en Indias* (Madrid: Editorial Reus, 1930), examines in documentary format one aspect of this diminishing autonomy.

16. Juan B. Iguíniz, *Los Gobernantes de Nueva Galicia: Datos y Documentos para sus Biografías* (Guadalajara: Unidad Editorial, 1981), p. 89. The position of highest rank at this time became *capitán general,* an official who also presided over the *audiencia.*

17. Lyle McAlister, *The "Fuero Militar" in New Spain, 1764–1800* (Gainesville: University of Florida Press, 1957), p. 15, maintains that the judicial privileges connected with the army formed the basis of later military dominance in the political life of nineteenth-century Latin America.

18. On the history of the collection under American sovereignty, see Henry Putney Beers, *Spanish and Mexican Records of the Southwest* (Tucson: University of Arizona Press, 1979), pp. 9–23.

19. Beers, *Spanish and Mexican Records,* 103–4.

20. Daniel Tyler, *Sources for New Mexican History, 1821–1848* (Santa Fe: Museum of New Mexico Press, 1984), pp. 126–28. See also Adán Benavides, Jr., "Loss by Division: The Commandancy General Archive of the Eastern Interior Provinces," *The Americas* 43 (October 1986): 203–19.

21. This became codified in the Constitution of 1812, art. 13, cap. 2, decreto of 9 October 1812, which dealt with judicial matters, cited in José María Alvarez, *Instituciones de Derecho Real de Castilla y de Indias,* tomo 4 (New York: Casa de Lanuza, Mendia, and Co., 1827; reprint, México: Universidad Nacional Autónoma de México, 1982), pp. 224–25.

22. ARAG Criminal 2–3-46. Certificación of Alcalde Ordinario Don Lope de la Vega. Chihuahua, 30 December 1809.

23. On the role of the law and legal professionals in shaping the expectations of the participants, see Steven Epstein, *Wills and Wealth in Medieval Genoa, 1150–1250* (Cambridge: Harvard University Press, 1984), pp. 13–21.

Chapter 1

1. Alejandro de Humboldt, *Ensayo Político Sobre el Reino de la Nueva España* (México: Editorial Porrúa, S.A., 1973), pp. 109–55, provides a contemporary description of the city at the turn of the nineteenth century.

2. Quote in John L. Kessell et al., eds., *Remote Beyond Compare: Letters of don Diego de Vargas to His Family from New Spain and New Mexico, 1675–1706* (Albuquerque: University of New Mexico Press, 1989), p. 168 (English) and p. 375 (Spanish).

3. Still the best work on Coronado is Herbert E. Bolton, *Coronado, Knight of Pueblos and Plains* (Albuquerque: University of New Mexico Press, 1949).

4. Bolton, *Coronado,* pp. 396—99, 381.

5. On the early institutional history of colonial Spanish America see C. H. Haring, *The Spanish Empire in America* (New York: Harbinger Books, 1963).

6. For early interest in New Mexico prior to colonization, see George P. Hammond and Agapito Rey, *The Rediscovery of New Mexico, 1580–1594: The*

Explorations of Chamuscado, Espejo, Castaño de Sosa, Morlete, and Leyva de Bonilla and Humaña (Albuquerque: University of New Mexico Press, 1966).

7. George P. Hammond and Agapito Rey, *Don Juan de Oñate: Colonizer of New Mexico, 1595–1628*, 2 vols. (Albuquerque: University of New Mexico Press, 1940). On the important mining center of Zacatecas, see Peter J. Bakewell, *Silver Mining and Society in Colonial Mexico: Zacatecas, 1546–1700* (Cambridge: Cambridge University Press, 1971). The apparent odd construction of "Nueva México," used commonly until the end of the eighteenth century, stems from the association with the city of Mexico. Thus, "nueva" is the implied modifier of "ciudad," a feminine noun.

8. *Recopilación de Indias*, 3.2.66.

9. The standard for the seventeenth century is the work of France V. Scholes, "Church and State in New Mexico," *New Mexico Historical Review* 11 (January 1936): 9–76; "Civil Government and Society in New Mexico in the Seventeenth Century," *New Mexico Historical Review* 10 (April 1935): 71–111; *Troublous Times in New Mexico, 1659–1670* (Albuquerque: University of New Mexico Press, 1942).

10. Robert S. Weddle, *Wilderness Manhunt: The Spanish Search for La Salle* (Austin: University of Texas Press, 1973). On mission activity in colonial Texas, see Carlos E. Castañeda, *Our Catholic Heritage in Texas*, 7 vols. (Austin: Von Boeckmann-Jones Company, 1936–58).

11. Archivo General de Indias (hereafter AGI) Guadalajara 129. King to Audiencia de México. Aranjuez, 23 May 1739.

12. For an idea of contemporary Spanish notions of the territorial limits of the province, see Charles Wilson Hackett, ed. and trans., *Pichardo's Treatise on the Limits of Louisiana and Texas*, 4 vols. (Austin: University of Texas Press, 1931–34). See also Donald E. Chipman, *Spanish Texas, 1519–1821* (Austin: University of Texas Press, 1992), pp. 2–5.

13. Geographer D. W. Meinig has pointed out the existence, even in colonial times, of "two lands with very different peoples and very different interests." D. W. Meinig, *Imperial Texas: An Interpretive Essay in Cultural Geography* (Austin and London: University of Texas Press, 1969), p. 28. For an overview of Texas geography in the colonial era, see Chipman, *Spanish Texas*, pp. 1–5.

14. Juan Agustín Morfi, *History of Texas, 1673–1779*, Carlos Eduardo Castañeda, ed. and trans. (Albuquerque: The Quivira Society, 1935), p. 49.

15. Lawrence Kinnaird, ed., *The Frontiers of New Spain: Nicolás de Lafora's Description, 1766–1768* (Berkeley: Quivira Society, 1958), p. 184.

16. Marc Simmons, "Settlement Patterns and Village Plans in Colonial New Mexico," in David J. Weber, ed., *New Spain's Far Northern Frontier: Essays on Spain in the American West, 1540–1821* (Albuquerque: University of New Mexico Press, 1979), pp. 102, 103, 110.

17. *Recopilación de Indias*, 4.7, incorporated Philip II's Ordenanzas de Pacificación (1573). See Zelia Nuttall, "Royal Ordinances Concerning the Laying Out of New Towns," *Hispanic American Historical Review* 5 (May 1922): 249–54. Later legislation included the important Plan de Pitic of 1789, a model for town planning on the northern frontier, which served to perpetuate the traditional Spanish municipality. A copy of the Plan de Pitic, dated Chihuahua, 20 Janu-

ary 1802, is found in SANM I:1265. See also Guillermo F. Margadant S., "El Plan de Pitic," *Boletín Mexicano de Derecho Comparado* 21 (Mayo–Agosto 1988): 699–715.

18. Simmons, "Settlement Patterns," pp. 99–115.

19. AGI Guadalajara 267, Desórdenes, n. 2.

20. Fray Francisco Atanacio Domínguez, *The Missions of New Mexico in 1776,* Eleanor B. Adams and Fray Angelico Chavez, trans. and eds. (Albuquerque: University of New Mexico Press, 1956), pp. 39–40.

21. Simmons, "Settlement Patterns," pp. 110–11.

22. A fuller discussion of the *cabildos* in New Mexico and Texas follows in Chapter 4.

23. See Marc Simmons, *Spanish Government in New Mexico* (Albuquerque: The University of New Mexico Press, 1968), pp. 193–99.

24. On the founding of San Antonio and its conformity to general town planning, see Gilbert R. Cruz, *Let There Be Towns: Spanish Municipal Origins in the American Southwest, 1610–1810* (College Station: Texas A&M Press, 1988).

25. Z[ebulon] M[ontgomery] Pike, *An Account of Expeditions to the Sources of the Mississippi, and the Western Parts of Louisiana, . . . And a Tour Through the Interior Parts of New Spain* (Philadelphia: C. & A. Conrad, 1810; facsimile reprint, n.p.: Readex Microprint, 1966), Appendix to Part III, p. 32.

26. Teodoro de Croix, General Report of 1781, in Alfred Barnaby Thomas, ed., *Teodoro de Croix and the Northern Frontier of New Spain, 1776–1783* (Norman: University of Oklahoma Press, 1941), p. 77.

27. Morfi, *History of Texas,* vol. 1, pp. 92—93.

28. France V. Scholes, "Royal Treasury Records Relating to the Province of New Mexico, 1596–1683," *New Mexico Historical Review* 50 (April 1975): 160. The crown spent about 55,000 pesos annually in the first years of the nineteenth century. Simmons, *Spanish Government,* p. 88. Writing in 1815, Governor Alberto Máynez noted that over the preceding century the government had spent 50,000 pesos annually to ensure Spanish control of New Mexico. John O. Baxter, *Las Carneradas: Sheep Trade in New Mexico, 1700–1860* (Albuquerque: University of New Mexico Press, 1987), p. 78. Similarly, Castañeda, *Our Catholic Heritage,* vol. 4, p. 44, notes that while it cost the king of Spain over 100,000 pesos per year to support the presidios and missions in Texas, "not one cent did he receive in return."

29. AGI Guadalajara 268. Relación Concisa y Exacta, Felipe de Neve (hereafter cited as Neve Report), p. 30. An *ordenanza* of 25 May 1653 for the *gobierno* of New Spain states: "Que los Mestizos, Mulatos y Negros libres, aunque sean Tributarios y paguen Tributo, no sean libres de Alcabala, y la paguen como los demas de todo lo que se debiere pagar." Eusebio Ventura Beleña, *Recopilación Sumaria de Todos los Autos Acordados de la Real Audiencia y Sala del Crímen de esta Nueva España* (México: Don Felipe de Zúñiga y Ontiveros, 1787; facsimile reprint, México: Universidad Nacional Autónoma de México, 1991), tomo 1, "Ordenanzas de Gobierno," III, p. 1. Indians also were subject to tribute, but not to the *alcabala* or tithe.

30. Not only was trade in New Mexico exempt from the *alcabala,* but the items that New Mexicans brought to Chihuahua were tax free at various times

in the late colonial period. See AGI Guadalajara 354, Conde de Revillagigedo to Antonio Valdés. México, 27 March 1790. On the *alcabala* in New Mexico see Simmons, *Spanish Government*, pp. 90–92. Jack Jackson, *Los Mesteños: Spanish Ranching in Texas, 1721–1821* (College Station: Texas A&M Press, 1986), p. 363, states that no *alcabala* was collected in Texas.

31. AGN Provincias Internas 103, exp. 1. Tomás Madrid and Francisco Esquibel to Marqués de Croix. Santa Fe, 14 September 1768. In this document, the two presidiales state that Croix's order to pay the soldiers in specie is impractical "por no haverlo ni correr en este País." Furthermore, they declare that in the past they have received their salaries in the form of supplies, and wish to continue to do so. Also, AGI Guadalajara 354, Testimonio de Expediente sobre los medios de fomentar la Industria y comercio del Nuevo México, f. 2. México, 17 September 1788. According to this document, "el soldado consuma todo su haver en solo mal vestirse, y que necesite de trabajar y cultivar personalmente sus tierras para comer, sin que jamás entre en su poder, ni en la Provincia el valor de medio real en moneda numeraria."

32. Baxter, *Las Carneradas*, p. 77, makes this suggestion, yet he emphasizes elsewhere in his work the scarcity of currency.

33. SANM II:79 "Causa Criminal contra Agustín Sáez y Luisa Varela por amanzebados," 4 October–20 October 1701. Simply stated, the system of *pesos de la tierra* consisted of assigning a monetary value to various exchangeable commodities, such as livestock, hides, or grains. AGI Guadalajara 267, Desórdenes, n. 13. Morfi claims that four different kinds of "money" were in use in colonial New Mexico, but other official reports refer to only two (AGI Guadalajara 354, Expediente sobre . . . la industria y el comercio, *passim*). Similarly, judicial records reveal only the *peso de la tierra* and the *peso de plata*. Although variable, the usual value of the *peso de la tierra* was half that of a *peso de plata*. This two-to-one ratio apparently continued well into the period of Mexican sovereignty. See University of New Mexico General Library, Special Collections (hereafter cited as UNMSC), New Mexico Documents, Archive 146P #20. In 1829, Antonio Suaso bought a certain tract of land in Taos for 56 "pesos al corriente de la tierra," and sold it nine years later for half that amount in cash.

34. AGI Guadalajara 354, Expediente sobre . . . la industria y el comercio, f. 1–1v.

35. SANM II:1284, Facundo Melgares to Alejo García Conde. Santa Fe, 19 June 1820.

36. SANM II:552, "Bando en qe. se Proibe qe. ninguno pueda comprar ni regalar a los Yndios Ynfieles nada sin qe. primero se han abierto los resgates p.r la R.l Justizia." Santa Fe, 7 January 1737. Also SANM II:402, "Causa criminal fulminada contra Diego de tores theniente de Alcalde Mayor de la Jurisdision de chama sobre hauer contrauenido a lo prohibido en los Resgates." 13 April–16 May 1735.

37. Some idea of the types of items exchanged in barter can be found in SANM II:470, "Autos de la Visita General . . . fechos por . . . D.n Joachín Codallos y Rabal . . . ," 20 June 1745.

38. Oakah L. Jones, Jr., *Los Paisanos: Spanish Settlers on the Northern Frontier of New Spain* (Norman: University of Oklahoma Press, 1979), pp. 133–34.

39. Jones, *Los Paisanos*, p. 134.

40. On this important facet of colonial New Mexico economy, see Baxter, *Las Carneradas*.

41. For a discussion of the partido system, see Baxter, *Las Carneradas*, p. 28.

42. AGI Guadalajara 354, Conde de Revillagigedo to Antonio Valdés. México, 27 March 1790.

43. For an overview of the economic history of colonial Texas, see Jones, *Los Paisanos*, pp. 51–54. Also, Odie B. Faulk, *The Last Years of Spanish Texas, 1778–1821* (The Hague: Mouton and Co., 1964), pp. 83–99.

44. Old, but unsurpassed in its sympathetic examination of the missions of Texas, is Carlos E. Castañeda, *Our Catholic Heritage in Texas.*

45. Documentation for land disbursement following secularization of the San Antonio area missions can be found in the Bexar County Archives (BCA), Mission Records.

46. On the early history of the cattle industry in Texas, see Jackson, *Los Mesteños*; also Sandra L. Myers, *The Ranch in Spanish Texas, 1691–1800* (El Paso: Texas Western Press, 1969).

47. Jackson, *Los Mesteños*, pp. 51–73, 87–107; *latifundia* more typical of the northern Mexican model were found in the so-called "Nueces strip," located in present-day Texas but at that time part of Nuevo Santander. The classic work on the Mexican hacienda is François Chevalier, *Land and Society in Colonial Mexico: The Great Hacienda*, trans. by Alvin Eustis, ed. by Lesley Byrd Simpson (Berkeley and Los Angeles: University of California Press, 1963).

48. Jones, *Los Paisanos*, p. 52. The 1777 census lists 1,141 men, including 332 *labradores* (just under 30 percent), 62 day laborers, 185 servants, 12 merchants, 98 artisans, and 237 with no specified occupation. The 1792 census reveals a similar composition. Of 295 adult males listed in 1820, there were 110 small farmers, 108 day laborers, 33 artisans, 3 merchants, a retired military officer, a curate, an employee of the Royal Treasury, a scribe, and a schoolmaster.

49. One particular case that exemplifies this point concerns the theft of 700 pesos, all in hard currency, from a visiting *mercader*. Béxar Archives (hereafter BA), r. 11 fr. 470, "Sumaria del Rovo hecho a D.n Santhiago Villa S.r, entrando por una bentana De su casa la noche de 24 al 25 De Oct.re Del 1774, De la Cantidad de 700 P.s En S.n Ant.o De Béxar." 28 October 1774–1 December 1778.

50. Pike, *Sources of the Mississippi*, Appendix to Part III, p. 20.

51. Information on demographics and ethnicity in late-colonial Texas is found in Alicia Vidaurreta Tjarks, "Comparative Demographic Analysis of Texas, 1777–1793," *Southwestern Historical Quarterly* 77 (January 1974): 291–338. For New Mexico see Antonio José Ríos-Bustamante, "New Mexico in the Eighteenth Century: Life, Labor and Trade in la Villa de San Felipe de Albuquerque, 1706–1790," *Aztlán* 7 (Fall 1976): 357–89; Janie Louise Aragón, "The People of Santa Fé in the 1790s," *Aztlán* 7 (Fall 1976): 391–417.

52. For examples of these prohibitions on free movement, see BCA, Protocolos 12, Petition of Joaquín Leal for José Leal. Trinidad, 4 January 1810; SANM II:183a, "Memoria de los Vez.os que estan fuera de este reino con liz.a." Santa Fe, 1 November 1712. See also *Recopilación de Indias*, 5.1.17. Some writers

have greatly emphasized the constraints placed upon freedom of movement on the northern frontier. See Jones, *Los Paisanos*, p. 254 and *passim*, and Chipman, *Spanish Texas*, pp. 8–9. On an individual basis, movement from one town or province to another was probably not so tightly controlled. Nevertheless, the contrast between the Anglo and Hispanic policies is striking.

53. D. A. Brading, "Government and Elite in Late Colonial Mexico," *Hispanic American Historical Review* 53 (August 1973): 389–414, presents a view of Mexican society that is fairly complex. See also John E. Kicza, *Colonial Entrepreneurs: Families and Business in Bourbon Mexico City* (Albuquerque: University of New Mexico Press, 1983), pp. 1–5.

54. In general, see John K. Chance, *Race and Class in Colonial Oaxaca* (Stanford: Stanford University Press, 1978); Kicza, *Colonial Entrepreneurs*, p. 14; Nicolás Sánchez Albornoz, *The Populations of Latin America* (Berkeley: University of California Press, 1974), p. 130; Magnus Mörner, *Race Mixture in the History of Latin America* (Boston: Little, Brown, and Company, 1967).

55. For New Mexico, see Adrian Bustamante, "'The Matter Was Never Resolved': The *Casta* System in Colonial New Mexico, 1693–1823," *New Mexico Historical Review* 66 (April 1991): 143–63.

56. Ventura Beleña, *Recopilación Sumaria*, t. 1, Autos Acordados, cxxxiii, 2 December 1574 and 31 July 1576. Mestizos and blacks, as well as Indians, comprised the so-called "*castas tributarias*" who by law were required to pay tribute. *Españoles*, of course, were exempt from tribute. As previously noted, commerce in the frontier areas was exempt from the *alcabala*.

57. SANM II:170, "Causa criminal contra don fernando de chaues por auer tratado mal de palabra a Ju.o Gonzales Alcalde ma.or," 20–26 January 1712. The slur of "*morisco*" is found in a Texas document. BA, r. 8 fr. 288, Juan Leal Goraz v. Patricio Rodríguez Galano. 6–7 September 1734. On the role of "fighting words" in other parts of New Spain, see William B. Taylor, *Drinking, Homicide, and Rebellion in Colonial Mexican Villages* (Stanford: Stanford University Press, 1979), pp. 81–83.

58. AGI Guadalajara 267, Desórdenes, n. 30; Fray Juan Agustín de Morfi, *Diario y Derrotero (1777–1781)* (Monterrey: Publicaciones del Instituto Tecnológico y de Estudios Superiores de Monterrey, 1967), p. 405 n. 419.

59. Gerald E. Poyo, "Immigrants and Integration in Late Eighteenth-Century Béxar," in Gerald E. Poyo and Gilberto M. Hinojosa, eds., *Tejano Origins in Eighteenth-Century San Antonio* (Austin: University of Texas Press, 1991), p. 88.

60. Jones, *Los Paisanos*, p. 134, notes that nearly 10 percent of all servants in New Mexico were *españoles*.

61. On the Pueblo Indians of New Mexico, consult Alfonso Ortiz, ed., *Handbook of North American Indians: The Southwest*, vol. 9 (Washington, D.C.: Smithsonian Institution, 1979).

62. The crucial role of the Pueblos in the defensive structure of New Mexico is described in Oakah L. Jones, Jr., *Pueblo Warriors and Spanish Conquest* (Norman: University of Oklahoma Press, 1966). For Pueblo involvement in the Spanish legal system, see Charles R. Cutter, *The Protector de Indios in Colonial New Mexico, 1659–1821* (Albuquerque: University of New Mexico Press, 1986).

On the altered relationship after reconquest, see John L. Kessell, "Spaniards and Pueblos: From Crusading Intolerance to Pragmatic Accommodation," in David Hurst Thomas, ed., *Columbian Consequences: Archaeological and Historical Perspectives on the Spanish Borderlands West*, vol. 1 (Washington, D.C.: Smithsonian Institution Press, 1989).

63. George P. Hammond and Agapito Rey, ed. and trans., *Narratives of the Coronado Expedition, 1540—1542* (Albuquerque: University of New Mexico Press, 1940), pp. 252–56.

64. Thomas H. Naylor and Charles W. Polzer, S.J., *Pedro de Rivera and the Military Regulations for Northern New Spain, 1724–1729: A Documentary History of His Frontier Inspection and the Reglamento de 1729* (Tucson: The University of Arizona Press, 1988), pp. 217–18.

65. AGI Guadalajara 267, Desórdenes, n. 7.

66. Angelico Chavez, "Genízaros," in Ortiz, *Handbook of North American Indians*, vol. 9, pp. 198–200; Simmons, "Settlement Patterns," p. 108.

67. On these two major groups see T. N. Campbell, "Coahuiltecans and Their Neighbors," and W. W. Newcomb, Jr., "Karankawa," both in Alfonso Ortiz, ed., *Handbook of North American Indians: Southwest*, vol. 10, pp. 343–58, 359–67.

68. Campbell, "The Coahuiltecans and Their Neighbors," p. 346.

69. On the mission experience of Indians in Texas, see Gilberto M. Hinojosa, "The Religious-Indian Communities: The Goals of the Friars," and Gilberto M. Hinojosa and Anne A. Fox, "Indians and Their Culture in San Fernando de Béxar," in Gerald E. Poyo and Gilberto M. Hinojosa, eds., *Tejano Origins in Eighteenth-Century San Antonio*.

70. ARAG Civil 161–9-1765. Isidro José de Cadelo Concha to M.P.S., Guadalajara, 6 February 1800. Fray Isidro José de Cadelo, who seems to have had a contentious nature, asserted that the Pueblos differed little from their heathen counterparts and lived "en estado de una bronca barbarie, y en camino de perder sus almas" (f. 86). Fray Francisco Atanacio Domínguez noted that the Indians of Taos and Picurís fled and hid when their missionary arrived. *The Missions of New Mexico in 1776*, p. 258.

71. Borderlands scholars have focused considerable attention on Spanish relations with the *indios bárbaros*. See Elizabeth A. H. John, *Storms Brewed in Other Men's Worlds: The Confrontation of Indians, Spanish, and French in the Southwest, 1540–1795* (College Station: Texas A&M University Press, 1975); Max L. Moorhead, *The Apache Frontier: Jacobo Ugarte and Spanish-Indian Relations in Northern New Spain, 1769–1791* (Norman: University of Oklahoma Press, 1968); and several collections of documents edited by Alfred B. Thomas.

72. Information on these groups can be found in Ortiz, ed., *Handbook of North American Indians*, vol. 10.

73. AGN Provincias Internas 73, exp. 2. "Papel Ynstructibo del exmo señor B.o Fr. D.n Antonio Bucarely y Ursua, Virrey de Nueva España, relatibo a las Provincias Ynternas, para el señor D.n Teodoro de Croix, Comandante de ellas." México, 20 March 1777.

74. AGI Guadalajara 268. Neve Report, p. 57.

Chapter 2

1. *Las Siete Partidas del Sabio Rey don Alonso el Nono* (Salamanca: Andrea de Portonaris, 1555; facsimile reprint, Madrid: Boletín Oficial del Estado, 1974), 2.1.1. See also Colin M. MacLachlan, *Spain's Empire in the New World: The Role of Ideas in Institutional and Social Change* (Berkeley: University of California Press, 1988), pp. 8–13; Benjamín González Alonso, *El Corregidor Castellano (1348–1808)* (Madrid: Instituto de Estudios Administrativos, 1970), p. 18. This notion of the monarchy persisted well into the late Bourbon period. See Lorenzo Guardiola y Sáez, *El Corregidor Perfecto y Juez Exactamente Dotado de las Calidades Necesarias y Convenientes para el Buen Gobierno Económico y Político de los Pueblos* (Madrid: Alfonso López, 1785), pp. 38–39, quote on p. 35.

2. Francisco Tomás y Valiente, *Manual de Historia del Derecho Español,* 4th ed. (Madrid: Tecnos, 1983), pp. 243–47. On the controversy surrounding the authorship and date of the *Partidas,* see pp. 237–42.

3. Tomás y Valiente, *Manual,* pp. 339–40.

4. García Gallo, *Metodología de la Historia del Derecho Indiano,* p. 60.

5. Tomás y Valiente, *Manual,* p. 341.

6. Benjamin Keen, *A History of Latin America* (Boston: Houghton Mifflin Company, 1992), pp. 101–2; Charles Gibson, *Spain in America* (New York: Harper, 1966), p. 109; Stanley J. Stein and Barbara H. Stein, *The Colonial Heritage of Latin America* (New York: Oxford University Press, 1970), p. 81. Some examples of nineteenth-century comments are found in Abelardo Levaggi, *Manual de Historia del Derecho Argentino* (Buenos Aires: Ediciones Depalma, 1991), t. 1, p. 203. Michael C. Meyer and William L. Sherman, *The Course of Mexican History* (New York and Oxford: Oxford University Press, 1991), p. 314. Commenting on New Mexico, Josiah Gregg, *Commerce of the Prairies* (Norman: University of Oklahoma Press, 1954), asserted that "there is scarcely one alcalde in a dozen who knows what a law is" (164–65). An almost identical assessment was offered by W. W. H. Davis, *El Gringo: New Mexico and Her People* (New York: Harper, 1857; reprint, Lincoln: University of Nebraska Press, 1982), who believed that "none of [the *alcaldes*] were ever accused of knowing any thing about law" (p. 105), and that "the decision of the *alcalde* was seldom made up according to the merits of the case" (p. 106). See also David J. Langum, *Law and Community on the Mexican California Frontier: Anglo-American Expatriates and the Clash of Legal Traditions, 1821–1846* (Norman: University of Oklahoma Press, 1987), especially pp. 131–52.

7. In *A New Pronouncing Dictionary of the Spanish and English Languages* (New York and London: D. Appleton and Company, 1900), Velázquez defines *derecho* as "right, justice, law, equity."

8. See Alfonso García Gallo, *Manual de Historia del Derecho Español,* 9th ed. (Madrid: AGESA, 1982), vol. 1, pp. 161–64 and vol. 2, pp. 40–48.

9. Although laws formulated specifically for the Indies always took precedence over Castilian law, the crown usually sought compatibility between the two systems. See, for example, *Recopilación de Indias,* 2.2.13; in a similar vein, 2.1.2. For a closer scrutiny of this issue see Bernardino Bravo Lira, "El

Derecho Indiano y sus Raíces Europeas: Derecho Común y Propio de Castilla," *Anuario de Historia del Derecho Español* 58 (1988), especially pp. 5–35; Tomás y Valiente, *Manual*, pp. 337–41.

10. Quote in SANM II:160, María Martín v. Luis López, 30 April–30 May 1710.

11. The idea of balance in approaching the art of jurisprudence appears as early as the *Partidas* and extends well into the nineteenth century. *Siete Partidas*, 3.3.3, for example, states that judges must be "de buena fama. E sin mala cobdicia. E que ayan sabiduria, para judgar los pleytos, derechamẽte, por su saber, o por vso de luengo tiẽpo. E que sean mãsos. E de buena palabra, a los que vinierẽ, ante ellos, a juyzio, E sobre todo, que teman a Dios."

12. *Equidad* should not be confused with the more narrowly defined "equity" of Anglo legal tradition. Especially important works in identifying the components of *derecho indiano* are Víctor Tau Anzoátegui, "La Noción de Ley en América Hispana durante los Siglos XVI a XVIII," *Anuario de Filosofía Jurídica y Social* 6 (1986): 193–232; and Abelardo Levaggi, "El Concepto del Derecho según los Fiscales de la Segunda Audiencia de Buenos Aires (1784–1810)," *Actas del VIII Congreso del Instituto Internacional de Historia del Derecho Indiano* (Santiago: Revista Chilena de la Historia del Derecho, 1987), pp. 245–59.

13. For a fuller treatment of the range and types of "laws," see Alfonso García Gallo, "La Ley como Fuente del Derecho en Indias en el Siglo XVI," *Estudios de Historia del Derecho Indiano* (Madrid: Instituto Nacional de Estudios Jurídicos, 1972), pp. 169–285.

14. See Víctor Tau Anzoátegui, "La Doctrina de los Autores como Fuente del Derecho Castellano-Indiano," *Revista de Historia del Derecho* 17 (1989): 351–408.

15. Important work has been done in this respect by Víctor Tau Anzoátegui and, earlier, Rafael Altamira. For the American Southwest under Spanish rule, Malcolm Ebright argues strongly for the importance of custom in Hispanic law. See, for example, Malcolm Ebright, "Introduction: Spanish and Mexican Land Grants and the Law," in Malcolm Ebright, ed., *Spanish and Mexican Land Grants and the Law* (Manhattan: Sunflower University Press, 1989), pp. 3–11; Malcolm Ebright, "New Mexican Land Grants: The Legal Background," in Charles L. Briggs and John R. Van Ness, eds., *Land, Water, and Culture: New Perspectives on Hispanic Land Grants* (Albuquerque: University of New Mexico Press, 1987), pp. 15–64.

16. The notion that the prime goal of justice was "dar a cada uno lo suyo" appears, even on the northern frontier of New Spain, repeatedly throughout the Hispanic world of the antiguo régimen. SANM II:316, Martín Hurtado v. Jacinto Sánchez, 23 April–26 April 1722. *Siete Partidas*, 3.1.3, "E los mandamientos de la Iusticia, e del derecho son tres. El primero, que ome biua honestamente, quanto en si. El segundo, que non faga mal, nin daño a otro. El tercero, que de su derecho a cada vno." Joseph Juan y Colom, *Instrucción Jurídica de Escribanos, Abogados, y Jueces Ordinarios de Juzgados Inferiores* (Madrid: Imprenta de la Viuda e Hijo de Marín, 1795), p. 1, "La justicia es una constante y perpetua voluntad de dar a cada uno lo que es suyo." José María Alvarez, *Instituciones de Derecho Real de Castilla y de Indias*, p. 21, "La

justicia, tomada en general, podemos decir que es: la observancia de todas las leyes que previenen no dañar a otro, dar a cada uno lo que es suyo y vivir honestamente."

17. See Abelardo Levaggi, "El Concepto del Derecho Según los Fiscales," pp. 245–59.

18. The trend in Latin American and Spanish law during the nineteenth century was toward codification that sought in large measure to eliminate the discretionary powers of the judiciary. See Bravo Lira, "El Derecho Indiano y sus Raíces Europeas," pp. 67–79; on the codification process in Spain, Tomás y Valiente, *Manual*, pp. 465–557.

19. *Recopilación de Indias*, 2.1.24 states that all royal provisions must be obeyed, "salvo siendo el negocio de calidad, que de su cumplimiento se seguiria escandalo conocido, ó daño irreparable, que en tal caso permitimos, que haviendo lugar de derecho, suplicacion, é interponiendo por quien, y como deba, puedã sobreseer en el cumplimiento." See also *Recopilación de Indias*, 2.1.22; *Nueva Recopilación*, 4.14.2; *Novísima Recopilación*, 3.4.4; *Siete Partidas*, 3.18.29–31. On other mechanisms for altering legislation, see Víctor Tau Anzoátegui, "La Ley 'Se Obedece pero no se Cumple.' En Torno a la Suplicación de las Leyes en el Derecho Indiano," *Anuario Histórico Jurídico Ecuatoriano* 6 (1980): 55–110. On the idea that laws must be reasonable, Levaggi, "El Concepto del Derecho," *passim*. Various texts that affirm this right can be found in García Gallo, *Manual de Historia del Derecho Español*, vol. 2, pp. 105–6.

20. In this respect, a most valuable collection of arguments of a prosecuting attorney (*fiscal*) for the Audiencia de Buenos Aires in the late eighteenth century is Abelardo Levaggi, *El Virreinato Rioplatense en las Vistas Fiscales de José Márquez de la Plata*, 3 vols. (Buenos Aires: Universidad del Museo Social Argentino, 1988). See also Levaggi, "El Concepto del Derecho," *passim*. Other valuable sources include the Colección Mata Linares housed at the Real Academia de Historia, Madrid; and the writings of a colonial Mexican jurist, Juan de Torquemada, found in the Biblioteca Nacional (Madrid), ms. 20311, "Varias Alegaciones Jurídicas que el Lic.do D. Juan Antonio de Torquemada, Abogado de la R.l Avdien.cia de esta Nueva España, Dixo En sus Reales Estrados, en los de su Real Sala de el Crimen, y en los de el Jusgado, y Avdiencia Ecclesiastica," 1724–1725.

21. María Paz Alonso Romero, *El Proceso Penal en Castilla (Siglos XIII–XVIII)* (Salamanca: Ediciones Universidad de Salamanca, 1982), p. 260; José Sánchez-Arcilla Bernal, *Las Ordenanzas de las Audiencias de Indias (1511–1821)* (Madrid: Dykinson, S.L., 1992), p. 315, Ordenanzas de Palafox, "Ordenanzas para la Rl. Audiencia desta Nueua España, Ministros y officiales della," tít. 1, n. 24. On the problems that this prohibition poses, see Francisco Tomás y Valiente, *El Derecho Penal de la Monarquía Absoluta (Siglos XVI-XVII-XVIII)* (Madrid: Tecnos, 1969), p. 182. Still, we can gain a fairly good idea of judicial reasoning by examining the arguments of the *fiscales* (state prosecutors) of the *audiencia*. Steeped in a common intellectual tradition, these officials no doubt shared with the *oidores* the underlying juridical assumptions that might decide a particular case.

22. Besides the above-mentioned works by Abelardo Levaggi, see Víctor

Tau Anzoátegui, "La Costumbre como Fuente del Derecho Indiano en los Siglos XVI y XVII: Estudio a Través de los Cabildos del Río de la Plata, Cuyo y Tucumán," *III Congreso del Instituto Internacional de Historia del Derecho Indiano* (Madrid: Instituto Nacional de Estudios Jurídicos, 1970), pp. 115–92; Tau Anzoátegui, "La Noción de Ley en América Hispana," pp. 193–232; especially Tau Anzoátegui, "La Doctrina de los Autores Como Fuente del Derecho Castellano-Indiano," pp. 351–408. See also Abelardo Levaggi, "El Derecho Romano en la Formación de los Abogados Argentinos del Ochocientos," *Derecho* 40 (1986): 17–33; Bernardino Bravo Lira, "El Derecho Indiano y Sus Raíces Europeas," pp. 5–80.

23. Explored more fully in Charles R. Cutter, "La Magistratura Local en el Norte de la Nueva España: El Caso de Nuevo México," *Anuario Mexicano de Historia del Derecho* 4 (1992): 29—39.

24. Joseph W. McKnight, "Law Books on the Hispanic Frontier," *Journal of the West* 27 (July 1988): 75. Ricardo Zorraquín Becú, *Organización Judicial Argentina en el Período Hispánico* (Buenos Aires: Editorial Perrot, 1981), pp. 82–83. Although the prominence of the *asesor letrado* rose in the eighteenth century, some gobernaciones had such a figure at an earlier date. See *Recopilación de Indias*, 5.2.37, 5.2.39.

25. Even on the peninsula, magistrates at the local level had little formal training in law. For contemporary comments on this state of affairs, see José Berní y Catalá, *Instrucción de Alcaldes Ordinarios, Que Comprehende las Obligaciones de Estos, y del Amotacén* (Valencia: Agustín Laborda, 1757), p. 1; Vicente Vizcaíno Pérez, *Tratado de la Jurisdicción Ordinaria para la Dirección y Guía de los Alcaldes de los Pueblos de España*, 4th ed. (Madrid: 1802; reprint, Madrid: Instituto de Estudios de Administración Local, 1979), pp. 33–34.

26. In addition to allusions noted in footnote #6, see Simmons, *Spanish Government*, p. 176; and more recently, David J. Langum, *Law and Community on the Mexican California Frontier*, p. 33, who cites Simmons.

27. McKnight, "Law Books on the Hispanic Frontier," pp. 75–78. For an extended essay on colonial juridical bibliography, see Javier Malagón Barceló, *La Literatura Jurídica Española del Siglo de Oro en la Nueva España* (México: Biblioteca Nacional de México, Instituto Bibliográfico Mexicano, 1959). Useful discussions of the evolution in styles of Hispanic juridical writing are found in Bravo Lira, "El Derecho Indiano y sus Raíces Europeas," pp. 36–77, and in Tomás y Valiente, *Derecho Penal*, pp. 85–151.

28. Volume 2 of this work was entitled *Instrucción Jurídica de Escribanos, Abogados, y Jueces Ordinarios de Juzgados Inferiores*. McKnight, "Law Books on the Hispanic Frontier," p. 78, finds a 1787 edition of this work in San Antonio, Texas. For New Mexico, SANM I:252, Settlement of estate of Manuel Delgado, "Inventario," 29 September 1815, lists this as "Colón de escrivanos." Governor Joaquín del Real Alencaster made a rather cryptic allusion to the "formulario de Colón" in ARAG Criminal 45–13–1023, Joaquín del Real Alencaster to Señores de la Real Audiencia [de Guadalajara]. Santa Fe, 1 July 1805. This may well be a reference not to the work of Joseph Juan y Colom, however, but to the manual composed by Félix Colón de Larriátegui, *Juzgados Militares de España y sus Indias* (Madrid: Repulles, 1797).

162 · NOTES TO PAGES 37–38

29. An example of some rather sophisticated notions of what constituted *derecho* appear in SANM I:464, Petition of Diego Torres, Bartolomé Truxillo, Antonio de Salazar, Manuel Valerio, and Manuel Martín, n.d. (but probably early to mid eighteenth century). These men argue that their position is supported by "Ley, Authoridad, Doctrina, e opinion, assi en el [derecho] Civil comun, o canonico." They also cite Juan de Solórzano Pereira's *De Indiarum Iure* by book, chapter, and number.

30. Rothrock List, "Books in Colonial New Mexico," manuscript in University of New Mexico General Library, Special Collections. McKnight, "Law Books on the Hispanic Frontier," *passim*. See also Eleanor B. Adams and France V. Scholes, "Books in New Mexico, 1598–1680," *New Mexico Historical Review* 17 (July 1942): 226–70; and by the same authors, "Two Colonial New Mexico Libraries, 1704, 1706," *New Mexico Historical Review* 19 (April 1944): 135–67. Basic texts such as these seem to have been readily available in all parts of the Spanish colonies. See, for example, Jorge Luján Muñoz, "Acerca de la Llegada y Aplicación de la Recopilación de las Leyes de Indias en el Reino de Guatemala, 1681–1699," in *Memoria del Simposio Hispanoamericano Sobre las Leyes de Indias* (San José, Costa Rica: Imprenta Nacional, 1984).

31. For example, SANM II:508, "Año de 1749. Demanda puesta p.r Manuel Sanz de Garuizu, En nom.re de d.n Antonio de tapia vez.o de la Ziudad de Mex.co de la Cantt.d que en ella se expresa, Conttra Jph Romo de Vera vez.o de estta villa." 3 November 1749–14 July 1751; SANM II:360, "Caussa Criminal Contra Ant.o Yuba yndio natural del Pu.o de tezuque y Asensio Povio Yndio natural del Pueblo de Nambé de la naz.n teguas." 25 June–2 August 1731; AGN Provincias Internas 32, exp. 10, "Año de 1730. Caussa Criminal hecha p.r muertte de Nicolas Pasqual conttra Philipe de Abila actor y reo en el." 12 April–18 May 1731. An allusion to Article 283 of the Constitution of 1812 in SANM I:216, Ursula Chaves v. Joaquín Pino, 1821.

32. See Joaquín Escriche, *Diccionario Razonado de Legislación y Jurisprudencia* (Paris: Librería de Garnier Hermanos, 1869), pp. 528–29.

33. The term consensual hegemony is an adaptation of Antonio Gramsci's social theory of cultural hegemony, in which he posited that dominant cultures or ideologies allowed sufficient input from below to afford to all a sense of belonging to the whole. On Gramsci's ideas that have been most useful for scholars, see Walter L. Adamson, *Hegemony and Revolution: A Study of Antonio Gramsci's Political and Cultural Theory* (Berkeley: University of California Press, 1980). Elaborations of the idea of cultural hegemony include T. J. Jackson Lears, "The Concept of Cultural Hegemony: Problems and Possibilities," *American Historical Review* 90 (June 1985): 567–93; Raymond Williams, "Base and Superstructure in Marxist Cultural Theory," *New Left Review* 82 (November–December 1973): 3–16.

34. On the regional variations, see Wistano Luis Orozco, *Los Ejidos de los Pueblos* (1914; reprint, México: Ediciones "El Caballito," 1975), pp. 59–72.

35. Discussed more fully in Charles R. Cutter, "El Indio Fronterizo ante la Justicia Española: La Creación de una Hegemonía Consensual," *IX Congreso del Instituto Internacional de Historia del Derecho Indiano: Actas y Estudios* (Madrid: Universidad Complutense de Madrid, 1991) 2: 19–28.

36. SANM I:78, "Pleyto de Xp.al Xaramillo con los Yndios de S Ph.e," 26 February 1704. The petition was denied by Governor Diego de Vargas.

37. SANM I:1351, "Autos Seguidos por los Yndios del Pueblo de S.n Yldefonso contra los Erederos de Juana Luján y de fran.co Gómez deel Castillo," 4 February 1763. SANM I:1354, Las Repúblicas de Santa Clara y San Yldefonso to Governor Juan Bautista de Anza, Santa Fe, 6 May 1786. See also Jenkins, "Spanish Land Grants in the Tewa Area."

38. Among the numerous other examples of recognition of the Pueblo league are ARAG Civil 267–17–3654, "El Común y Pueblo de Cochití diciendo de nulidad a la venta de un Rancho cituado en su fundo legal, y reclamando la usurpación de otro." 6 September 1816; SANM I:703, Felipe Sandoval to governor. 17 August 1814; SANM I:1339, "Petizion a fauor de los Yndios teguas contra Ynacio de Roybal," 16 September 1704.

39. Jones, *Los Paisanos*, pp. 136–39 and 55–57, points out the absolute lack of primary schools in New Mexico until the end of the eighteenth and beginning of the nineteenth centuries. Texas also faced a shortage. Neither province boasted institutions of higher learning.

40. For more on Felipe Tafoya, see Chapter 4.

41. Quote from ARAG 261–15–3564, "El Común del Pueblo de Cochití," f. 95. Archival holdings in Mexico City and in Guadalajara indicate that the crown routinely permitted this simplified form throughout New Spain. See Cutter, "La Magistratura Local." For central Mexico, see María del Refugio González and Teresa Lozano, "La Administración de Justicia," in Woodrow Borah, coordinator, *El Gobierno Provincial en la Nueva España, 1570–1787* (México: Universidad Nacional Autónoma de México, 1985), pp. 77, 78, 83.

42. On the *juicio sumario* or *extraordinario*, Juan Sala, *Ilustración del Derecho Real de España* (Valencia: Joseph de Orga, 1803), t. 2, lib. 3, tít. 2; Pedro Carrillo Sánchez, *Prontuario Alfabético de Legislación y Práctica* (Madrid: Boix Editor, 1840), p. 158; Alvarez, *Instituciones de Derecho Real de Castilla y de Indias*, lib. 4, p. 212.

43. SANM II:369, "Pleyto y demanda q.e puso Antonio de Cárdenas contra los herederos de Juan Luxan sobre los salarios q se le deuian," 5 June–11 September 1732.

44. SANM II:465, "Queja que dio Antonio Baca Alc.e may.r y cap.n a Guerra del Pueblo de Xemes y su Juridicion, contra Hernando chabez ambos Vecinos de la V.a de S.n Phelipe de Alburquerque sobre hauerle probocado con palabras indecorosas en la forma que adentro se percive," 12–25 June 1745.

45. SANM II:465c, "Causa criminal, a pedimento de Juan Antonio Salazar, contra Manuel Valerio, ambos vecinos de la Villa de Santa Cruz de la Cañada, sobre una herida que le hizo, y malos tratamientos de palabras, en la forma que adentro se contiene," 31 July–6 September 1745. The five "palabras de injuria" were "gafo ó sodomético, ó cornudo, ó traidor, ó herege." For married women, "puta." *Novísima Recopilación*, 12.25.1.

46. Illuminating the peninsular viewpoint is José Berní y Catalá, *Práctica Criminal* (Valencia: Simón Faure, 1749), pp. 7–8, 16.

47. BA, r. 14 fr. 921, Proceedings against Juan José Vergara. 4 February–30 June 1782.

48. BA, r. 14 fr. 800, José Miguel Sales Games, Francisco Sales Games, Pedro Hernández, and Carlos Hernández v. Urbano Ynojosa and Ana María Trinidad Games. 4 June–29 November 1781.

49. SANM II:574, "Diligencias seguidas por querella de dos Yndias Genízaras sirbientes contra sus amos," 12–15 October 1763.

50. BA, r. 8 fr. 369, Antonia Lusgardia Hernández v. Miguel Núñez Morillo. 9 August 1735.

Chapter 3

1. *Recopilación de Indias*, 2.2.13; in a similar vein see 2.1.2.

2. *Siete Partidas*, 2.1.1.

3. Juan de Solórzano Pereira, *Política Indiana* (Madrid: 1647; reprint, Madrid and Buenos Aires: Compañía Ibero-Americana de Publicaciones, S.A., 1930), 5.6.4. On the notion of the monarch as God's representative on earth, see *Siete Partidas*, 2.1.5; Solórzano Pereira, *Política Indiana*, 5.8.1; José María Ots Capdequí, *Instituciones* (Barcelona: Salvat Editores, S.A., 1959), p. 307.

4. González Alonso, *Corregidor Castellano*, p. 18. A late eighteenth-century jurist, Lorenzo Guardiola y Sáez, *El Corregidor Perfecto* (1785), pp. 35, 38–39, wrote "el Rey se debe mostrar liberal en oir peticiones y querellas a todos los que pidieren Justicia, porque su propio oficio es hacer juicio y Justicia, y que este poderío temporal lo recibe de la Celestial Magestad." See also *Nueva Recopilación de Castill*a, 2.2.1, 2, 3, 4, 5; MacLachlan, *Spain's Empire in the New World*, pp. 8–13.

5. González Alonso, *Corregidor Castellano*, p. 77. Still, the notion of the *rey justiciero* held strong appeal—at the end of the fifteenth century, Fernando and Isabel still held public court in which they personally administered justice. See Henry Kamen, *Spain, 1469–1714: A Society of Conflict* (London: Longman, 1983), p. 30.

6. See John L. Phelan, *The People and the King: The Comunero Revolution in Colombia, 1781* (Madison: University of Wisconsin Press, 1977), pp. xvii, 77–78, and *passim*. In a similar vein, Taylor, *Drinking, Homicide, and Rebellion*, pp. 133–34.

7. The standard study of this institution is Ernesto Schäfer, *El Consejo Real y Supremo de las Indias*, 2 vols. (Sevilla: Escuela de Estudios Hispano-Americanos, 1935–47). See also Haring, *Spanish Empire in America*, pp. 94–109.

8. *Recopilación de Indias*, 2.2–14, deals with matters of the Consejo de Indias and its functionaries. On the late-colonial role of the Council of the Indies, see Mark A. Burkholder, "The Council of the Indies in the Late Eighteenth Century: A New Perspective," *Hispanic American Historical Review* 56 (1976): 404–23.

9. On León Pinelo, Juan Manzano Manzano, "El Proceso Recopilador de las Leyes de Indias Hasta 1680: Estudio Preliminar," in *Recopilación de Leyes de los Reynos de las Indias*. Ismael Sánchez Bella et al., "El Proyecto de Recopilación de Leyes de León Pinelo," *IX Congreso del Instituto Internacional de*

Historia del Derecho Indiano (Madrid: Universidad Complutense de Madrid, 1991) vol. 1, pp. 61–107.

10. Antonio Rodríguez de León Pinelo, *Tratado de Confirmaciones Reales* (Madrid: Juan González, 1630; facsimile reprint, Caracas: Biblioteca de la Academia Nacional de la Historia, 1979), Parte I, cap. viii, ff. 49v–50.

11. AGI Guadalajara 142, "Expedientes relativos a Diego de Vargas, gobernador de Nuevo México: pleito con la villa de Sta. Fé y sucesión de su hija en el título nobiliario que ostenta de marqués de la Nava de Brazinas, 1699–1719."

12. AGI Guadalajara 333, "Expediente sobre la causa formada en México contra el Coronel d.n Jacinto de Barrios y Jáuregui sobre trato ilícito que tuvo siendo Governador de la Provincia de los Texas con los Franceses, y Indios fronterizos no sugetos." Before the creation in the late eighteenth century of a special Junta de Competencias, the Council of the Indies apparently served as supreme arbiter in such matters. Relatively unimportant cases, but ones that involved jurisdictional squabbles frequently came before the council. See, for example, AGI Guadalajara 342, "Año de 1777. Testim.o del Expediente formado sobre que se declare a quien toque el conocimiento de las causas y negocios del distrito de San Luis Colotlán." This case, involving the rape of a young woman in Santiago Totatiche (near Nayarit), came before the Council of the Indies because of a jurisdictional dispute between the Viceroy and the Real Audiencia.

13. Haring, *Spanish Empire*, p. 121, states that the minimum stayed at 10,000 pesos "into the eighteenth century."

14. AGI Guadalajara 142, "Expedientes relativos a Diego de Vargas," ff. 81, 15.

15. J. M. Ots Capdequí, *El Estado Español en las Indias* (México: Fondo de Cultura Económica, 1946), p. 65, points out that the monarchs entrusted the *audiencias* with these attributes of government because of the great distances involved. Some debate lingers as to the nature of the *audiencias'* duties. While some scholars emphasize its administrative functions, others see it as primarily a judicial body. See Fernando Muro Romero, *Las Presidencias-Gobernaciones en Indias (Siglo XVI)* (Sevilla: Escuela de Estudios Hispano-Americanos de Sevilla, 1975), pp. 1–2, n. 1.

16. The classic, and most complete, study of the Audiencia of Guadalajara remains J. H. Parry, *The Audiencia of New Galicia in the Sixteenth Century* (Cambridge: Cambridge University Press, 1948). Surprisingly, there exists no comprehensive study of the Audiencia of Mexico.

17. Haring, *Spanish Empire*, p. 122.

18. *Recopilación de Indias*. 2.15.3, 2.15.7.

19. Haring, *Spanish Empire*, p. 120.

20. Guillermo F. Margadant S., *Introducción a la Historia del Derecho Mexicano* (México: Editorial Esfinge, S.A., 1986) 7th ed., p. 55.

21. *Recopilación de Indias*. 2.24.1.

22. Examinations for *escribanos de cámara*, in Sanchez-Arcilla Bernal, *Las Ordenanzas de las Audiencias de Indias*, pp. 362–71; *escribanos de provincia* and *escribanos públicos*, p. 427. On the important role of the *escribano*, see Jorge Luján Muñoz, *Los Escribanos en las Indias Occidentales, y en Particular en el Reino de Guatemala* (Guatemala: Instituto Guatemalteco de Derecho Notarial, 1977).

23. Richard L. Kagan, *Lawsuits and Litigants in Castile, 1500–1700* (Chapel Hill: University of North Carolina Press, 1981), notes that business in royal courts in Castile had begun to fall off by the mid seventeenth century.

24. AGI Guadalajara 319, "Diario Despacho de los negocios Civiles y Criminales . . . 1819." Also AGI Guadalajara 365, "Lista de negocios despachados, 1798." Similar hours (7 to 12; 3 to 7, six days a week) held sway in the Real Consejo de Castilla in the mid eighteenth century. BN ms. 905, "Distribución, y despacho, en los dias, y horas que les corresponde, del Real Consejo de Castilla, y repartimiento de sus Salas." *Recopilación de Indias*, 2.15.21, gives the hours at which the oidores were to be in attendance.

25. For obligations of audiencia personnel, see *Recopilación de Indias*, libro 2, various títulos.

26. Haring, *Spanish Empire*, p. 121.

27. AGI Guadalajara 276, Croix to Gálvez. Chihuahua, 3 April 1778. At this time, Croix suggested the convenience and efficiency of such a change. The formal transfer of jurisdiction came shortly thereafter. AGN Provincias Internas 59, exp. 3, Real Orden. El Pardo, 12 March 1779 (copy made at Mexico City, 28 June 1779). Also in Ventura Beleña, *Recopilación Sumaria*, t. 1, Providencias, DCXVI, 12 March 1779, p. 291.

28. Antonio Javier Pérez y López, *Teatro de la Legislación Universal de España e Indias* (Madrid: Manuel González, 1791–98), t. 3, p. 482, voz "apelación," makes reference to law 163 of the Leyes de Estilo, "No se admite apelación de sentencia de muerte o perdimiento de miembro, ni tampoco de definitiva o interlocutoria en pleito criminal." Also Ventura Beleña, *Recopilación Sumaria*, t. 1, Autos Acordados, XIII, 29 August 1778.

29. For example, ARAG Criminal s/n s/c, "Provincia del N.o México. Jurisdicción de Alburquerque. Año de 1806. Causa criminal formada contra Juan Christóbal García, por haver dado muerte en riña a Antonio Josef Baca, vecinos de dicha Jurisdicción. Juez el Alcalde de Alburquerque Don Manuel de Arteaga = actuando p.r receptoría." 3 November 1806–24 January 1810; ARAG Criminal 34–7-761, "San Antonio de Béxar. Año de 1801. Prov.a de Coahuila. Causa contra Rafael Gutiérrez, alias quemaculos, por Lad.on muerte y otros excesos." 26 September 1801–10 October 1810; SANM II:673, "Causa Criminal contra las reas M.a Fran.ca y M.a su madre sentenciadas a muerte con parecer de asesor." 22 April 1773.

30. SANM II:611. In a suit involving slander, for example, Asesor Licenciado Antonio Lavandera's *dictamen* called for the defendant, Mariano Baca, to be set free and for the plaintiff, María Manuela de la Luz Romero, to pay court costs. The provincial governor, however, charged the court costs to the defendant and ordered him to stay away from the *paraje* of Atrisco. For a different reading and interpretation of this case, see Gutiérrez, *When Jesus Came*, pp. 224–25.

31. On the destruction and dispersal of the sources, see the discussion in the Introduction.

32. The primary responsibility of the *relator* was to summarize in an accurate manner for the judges all formal proceedings in civil or criminal cases. On other obligations, see *Recopilación de Indias*, 2.22.

33. ARAG Criminal 3–13–80. "Año de 1816. Quad.no de las providencias del relator, civiles y criminales." The list runs only through 19 December of that year.

34. The most detailed work on the administrative and military aspects of the Provincias Internas is Luis Navarro García, *Don José de Gálvez y la Comandancia General de las Provincias Internas del Norte de la Nueva España* (Sevilla: Escuela de Estudios Hispano-Americanos, 1964). See also Herbert Ingram Priestley, *José de Gálvez, Visitor-General to New Spain, 1765–1771* (Berkeley: University of California Press, 1916); Thomas, *Teodoro de Croix*; Simmons, *Spanish Government*, especially pp. 3–50.

35. Simmons, *Spanish Government*, pp. 12–16.

36. See McAlister, *Fuero Militar*.

37. For similarity of form, see the contemporary legal handbook, Colón de Larriátegui, *Juzgados Militares de España y sus Indias*. Also Title 8, Article 16 of the Ordenanza de Milicias (Aranjuez, 30 May 1767) stipulates that the military must follow the same procedure as magistrates of ordinary royal jurisdiction. Cited in Vizcaíno Pérez, *Tratado de la Jurisdicción Ordinaria*, p. 187.

38. For example, BA, r. 11 fr. 835, "Año de 1778. Prov.a de Texas. Causa formada p.r el Gov.or deesta Provinc.a Barón de Ripperdá, contra Francisco Xavier Rodríguez, Juan Josef Flores, y Nepomuceno Travieso, vecinos de la Villa de S.n Fernando, sobre extracción de Reses orejanos." 27 March 1777.

39. After his tenure as commandant general, for example, Teodoro de Croix served as Viceroy of Peru. Thomas, *Teodoro de Croix*, p. 67. Similarly, Jacobo Ugarte y Loyola had an exemplary tenure as Commandant General of Guadalajara and president of that *audiencia*. See Iguíniz, *Gobernantes de Nueva Galicia*, pp. 135–51.

40. AGI Guadalajara 239, *Real Reglamento Para las Milicias Provinciales de Nueva Vizcaya* (Madrid: Pedro Marín, 1782), especially título 6, "Gobierno Interior de los Cuerpos."

41. SANM II:837, Caballero de Croix to Juan Bautista de Anza. Arizpe, 21 February 1782.

42. AGI Guadalajara 268, "Instrucción formada en virtud de Real Orden de S.M., que se dirige al Señor Comandante General de Provincias internas Don Jacobo Ugarte y Loyola para gobierno y puntual observancia de este Superior Gefe y de sus inmediatos Subalternos." México, 26 August 1786.

43. AGI Guadalajara 268, Pedro de Nava to Eugenio de Llaguno. Chihuahua, 9 September 1795; AGI Guadalajara 270, Pedro Galindo Navarro to King. Chihuahua, 18 November 1778. Joseph W. McKnight, "Law Without Lawyers on The Hispano-Mexican Frontier," *The West Texas Historical Association Year Book* 66 (1990): 57, gives Galindo's date of service as 1776 to 1804.

44. AGI Guadalajara 270, Caballero de Croix to José de Gálvez. Chihuahua, 30 November 1778.

45. AGI Guadalajara 272, Caballero de Croix to José de Gálvez. Arizpe, 26 March 1781.

46. AGI Guadalajara 272, Real Orden (triplicado). El Pardo, 8 February 1782. Galindo's 3,000 pesos compares well with the 2,000 peso salary of New Mexico Governor Juan Bautista de Anza (1777), or the 4,000 peso salary of

Governor Fernando de la Concha (1786). AGI México 1216, Títulos. 19 May 1777, 10 December 1786. In 1777 the Regente, Presidente, Gobernador, and Comandante General of Nueva Galicia, Eusebio Sánchez Pareja, received an annual salary of 6,600 pesos.

47. AGI Guadalajara 268, Pedro de Nava to Eugenio de Llaguno. Chihuahua, 9 September 1795.

48. See, for example, AGI Guadalajara 268, "Cuenta General de Cargo, y Data que rinde el Oficial mayor de esta Secretaría de todas las cantidades que han entrado en su poder desde 13 de Abril de 78 hasta fin de Diciembre del de 80," which states "recibí de D. Juan Umaran del Comercio de la Villa de Chihuahua 900 pesos que de orden del Señor Comandante General, se exigieron de multa al cabildo del Saltillo de los cuales deducidos 100 pesos al Asesor. quedan al cargo . . . 800 pesos." Examples of Galindo's outside activities include ARAG Civil 121-1-1310, Pedro Nicolás Cadrecha v. Francisco Antonio de Trespalacios for María Ana García Villegas. Chihuahua, 1 July-10 November 1778. In this case Galindo served at the request of both parties as a legal mediator ("juez árbitro, arbitrador, y amigable componedor").

49. AGI Guadalajara 268, "Cuenta General de Cargo."

50. AGI Guadalajara 268, Bruno Díaz de Salcedo to [Viceroy]. San Luis Potosí, 31 March 1789; AGI Guadalajara 268, Manuel Antonio Flórez to Antonio Valdés. México, 27 March 1789.

51. AGI Guadalajara 268, Croix to Gálvez. Arizpe, 30 November 1781.

52. AGI Guadalajara 268, Real Orden. San Ildefonso, 7 July 1782.

53. AGI Guadalajara 268, Real Orden. El Pardo, 8 March 1782. AGI Guadalajara 268, Real Orden (triplicado). San Ildefonso, 7 July 1782.

54. ARAG Criminal 45–13–1023. Joachin del Real Alencaster to Señores de la Real Audiencia. Santa Fe, 1 July 1805.

55. AGI Guadalajara 268, Neve Report, p. 24.

56. The bibliography for this period has seen a marked increase in recent years. See, for example, Henry Kamen, *Spain in the Later Seventeenth Century* (London: Longman, 1980); J. H. Elliot, *The Count-Duke of Olivares* (New Haven: Yale University Press, 1988); J. H. Elliot, *Spain and its World, 1500–1700: Selected Essays* (New Haven: Yale University Press, 1989); Antonio Domínguez Ortiz, *El Antiguo Régimen: Los Reyes Católicos y los Austria* (Madrid: Alianza Editorial, 1983); R. A. Stradling, *Europe and the Decline of Spain: A Study of the Spanish System, 1580–1720* (London: Allen & Unwin, 1981).

57. On the Bourbon regime in eighteenth-century Spain, see Richard Herr, *The Eighteenth-Century Revolution in Spain* (Princeton: Princeton University Press, 1958); Antonio Domínguez Ortiz, *Carlos III y la España de la Ilustración* (Madrid: Alianza Editorial, 1988); Gonzalo Anes, *El Antiguo Régimen: Los Borbones* (Madrid: Alianza Editorial, 1975). On the essential Spanishness of the Bourbon reforms, Kamen, *Spain, 1469–1714*, p. 270.

58. Literature on the intendancy system abounds. For generalized treatments, see Gisela Morazzani de Pérez Enciso, *La Intendencia en España y en América* (Caracas: Consejo de Desarrollo Científico y Humanístico, 1966); Luis Navarro García, *Intendencias en Indias* (Sevilla: Escuela de Estudios Hispano-Americanos de Sevilla, 1959); Lillian Estelle Fisher, *The Intendant System in*

Spanish America (Berkeley: University of California Press, 1929). For more specific treatment of the various intendancies, see María Laura San Martino de Dromi, *Intendencias y Provincias en la Historia Argentina* ([Buenos Aires]: Editorial Ciencias de la Administración S.R.L., n.d).; John R. Fisher, *Government and Society in Colonial Peru: The Intendant System, 1783–1814* (London: Athlone, 1970); Ricardo Rees Jones, *El Despotismo Ilustrado y los Intendentes de la Nueva España* (México: Universidad Nacional Autónoma de México, 1983).

    59. Quote in Kessell et al., *Remote Beyond Compare*, p. 168 (English) and p. 375 (Spanish).

    60. AGI Guadalajara 332, Real Cédula. San Ildefonso, 26 August 1764. This *cédula* established monthly packetboat service from the port city of La Coruña, in northwestern Spain, to Havana. Luis Navarro García, *Don José de Gálvez*, p. 318, asserts that in 1779 northern New Spain linked up with this network of regular mail service. New Mexico, however, apparently never became a part of this regular monthly service. In 1805 Governor Joaquín del Real Alencaster stated that there were only four annual *correos*. ARAG Criminal 45–13–1023, Real Alencaster to Real Audiencia, Santa Fe, 1 July 1805.

    61. Navarro García, *Don José de Gálvez*, pp. 90–91; also Charles Edward Chapman, *The Founding of Spanish California: The Northwestward Expansion of New Spain, 1687–1783* (New York: 1916; reprint, New York: Octagon Books, 1973), pp. 35–40.

    62. Navarro García, *Don José de Gálvez*, p. 92.

    63. AGI Guadalajara 276, Croix to Gálvez. Chihuahua, 29 June 1778. Navarro García, *Don José de Gálvez*, pp. 314–15.

    64. Navarro García, *Don José de Gálvez*, p. 315.

    65. AGI Guadalajara 268, Neve Report, pp. 22–24. By way of comparison, proponents of an *audiencia* at Caracas employed almost identical images in portraying the ultimate benefits that such a tribunal would bring. See Alí Enrique López Bohórquez, "La Real Audiencia de Caracas: Razones de su Creación y Ejemplo de Reorganización Judicial Borbónica," in López Bohórquez, ed., *La Real Audiencia de Caracas en la Historiografía Venezolana* (Caracas: Biblioteca de la Academia Nacional de la Historia, 1986), p. 528.

    66. Ricardo Zorraquín Becú, *La Función de Justicia en el Derecho Indiano* (Buenos Aires: Imprenta de la Universidad, 1948), p. 13.

    67. AGI Guadalajara 268, Neve Report, pp. 25–29.

    68. See Simmons, *Spanish Government*, pp. 27–29.

    69. AGN Provincias Internas 255, "Un oficio num.o 98 de 2 de Junio de 1787, proponiendo la creación de una R.l Audiencia en Provincias Internas," f. 79.

    70. AGN Provincias Internas 255, "Un oficio num.o 98 de 2 de Junio de 1787," f. 80. The *audiencia* at Caracas, which functioned from 1786 to 1810, was a modest tribunal with only one *regente* and four other *ministros*. See Alí Enrique López Bohórquez, *Los Ministros de la Audiencia de Caracas (1786–1810)* (Caracas: Biblioteca de la Academia Nacional de la Historia, 1984), pp. 42–43.

    71. AGN Provincias Internas 255, "Un oficio num.o 98 de 2 de Junio de 1787," ff. 80–80v.

72. AGI Guadalajara 287, Jacobo Ugarte to Marqués de Sonora. Arizpe, 2 June 1787; also in AGN Provincias Internas 255, "Un oficio num.o 98 de 2 de Junio de 1787," ff. 80v–81.

73. AGN Provincias Internas 254. Informe de Jacobo Ugarte y Loyola. Arispe, 10 December 1787.

74. Navarro García, *Don José de Gálvez*, p. 460. See also Christon I. Archer, *The Army in Bourbon Mexico, 1760–1810* (Albuquerque: University of New Mexico Press, 1977), pp. 20–21.

75. See H. Bailey Carroll and J. Villasana Haggard, eds. and trans., *Three New Mexico Chronicles* (Albuquerque: The Quivira Society, 1942), p. 56.

76. David J. Weber, *The Mexican Frontier, 1821–1846: The American Southwest Under Mexico* (Albuquerque: University of New Mexico Press, 1982), pp. 17–18. See also Charles R. Berry, "The Election of the Mexican Deputies to the Spanish Cortes, 1810–1822," in Nettie Lee Benson, ed., *Mexico and the Spanish Cortes, 1810–1822: Eight Essays* (Austin: University of Texas Press, 1966), p. 16.

77. The Spanish text in Pedro Bautista Pino, *Exposición Sucinta y Sencilla de la Provincia del Nuevo México* (Cádiz: Imprenta del Estado Mayor General, 1812), pp. 23–24, 28–29. Approval by the Cortes found in *Colección de los Decretos y Órdenes que Han Expedido las Cortes Generales y Extraordinarias* (Cádiz: En la Imprenta Nacional, 1813; facsimile reprint, Madrid: Cortes Generales, 1987), t. 2, pp. 748–49. Decree 217 of 26 January 1813, "Erección de Obispado y Seminario en la capital del Nuevo-México."

78. The Provincias Internas experienced a variety of territorial changes. The first restructuring, which created the Command of the West and the Command of the East, occurred by virtue of a decree of 3 December 1787. Simmons, *Spanish Government*, p. 30. Also in Ventura Beleña, *Recopilación Sumaria*, t. 1, Providencias, Nota VIII, pp. 370–71.

79. Pino, *Exposición*, pp. 6–7.

80. Cited in Carroll and Haggard, *Three New Mexico Chronicles*, p. xix.

81. Luis Navarro García, *Las Provincias Internas en el Siglo XIX* (Sevilla: Escuela de Estudios Hispano-Americanos, 1965), pp. 129–30.

82. Another attempt was made during the short-lived reign of Emperor Agustín de Iturbide, which proposed a similar remedy for the perceived defects of judicial administration in the Western Interior Provinces. See Juan Miguel Riezgo et al., *Memoria Sobre las Proporciones Naturales de las Provincias Internas Occidentales: Causas de que Han Provenido sus Atrasos, Providencias Tomadas con el Fin de Lograr su Remedio, y las que por Ahora Se Consideran Oportunas para Mejorar su Estado, e Ir Proporcionando su Futura Felicidad* (México: Imprenta de D. José Ramos Palomera, 1822). Copy located at the Lilly Library, Indiana University.

83. On Ramos Arizpe as a delegate, see *Idea General sobre la Conducta Política de D. Miguel Ramos de Arizpe, Natural de la Provincia de Coahuila, Como Diputado que Ha Sido por Esta Provincia en las Cortes Generales y Extraordinarias, y en las Ordinarias de la Monarquía Española desde el Año de 1810 hasta el de 1812* (México: Doña Herculana del Villar y Socios, 1822). Copy at Rare Books Section, Huntington Library, San Marino, California. Other biographical informa-

tion in Miguel Ramos Arizpe, *Memoria sobre el Estado de las Provincias Internas de Oriente Presentada a las Cortes de Cádiz*, Vito Alessio Robles, ed., (México: Bibliófilos Mexicanos, 1932), pp. 9–54. The influence of Ramos Arizpe also in Mario Rodríguez, *The Cádiz Experiment in Central America, 1808–1821* (Berkeley: University of California Press, 1978), p. 59; Berry, "The Election of the Mexican Deputies," p. 16.

84. Miguel Ramos Arizpe, *Report That Dr. Miguel Ramos de Arizpe, Priest of Borbon and Deputy in the Present General and Special Cortes of Spain for the Province of Coahuila, One of the Four Eastern Interior Provinces in the Kingdom of Mexico, Presents to the August Congress on the Natural, Political, and Civil Conditions of the Provinces of Coahuila, Nuevo Leon, Nuevo Santander, and Texas of the Four Eastern Interior Provinces of the Kingdom of Mexico*, trans. and intro. by Nettie Lee Benson (Austin: The University of Texas Press, 1950), p. 1.

85. For Ramos's concern regarding the United States, see Ramos Arizpe, *Report*, especially pp. 38–40.

86. Ramos Arizpe, *Report*, p. 31.

87. Ramos Arizpe, *Report*, p. 33.

88. Ramos Arizpe, *Report*, p. 35.

89. Ramos Arizpe, *Report*, p. 35.

90. Ramos Arizpe, *Report*, p. 36.

91. *Colección de los Decretos y Ordenes*, t. 2, pp. 662–85, Decree 201, 9 October 1812, "Reglamento de las Audiencias y Juzgados de primera instancia," capítulo 1, nn. 3–7; Ramos Arizpe, *Report*, p. viii. On the question of local self-governance see José Barragán Barragán, *Temas del Liberalismo Gaditano* (México: Universidad Nacional Autónoma de México, 1978), pp. 51–75.

92. Rodríguez, *The Cádiz Experiment*, p. 124.

93. Navarro García, *Provincias Internas*, pp. 128–29. Rees Jones, *El Despotismo Ilustrado*, p. 114, however, believes that Viceroy Calleja was hostile to the idea of a Saltillo intendancy and actively sought to thwart implementation.

94. Navarro García, *Provincias Internas*, pp. 128–29.

95. AGI Guadalajara 322, Vicente Cano Manuel to Juan Madrid Dávila. Palacio [Real], 8 April 1821. AGI Guadalajara 322, Manuel García Herrero to Secretario del Consejo de Estado. Palacio [Real], 24 January 1821.

96. AGI Guadalajara 322, Vicente Cano Manuel to Secretario del Despacho de la Gobernación de Ultramar. Palacio [Real], 21 September 1821.

97. AGI Guadalajara 322, "Lista de los Pretendientes a las Plazas de Regente, 9 Magistrados, y 2 fiscales de la Audiencia del Saltillo mandada crear por las Cortes." Palacio [Real], 18 April 1821.

98. AGI Guadalajara 322, Vicente Cano Miguel to Secretario del Despacho de la Gobernación de Ultramar. Palacio [Real], 21 September 1821.

99. Alvarez, Instituciones de Derecho Real. lib. 4, pp. 320–21.

100. Weber, *The Mexican Frontier*, pp. 38–39. For judicial practice in Mexican California, see Langum, *Law and Community on the Mexican California Frontier*. The role of the judiciary in colonial New Mexico is examined in Cutter, "La Magistratura Local en el Norte de la Nueva España."

101. AGI Guadalajara 268, Neve Report, p. 24.

Chapter 4

1. Alfonso García Gallo, "Los Orígines de la Administración Territorial de las Indias, el Gobierno de Colón," in *Estudios de Historia del Derecho Indiano* (Madrid: Instituto de Estudios Jurídicos, 1972), pp. 594–609.

2. Hammond and Rey, *Don Juan de Oñate*, vol. 1, pp. 42–57, pertains to his privileges and obligations as *adelantado*.

3. A list of colonial officials in the borderlands is found in Thomas C. Barnes, Thomas H. Naylor, and Charles W. Polzer, *Northern New Spain: A Research Guide* (Tucson: University of Arizona Press, 1981), pp. 94–120.

4. For contemporary views, see Solórzano Pereira, *Política Indiana*, 5.2.1, and *Recopilación de Indias*, 5.2. Modern assessments include Haring, *Spanish Empire*, pp. 128–29; Gibson, *Spain in America*, p. 95; Mario Góngora, *Studies in the Colonial History of Spanish America* (Cambridge: Cambridge University Press, 1975), pp. 94–95. Recent scholarship on Spanish legal history suggests that the various titles indicated the way in which the crown perceived the function of these officials. See García Gallo, "Alcaldes Mayores y Corregidores en Indias," p. 717. Also Alberto Yalí Román, "Sobre Alcaldías Mayores y Corregimientos en Indias: Un Ensayo de Interpretación," *Jahrbuch für Geschichte von Staat, Wirtschaft und Gesellschaft Lateinamerikas* 9 (1972): 10–15 and *passim*.

5. *Recopilación de Indias*, 5.1.1, "proveyendo en las menores Gobernadores particulares, que por estar más distantes de las Audiencias, las rijan, y gobiernen en paz, y justicia." Edmundo O'Gorman, *Historia de las Divisiones Territoriales de México* (México: Editorial Porrúa, S.A., 1966), 3rd ed., differs on what constituted *provincias mayores* and *provincias menores*, but appears to have imposed presentist criteria on what the differences were. The pertinent section of the *Recopilación* states: "Para mejor, y más fácil gobierno de las Indias Occidentales están divididos aquellos Reynos, y Señoríos en Provincias mayores, y menores, señalando las mayores, que incluyen otras muchas, por distritos a nuestras Audiencias Reales: proveyendo en las menores Gobernadores particulares, que por estar más distantes de las Audiencias, las rijan, y gobiernen en paz, y justicia: y en otras partes, donde por la calidad de la tierra, y disposición de los Lugares no ha parecido necesario, ni conveniente hacer Cabeza de Provincia, ni proveer en ella Governador, se han puesto Corregidores, y Alcaldes mayores para el govierno de las Ciudades, y sus Partidos, y lo mismo se ha observado, respecto de los Pueblos principales de Indios, que son Cabeceras de otros." This definition dates from about the time of the *Recopilación de Indias* of 1681.

6. Muro Romero, *Las Presidencias-Gobernaciones*, pp. 122–23.

7. Kessell et al., *Remote Beyond Compare*, pp. 25–41, 88–89. Definitions of *presidencia-gobernación* in Haring, *Spanish Empire*, p. 71; Muro Romero, *Las Presidencias-Gobernaciones*, pp. 122–23.

8. For example, AGI Guadalajara 506, "Don Facundo Melgares nombramiento de Segundo Alférez de la Compañía del Presidio del Norte." San Ildefonso, 10 September 1798. Melgares later became governor of New Mexico

(1818–22). Faulk, *Last Years of Spanish Texas*, pp. 23–37, reveals the predominantly military background of the governors of Texas.

9. The Spanish Archives of New Mexico, the Béxar Archives, the Archivo General de la Nación (ramo Provincias Internas), and the Archivo General de Indias (Guadalajara) all are replete with correspondence of this nature.

10. *Recopilación de Indias*, 5.2.7 provides a sample formulario of the oath of office, in which the general duties of office are listed. See also *Recopilación de Indias*, 5.2.22.

11. AGI México 1217, Título of Ju.o Boneo y Morales. Aranjuez, 23 May 1739. According to Velázquez's *New Pronouncing Dictionary of The Spanish and English Languages*, a *cadete* is "a volunteer in the army who serves in expectation of a commission."

12. Félix D. Almaráz, Jr., *Tragic Cavalier: Governor Manuel Salcedo of Texas, 1808–1813* (Austin: University of Texas Press, 1971), p. 24 n.7.

13. Quote in Ovidio Casado Fuente, *Don Francisco Cuerbo y Valdés, Gobernador de Nuevo México, Fundador de la Ciudad de Alburquerque* (Oviedo: Instituto de Estudios Asturianos, 1983), p. 40.

14. On this incident, see Alfred B. Thomas, *Forgotten Frontiers: A Study of the Spanish Indian Policy of Don Juan Bautista de Anza, Governor of New Mexico, 1777–1787* (Norman: University of Oklahoma Press, 1932), pp. 134–36; also John, *Storms Brewed in Other Men's Worlds*, pp. 584–90, 672–76.

15. A similar shift in emphasis occurred throughout New Spain. The president of the Audiencia of Guadalajara, for example, now was primarily a military figure, unlike his sixteenth- and seventeenth-century counterparts who were jurists. Iguíniz, *Gobernantes de Nueva Galicia*, p. 89.

16. *Recopilación de Indias*, 5.2.11.

17. AGI Guadalajara 1216, Título of Governor Juan Bautista de Anza, 19 May 1777, indicated the change in name.

18. Zorraquín Becú, *La Organización Judicial Argentina*, notes this three-part division of judicial authority.

19. Archer, *Army in Bourbon Mexico*, pp. 125–28.

20. See, for example, AGI Guadalajara 268, Neve Report, pp. 48–57 and *passim*. Simmons, *Spanish Government*, pp. 12–16, describes the commandant's fiscal duties.

21. For example, BA, r. 11 fr. 835. "Causa formada . . . contra Francisco Xavier Rodríguez, Juan Josef Flores, y Nepomuceno Travieso," 27 March 1777. On the *mesteña* fund, see Faulk, *Last Years of Spanish Texas*, p. 85, and Jackson, *Los Mesteños*, *passim*. BA, Cabello to Croix. San Antonio, 8 October 1779; BA, Decree of Cabello. San Antonio, 27 October 1779.

22. Chipman, *Spanish Texas*, pp. 164, 182.

23. The Bexar Archives show a marked increase in the number of contraband cases during this period. See also Faulk, *Last Years of Spanish Texas*, pp. 97–98.

24. Ordinarily, the *cabildo* chose two *alcaldes ordinarios* who exercised judicial functions within a five league radius of the municipality. Both groups, however, adjudicated matters of ordinary royal jurisdiction. In many areas of Spanish America, these conflicting jurisdictions often led to friction among

various local power groups. Typical was the struggle between the *gobernador* and the *alcaldes ordinarios* of Durango in 1750, which came before the Audiencia of Guadalajara and ultimately was sent to Spain. AGI Guadalajara 110, "Año 1750. Testimonio de diligencias executadas en la Ciu.d de Durango sobre Jurisdición que perteneze a los Alc.es ordinarios de dicha Ciudad."

25. García Gallo, "Alcaldes Mayores y Corregidores," p. 729, prefers the term *justicia* in order to underscore the multiple powers and lack of judicial training of these officials. The eighteenth-century Valencian jurist José Berní y Catalá, on the other hand, employed the term *alcalde lego* in referring to untrained *alcaldes ordinarios*. See Berní y Catalá, *Instrucción*, p. 5. Berní refers to a trained judge as a *juez de letras*. See *Práctica Criminal*, p. 91. In New Mexico, where the term *juez comisionado* was used consistently, the word *juez* carried no connotation of legal training.

26. Zorraquín Becú, *La Organización Judicial*, pp. 82–83. Some *gobernaciones*, of course, had at a much earlier time lieutenant governors who served primarily as legal advisers. See *Recopilación de Indias*, 5.2.37, 39.

27. Lansing B. Bloom, transcriber, "Ynstrucción a Peralta por Vi-Rey," *New Mexico Historical Review* 4 (April 1929): 178–87. *Recopilación de Indias*, 5.10.13, (heading) states "que la facultad dada a los Virreyes para conocer en primera instancia en causas de Indios, se entienda con los demás Gobernadores de Indias."

28. This close relationship between the governor and the Pueblos continued into the first several decades of American rule. See Kessell, "Spaniards and Pueblos: From Crusading Intolerance to Pragmatic Accommodation," pp. 127–38. See also Annie Heloise Abel, *The Official Correspondence of James S. Calhoun* (Washington, D.C.: Government Printing Office, 1915), pp. 88, 293. For this relationship in other parts of Spanish America, see Daisy Ripodas Ardanaz, "Los Indios y la Figura Jurídica del Rey Durante el Quinientos," in *Justicia, Sociedad, y Economía en la América Española* (Valladolid: Casa-Museo de Colón and Seminario Americanista de la Universidad de Valladolid, 1983), pp. 275–322. In many areas, Indians adapted readily to Spanish legal institutions. See Steve J. Stern, *Peru's Indian Peoples and the Challenge of Spanish Conquest: Huamanga to 1640* (Madison: University of Wisconsin Press, 1982); William B. Taylor, *Landlord and Peasant in Colonial Oaxaca* (Stanford: Stanford University Press, 1972); Cutter, *Protector de Indios*.

29. SANM II:673, "Causa Criminal contra las reas M.a Fran.ca y M.a su madre sentenciadas a muerte con parecer de asesor," 22 April 1773. SANM II:477, "Causa criminal de oficio de la R.l Justicia Contra Pedro de la Cruz Indio por hauer intentado fuga, pasandose a la gentilidad de la nación Cumanches," 22 February 1747.

30. AGI México 1216. "Título de Gobernador de lo Político y militar de la Provincia de Nuebo México," Tomás Vélez Cachupín. Buen Retiro, 5 March 1761.

31. Bakewell, *Silver Mining and Society in Colonial Mexico*, p. 84, notes that the appointment of the *corregidor* of Zacatecas was vague and ill-defined, and that the appointment stipulated only that the new *corregidor* should act with all the prerogatives of his predecessors.

32. García Gallo, "Alcaldes Mayores y Corregidores," p. 700. "En todo caso, el estudio se hace sumamente difícil porque los contemporáneos no se preocuparon de definir o caracterizar unas u otras instituciones [speaking of *alcaldías* and *corregimientos*]. Estas se dan por conocidas, sin duda lo eran para ellos, y las disposiciones legales o los documentos administrativos ordenan sobre aspectos concretos, se remiten a lo establecido, modifican preceptos singulares, y en todo caso dan por supuesta una ordenación legal o consuetudinaria que no ha llegado a nosotros y que en consecuencia desconocemos."

33. *Recopilación de Indias*, 5.2.7. The formulario for the oath of office stated "guardaréis, y cumpliréis los capítulos de buena gobernación, y leyes de el Reyno, cédulas, y provisiones de su Magestad, y las que están hechas y dadas, y se hizieren y dieren para el buen gobierno del Estado de las Indias."

34. Biblioteca Nacional, Madrid (hereafter BN) MS 7967. "Ordenanza General de Yntendentes de Yndias formada de orden de S.M. Año de 1802." While this particular ordinance never took effect, this passage exemplifies the admonitions to be familiar with the laws of the Indies.

35. BN MS 19252, "Reales decretos, órdenes y cédulas," "Instrucz.on que se da p.r las secret.s del consejo a los corregidores y Alcaldes mayores q.e van a las Ynd.s." This document bears no date, but internal evidence suggests that it pre-dates the intendancy system in the Indies.

36. AGI Guadalajara 273, *Instrucción para formar una linea o cordón de quince presidios sobre las Fronteras de las Provincias Internas de este Reino de Nueva España, y Nuevo Reglamento* (México: Imprenta del Br. D. Joseph Antonio de Hogal, 1771).

37. AGI Guadalajara 239, *Real Reglamento para las Milicias Provinciales de Nueva Vizcaya* (Madrid: Pedro Marín, 1782).

38. Vizcaíno Pérez, *Tratado de la Jurisdicción Ordinaria*, p. 187.

39. *Recopilación de Indias*, 8.7.34.

40. AGI Guadalajara 129, Gaspar Domingo de Mendoza to King, n.p., n.d.; Respuesta del Consejo, 7 May 1737. It should be noted that while this document seems to indicate that the newly appointed governor should have in his possession the compilation of Castilian law of 1567 known as the *Nueva Recopilación de Castilla*, the allusion clearly is to the *Recopilación de Indias*, for contemporaries did not always refer to the New World compilation by that title. Use of the word "new" simply meant that the *Recopilación de Indias* was more recent than the *Recopilación de Castilla*. One reads, for example, that the *alcalde mayor* of Verapaz (Guatemala) received his "four volumes of the *Recopilación*" before embarking for the Indies. The document that carries this information is entitled "Comprobante de la cuenta rendida por los jueces oficiales reales de la venta de la nueva recopilación." See Luján Muñoz, "Acerca de la Llegada y Aplicación de la Recopilación de las Leyes de Indias," p. 173. Similarly, in describing damage to a shipment of the *Recopilación de Indias*, an official of the Casa de Contratación reported that "two sets of the *Nueva Recopilación*" had suffered water damage. Quoted in Manzano Manzano, "El Proceso Recopilador de las Leyes de Indias Hasta 1680," p. 66.

41. Malagón-Barceló, *La Literatura Jurídica Española del Siglo de Oro en la Nueva España*. With respect to the eighteenth century, AGN Inquisición con-

tains lists prepared by the Holy Office of local booksellers' stocks, which indicate that legal literature continued to be readily available.

42. AGI Guadalajara 344, "Copia de Ynventario de los Bienes y Papeles del P.e Cueva que se encontraron en la Mision de S.n Gerónimo y en la Villa de Chihuahua." 21 November 1778.

43. Rothrock List of books in colonial New Mexico, typescript original in UNMSC.

44. Complete bibliographic data is found in Antonio Paláu y Dulcet, *Manual del Librero Hispanoamericano* (Barcelona: A. Paláu, 1948).

45. McKnight, "Law Books," pp. 74–84. Information on Muñoz's library on pp. 77–78, 82 nn. 20, 21.

46. AGI Guadalajara 330, Francisco Marín del Valle to Joseph Ignacio de Goyeneche. Santa Fe, 21 January 1760.

47. *Recopilación de Indias.* 8.7.34.

48. For example SANM I:1159, "Ymbenttario de los Papeles pertene-zienttes al archivo de estta Gouernaz.on del tpo que ha sido Gou.or y Capp.n Gen.l de estte Reino de la N.a Mex.co el Coronel d.n Geruazio Cruzatte y Góngora, y de los que an passado ante su th.e Gen.l d.n J.o Páez Vrttado, y Alcaldes Maiores de las jurisdiz.s de su dho reino, etc." Santa Fe, 20 November 1736. Similar inventory found in SANM I:1258. For Texas, the transfer of archives to Justo Boneo y Morales upon Tomas Felipe de Winthuysen's leaving the governorship of Texas in 1743, in AGN Provincias Internas 32 exp. 2, ff. 57–62. "Entrega de los autos y papeles del archibo de este Gobierno." Los Adaes, 17 January 1743.

49. *Recopilación de Indias,* 2.1.31, 8.7.34.

50. *Recopilación de Indias,* 5.2.44, 45.

51. Kicza, *Colonial Entrepreneurs,* pp. 36–40; Parry, *Audiencia of New Galicia,* pp. 72 and *passim.*

52. The several examples range from Diego de Vargas at the beginning of the period under study to Manuel Salcedo in Texas, who initially brought his wife and daughter to San Antonio but later sent them to New Orleans because of civil unrest in Texas. Also, Governor Juan María de Ripperdá brought his wife and six children to Texas. In New Mexico, Governor Juan Domingo Bustamante y Tagle did not marry, but his daughter married into a local family of note. See Angelico Chavez, *Origins of New Mexico Families,* pp. 150–51.

53. *Recopilación de Indias,* 5.2.10, stipulated that the term of appointment be for three years if the individual were currently residing in the Indies, and five years if in Spain. In practice tenure in office in New Mexico usually ranged from about six to eight years in the middle and late eighteenth century. In Texas, the duration of governorship conformed more to prescription.

54. See, for example, J. H. Parry, *The Sale of Public Office in the Spanish Indies Under the Hapsburgs* (Berkeley: University of California Press, 1953). Haring, *Spanish Empire,* pp. 270–73. The early laws governing the sale, transfer, and confirmation of offices are found in *Recopilación de Indias,* 8.20, 21, 22. See also Rodríguez de León Pinelo, *Tratado de Confirmaciones Reales,* pp. 261–378.

55. For a detailed treatment see Fernando Muro Romero, "El 'Beneficio' de

Oficios Públicos con Jurisdicción en Indias. Notas Sobre Sus Orígines," *Anuario de Estudios Americanos* 35 (1978): 1–67.

56. Those who purchased the title of Gobernador y Capitán General of New Mexico were: Diego de Vargas, 2,500 pesos; Pedro Rodríguez Cubero, 2,000 pesos; José Chacón Medina y Salazar, 4,000 pesos; Juan Ignacio Flores Mogollón (who believed he purchased the governorship of Nuevo León, but instead received that of New Mexico), 3,500 pesos; Manuel de Soldevilla, 1,000 doblones de a dos; Plácido de Porras, 5,000 pesos. In the 1740s Agustín Moreno de Castro and Antonio de Herrero, neither of whom served, bought their offices for 16,000 and 13,800 pesos fuertes, respectively. AGI México 1216, Títulos.

57. For a short period, the governors were also subject to the *media anata*, which Haring, Spanish Empire. p. 273, explains consisted of "half of the first year's salary and a third of all other emoluments of the recipient of a public office, favor, or concession." This was an obligatory deduction from salary and should not be considered as a purchase of office. This practice ended, however, pursuant to the Royal Order of 1 February 1779. From that time, apparently, the governors of New Mexico and Texas were not subject to the *media anata*. For New Mexico, see AGI México 1216, Títulos, and AGI México 1217, Títulos. The practice may have ended earlier in New Mexico, as indicated in AGI Guadalajara 276. Croix to Gálvez, Chihuahua, 24 August 1778. Croix stated that Juan Bautista de Anza was to receive 4,000 pesos annually, was exempt from the *media anata*, "y que no hay constancia segura de que los antecesores de Ansa hayan pagado la Media Anata." The appointments for the Texas governorship also indicate an exemption from the *media anata*. For a differing view on the chronology of the *media anata* exemption in New Mexico, see Simmons, *Spanish Government*, p. 58.

58. AGI Guadalajara 302, "Año de 1745, Exp.te sre la concesion del Gov.no de las Texas a d.n Thomas Cantelmi por el servicio de 60,000 rr.s qe ofrecio por el; en razon de que se le debuelva aq.a cantidad, respecto de haver resuelto el Rey no se beneficie aquel Gov.no."

59. A good indication of the range of alcaldes found under the Spanish system can be seen in Joaquín Escriche, *Diccionario Razonado*, and other such texts, under the general heading "alcalde."

60. The word *alcalde* is derived from the Arabic *al-kadi*, meaning "the judge." Yalí Román, "Sobre Alcaldías Mayores," p. 1.

61. *Recopilación de Indias*, 5.2, which treats legislation pertaining to these three officials, comes under the general heading "De los Gobernadores, Corregidores, Alcaldes mayores, y sus Tenientes, y Alguaciles." In his chapter on governors and corregidores, Juan de Solórzano Pereira, *Política Indiana*, 5.2.1, states that the same officials "in Peru are called *Corregidores*, and in Nueva España *alcaldes Mayores*, and those in some of the more distant provinces have the title of *Gobernadores*."

62. ARAG Civil s/c n.4, 1720–29. *Reglamento Para Todos los Presidios de las Provincias Internas de Esta Gobernación . . . Hecho por el Exc.mo Señor Marqués de Casa-Fuerte* (México: Herederos de la Viuda de Miguel de Rivera Calderón,

1729), n.155. García Gallo, "Alcaldes Mayores y Corregidores," p. 717, points out that sixteenth-century *gobernadores* also had the privilege of appointing their own *alcaldes mayores*. For later evidence that the governor appointed his *alcaldes mayores*, AGN Provincias Internas 152, exp. 2, f. 228v. Informe of Pedro Fermín de Mendinueta, Santa Fe, 8 January 1773.

63. AGI Guadalajara 268, Neve Report, p. 2. At least this was the situation at the time of this particular report. This information contrasts with Simmons, *Spanish Government*, p. 170, who states that the appointments of *alcaldes mayores* required the approval of the commandant. On what evidence he makes this assertion is unclear, since he provides no citation, but perhaps he has in mind *Recopilación de Indias*, 2.16.8, which states that *tenientes de alcaldes mayores* must have the confirmation of the viceroy.

64. Fuller treatment of the *alcalde's* military duties is in Simmons, *Spanish Government*, pp. 180–82.

65. On the *alcaldías* of the seventeenth century, see Scholes, "Civil Government and Society in New Mexico," pp. 91–93.

66. SANM II:1593, Chacón to Real Audiencia. Santa Fe, 28 March 1802.

67. Berní y Catalá, *Instrucción de Alcaldes Ordinarios*, p. 1.

68. Vizcaíno Pérez, *Tratado de la Jurisdicción Ordinaria*, p. 33.

69. Both quotes in Simmons, *Spanish Government*, p. 173; AGI Guadalajara 267, Desórdenes, n. 40.

70. For example, AGN Historia 25, ff. 332–37v. "Gobierno de las Misiones de S. Diego de Xemes, y S.S. Agustín de la Isleta, que observó el P. Fr. Joaquín de Jesús Ruiz, Ministro que fué de ellas." AGI Guadalajara 267, Desórdenes, n. 41 and *passim*.

71. See SANM II:1977, 1 April 1806; Quote in Simmons, *Spanish Government*, p. 174. Evidence of Real Alencaster's unpopularity in John L. Kessell, *Kiva, Cross, and Crown: The Pecos Indians and New Mexico, 1540–1840* (Washington, D.C.: National Park Service, 1979), pp. 434–35.

72. Most writers on colonial New Mexico have simply followed the tenor of contemporary writers. Beginning with Hubert Howe Bancroft the list of modern historians who have perpetuated a negative image of the *alcaldes mayores* is impressive. Hubert H. Bancroft, *History of Arizona and New Mexico, 1530–1888* (San Francisco: The History Company, 1889), pp. 272–73; Myra Ellen Jenkins, "The Baltasar Baca 'Grant'," p. 53, describes the *alcalde mayor* as "probably the weakest link in the Spanish government of New Mexico" who honored legislation "more in the breach than in the observance. The most influential Spaniard in the area was generally given the post of *alcalde mayor* for political favor and he in turn, especially if there were more than one pueblo in his jurisdiction, would appoint another member of his family or a close friend as assistant"; Simmons, *Spanish Government*, pp. 188–89.

73. Jorge Juan y Santacilia and Antonio de Ulloa, *Discourse and Political Reflections on the Kingdoms of Peru*, ed. and intro. John J. TePaske, trans. John J. TePaske and Bessie A. Clement (Norman: University of Oklahoma Press, 1978).

74. The most complete study in English of this topic is Farriss, *Crown and Clergy in Colonial Mexico*.

75. Richard E. Greenleaf, "The Inquisition in Eighteenth-Century New Mexico," *New Mexico Historical Review* 60 (January 1985): 29–60.

76. Royal legislation, in fact, barred the poorer elements of society from holding such offices. The Ordenamiento de Alcalá (l. 43, tít. 32), for example, stipulated that a servant (*hombre siervo*) could not be a magistrate. This prohibition was repeated in the *Nueva Recopilación* (3.9.8) and the *Novísima Recopilación* (11.1.5); the prohibitions continued at a later time. See Francisco de Paula Miguel Sánchez, *Dirección Teórico-Práctica de Alcaldes Constitucionales* (reprint, Madrid: Instituto de Estudios de Administración Local, 1979), p. 270.

77. AGI Guadalajara 267, Desórdenes, n. 43.

78. AGI Guadalajara 278, Caballero de Croix to José de Gálvez. Arizpe, 23 January 1780.

79. Chavez, *Origins of New Mexico Families*, p. 189, believes that Durán y Chaves used the term "griego" because González Bas came from the Bernal-Griego family. While this may be true, don Fernando may have just as well used the term in the sense of "cheat" or "liar" (*fullero*). The incident is found in SANM II:170, "Caussa criminal contra don fernando de chaues." 20–26 January 1712.

80. His daughter Prudencia, for example, married Antonio de Tafoya, son of another prominent recolonizer, Cristóbal de Tafoya Altamirano. Chavez, *Origins of New Mexico Families*, pp. 189–90.

81. AGI Guadalajara 276, Appointment of Carlos Fernández (copy), Chihuahua, 29 June 1778. Chavez, *Origins of New Mexico Families*, pp. 175–76.

82. SANM II:508, "Año de 1749. Demanda puesta p.r Manuel Sanz de Garuizu, En nom.re de d.n Antonio de tapia vez.o de la Ziudad de Mex.co de la Cantt.d que en ella se expresa, Conttra Jph Romo de Vera vez.o deestta villa." 3 November 1749–14 July 1751. The *alcalde mayor* of Santa Fe, Joseph Bustamante y Tagle, carried out a judicial auction (*remate*) "con zitacion de partes quienes se allaron presentes segun lo dispuesto Por las leyes de la Nueba Recupilazion de estas hindias liuro 2.o n.o 1 f. 102." SANM II:360, "Caussa Criminal Contra Ant.o Yuba yndio natural del Pu.o de tezuque y Asensio Povio Yndio natural del Pueblo de Nambe de la naz.n teguas." 25 June–2 August 1731.

83. For example, SANM II:883, proclamation of Superior Orden, Santa Fe, 10 March 1784; Simmons, *Spanish Government*, p. 186.

84. The important role of the family in overseeing the education of children is described by Bernardo P. Gallegos, *Literacy, Education, and Society in New Mexico, 1693–1821* (Albuquerque: University of New Mexico Press, 1992), pp. 21–22, 37–39, and *passim*. Jones, *Los Paisanos*, pp. 137–39, describes the meager educational opportunities available to New Mexicans in the colonial period.

85. Chavez, *Origins of New Mexico Families*, p. 291. As "*notario nombrado*" for Juez Eclesiástico Vicario Santiago Roibal, SANM II:531a, "Año de 1755. Una pettiz.on presentada antte el S.r Vicario y Juez eclesiastico p.r Domingo Luxan de este real Presidio contra christobal xaramillo hasi mismo soldado y Probidenzia que se dio"; activity as procurador, SANM I:571, "Año de 1766. Autos seguidos a petición de Miguel y Santiago Montoya Contra Juan Pablo Martín sobre vn sitio de tierras"; and SANM I:1351, "Autos Seguidos por los

Yndios del Pueblo de S.n Yldefonso contra los Erederos de Juana Luján y de fran.co Gómez deel Castillo." 4 February 1763. Activity as *alcalde mayor*, SANM I:44, "Año de 1769. Merced de tierra hecha a Antonio Armijo."

86. For Sandoval's activities as protector de indios, see Cutter, *Protector de Indios*, pp. 83–89.

87. Real Academia de la Historia, Colección Muñoz, Grupo III, tomo 25, Documentos para la historia del Nuevo México. "Noticias lamentables acaecidas en la Nueva Mexico y atrasos que cada día se experimentan asi en lo espiritual como en lo temporal escritas por el P. Fr. Juan Sanz de Lezaun en el Año 1760," f. 43. Text reads: "tambien las ventas de las Alcaldías estas el las consigue, es el que más mulas, y carneros dá, esto es tán sabido que ni los parvulitos no ignoran. ¿Que justicia pueden hacer estos?"

88. AGI Guadalajara 274, "Lista de los Alcaldes maiores, y Tenientes, que he nombrado con Títulos en el Distrito de esta Provincia de mi mando de la Nueva Vizcaya, con la nota de las cantidades, que me contribuien algunas [sic] anualmente por razon de sus empleos sacada a la margen." Durango, 8 November 1777.

89. Ralph Emerson Twitchell, *The Spanish Archives of New Mexico* (Cedar Rapids, Iowa: The Torch Press, 1914), vol. 2, pp. 254–55.

90. AGN Reales Cédulas Originales 104, exp. 97. Petition of Eusebio Durán y Chaves. Aranjuez, 18 April 1774. Copy in SANM II:675.

91. AGN Reales Cédulas Originales 104, exp. 97. Real Orden. Aranjuez, 28 April 1774.

92. AGN Reales Cédulas Originales 106, exp. 19. Julián de Arriaga a Virrey de Nueva España. El Pardo, 31 January 1775.

93. SANM II:686. Mendinueta to Bucareli y Ursúa. Santa Fe, 12 May 1775.

94. SANM II:1510, Nava to Chacón. Chihuahua, 6 October 1800; SANM II:1875, Petition of Juan Andrés Tafoya. Santa Fe, 16 August 1805. Also cited in Simmons, *Spanish Government*, p. 171 n. 38, p. 170 n. 37.

95. SANM II:1875, Petition of Juan Andrés Tafoya. Santa Fe, 16 August 1805.

96. Examples of these remarkably detailed *aranceles*, which existed for every non-salaried functionary of the various audiencias can be found in AGI Guadalajara 321. The fees for "Subdelegados de Justicia, Alcaldes, y demas Juezes ordinarios del Distrito de la R.l Aud.a [de Guadalajara]" are found in the same legajo, carpeta 15. The use of such schedules had long been the practice in the empire. Functionaries of ecclesiastical courts also were subject to similar *aranceles*. See BN 2/49606. *Constitutiones Synodales . . . de Coria*. Salamanca: 1606.

97. SANM II:335, Publication of viceregal order [relative to fees of legal proceedings for New Spain, New Galicia, and Nueva Vizcaya]. 12 July 1725.

98. For example, SANM II:228, "Causa Criminal Contra Diego Martin Moraga Vez.o de la Jurisdiz.on de la Cañada por hauer dado vnas Heridas a Joseph Uasq.z." 27 July–10 September 1715.

99. An example of the apparent discretionary power in assigning fees is SANM II:498, "Causa criminal de querella de Joseph Man.l Truxillo Contra Antonio Balberde y dos hijos suios, todos Vecinos de la Juridicion de la Villa

de S.ta Cruz de la Cañada, por vnas heridas, que dieron al dho Joseph Man.l Truxillo consta de sanidad, y esta determinada esta causa." 10 September–30 September 1748.

100. SANM II:591, "Año de 1765. Autos seguidos contra Bartholomé Garduño a petición de su muger." 12 June–8 October 1765.

101. SANM II:2140, Ignacio Sánchez Vergara to Alberto Máynez. Santa Ana, 3 August 1808.

102. Vito Alessio Robles, ed., *Diario y Derrotero de lo Caminado, Visto y Observado en las Visita que hizo a los Presidios de la Nueva España Septentrional el Brigadier Pedro de Rivera* (México: Archivo Histórico Militar Mexicano, 1946), p. 106.

103. Alessio Robles, *Diario y Derrotero.* p. 153.

104. AGI Guadalajara 276, Caballero de Croix to José de Gálvez. Chihuahua, 29 June 1778 (duplicado).

105. SANM II:137, Indians of San Juan v. Roque Madrid. 29 December 1707. Also Cutter, *Protector de Indios*, p. 67. I refer here to specific charges against various *alcaldes* that I have found in the judicial records of the Spanish Archives of New Mexico, and not to non-specific, and unsubstantiated, blanket indictments found in some contemporary accounts.

106. Simmons, *Spanish Government*, p. 171.

107. For example, Kessell, *Kiva, Cross, and Crown*, pp. 504–6, provides a list of *alcaldes* for the jurisdiction of Pecos that shows frequent turnover in the office.

108. For warrants and writs, see SANM II:526, José Fresques v. Antonio Gallegos. 9 May 1753.

109. SANM II:590, "Año de 1765. Autos Criminales seguidos contra evsebio chabes vecino de la Lameda por vnos golpes que dió a su suegro Andrés Martín." 3 June–12 July 1765. Baltasar Griego states that he is *teniente alcalde* "de toda esta jurisdición" of Albuquerque. Simmons, *Spanish Government*, p. 168, suggests that the *tenientes* operated only within their particular subdivisions.

110. New Mexico State Archives and Records Center, Records of the U.S. Surveyor General (hereafter SG):109, Conveyance, Baltasar Romero to Juan José Romero, Ana María Romero, Antonia Romero, and Domingo Mariano de los Dolores. San Gerónimo de los Taos, 14 August 1732. In this particular document, Teniente Alcalde Mayor y Capitán a Guerra Diego Romero stated he "did not sign this deed because I do not know how." His "*escribano*," Diego Velasco, signed for him. Velasco was not an *escribano* in the true sense of a trained professional. His orthography and penmanship leave much to be desired. He signed the document, in very scratchy hand: "Aruego de die goromero, Dye Go velasco (rubric)."

111. Several outstanding studies of the *cabildo* exist. A starting point, and still authoritative, is Haring, *Spanish Empire*, pp. 147–65. A more detailed examination is Constantino Bayle, *Los Cabildos Seculares en la América Española* (Madrid: Sapienta, S.A. de Ediciones, 1952). Case studies include John Preston Moore, *The Cabildo in Peru Under the Habsburgs: A Study in the Origins and Powers of the Town Council in the Viceroyalty of Peru, 1530–1700* (Durham: Duke

University Press, 1954), and by the same author, *The Cabildo in Peru Under the Bourbons: A Study in the Decline and Resurgence of Local Government in the Audiencia of Lima* (Durham: Duke University Press, 1966). Scholars in most Latin American countries have produced studies of their respective *cabildos*. General legislation relative to the *cabildo* is found in *Recopilación de Indias*, 4.9.

112. BA, r. 9 fr. 675, Representación of Cabildo, Justicia, y Regimiento to [Governor]. San Fernando, 26 August 1756; SANM II:186, Auto de Elección. Santa Fe, 1 January 1713.

113. Julio Alemparte R., *El Cabildo en Chile Colonial (Orígenes Municipales de las Repúblicas Hispanoamericanas)* (Santiago: Ediciones de la Universidad de Chile, 1940), p. 239.

114. In this regard, see Reinhard Liehr, *Ayuntamiento y Oligarquía en Puebla, 1787–1810* (México: Sep/Setentas, 1976), trad. de Olga Hentsche, t. 1, p. 8. Also Tomás y Valiente, *Manual*, p. 341.

115. On this local dimension of lawmaking, see Víctor Tau Anzoátegui, "Los Bandos de Buen Gobierno de Buenos Aires en la Epoca Hispánica," in *Justicia, Sociedad y Economía en la América Española (Siglos XVI, XVII y XVIII)* (Valladolid: Casa-Museo de Colón, Seminario Americanista de la Universidad de Valladolid, 1983).

116. Moore, *Cabildo . . . Bourbons*, p. 49; *Recopilación de Indias*, 4.10.1, 2.

117. *Recopilación de Indias*, 4.10.6. Quote in Francisco Domínguez Compañy, "La Condición del Vecino," in *Estudios Sobre las Instituciones Locales Hispanoamericanas* (Caracas: Biblioteca de la Academia Nacional de la Historia, 1981), p. 112.

118. María Alvina Gallaga, for example, referred to herself as a "vecina de esta ciudad" of Guadalajara, although she was the slave of Doña Máxima Argüelles. ARAG Civil s/c #1. Another slave, Antonia Bueno, averred that she was a "vecina en esta corte [Guadalajara]." ARAG Civil s/c n.o 9, 1731–35. Liehr, *Ayuntamiento y Oligarquía*, t. 1, p. 96, notes that in Puebla, a *vecino* was "aquel que tuviera su domicilio fijo en la ciudad, ya fuera blanco, mulato o indígena, bajando hasta los esclavos negros." Domínguez Compañy, "Condición del Vecino," pp. 121–22, also points out that the term *vecino* was used in the sense of "inhabitant" in many parts of Spanish America.

119. For a look at these important responsibilities see Liehr, *Ayuntamiento y Oligarquía*, pp. 146–70.

120. No clear explanation for its decline has surfaced from contemporary documents, but this probable explanation is found in SANM II:407, Cabildo to Visitador General [draft]. Santa Fe, [July?] 1725. See also Simmons, *Spanish Government*, pp. 193–95.

121. Simmons, *Spanish Government*, p. 207, citing SANM II:2560.

122. In the absence of a definitive study of the *cabildo* in San Antonio, consult Mattie Alice Austin, "The Municipal Government of San Fernando de Béxar, 1730–1800," *Southwestern Historical Quarterly* 8 (April 1905): 277–352; also Cruz, *Let There Be Towns*, pp. 144–64.

123. For example, BA, decrees of buen gobierno issued by Juan Leal Goraz. San Fernando, 14 April 1735. Manuel Muñoz, governor in 1798, described the duties of the *cabildo* as being "the administration of justice, and the protection

of the interests of the commonwealth." Quoted in Austin, "Municipal Government," p. 308.

124. Another major area of New World settlement was Montevideo.

125. Gerald E. Poyo, "The Canary Island Immigrants of San Antonio: From Ethnic Exclusivity to Community in Eighteenth-Century Béxar," in Poyo and Hinojosa, eds., *Tejano Origins in Eighteenth-Century San Antonio*, pp. 41–58.

126. See Scholes, "Civil Government in New Mexico."

127. SANM II:240. Santa Fe, 1 January 1716.

128. The term *villa* designated a community of some importance and gave it the legal right to form a *cabildo*. Only four *villas* existed in New Mexico during the colonial period—Santa Fe, Santa Cruz de la Cañada, Albuquerque, and El Paso (which itself at times fell within the jurisdiction of Nueva Vizcaya). Royal legislation allowed for six *regidores*. *Recopilación de Indias*, 4.10.2.

129. Austin, "Municipal Government," pp. 298–99.

130. Moore, *Cabildo . . . Habsburgs*, pp. 79–80, indicates that elections in Peru were carried out by either vocal or secret ballot.

131. SANM II:186, Auto de Elección. Santa Fe, 1 January 1713.

132. Austin, "Municipal Government," p. 306.

133. BA, "Posesiones de Oficios 1778–1784." Domingo Cabello to cabildo, 22 December 1784; Manuel Muñoz to *cabildo,* 29 December 1794. Austin, "Municipal Government," p. 308–9.

134. On these two individuals consult Chavez, *Origins of New Mexico Families*, p. 254 (Páez Hurtado), p. 183 (García de las Rivas).

135. AGN Provincias Internas 32, exp. 11, "Títulos de regidores." San Fernando, 20 July 1731; BA, "Auto de elecciones." 2 August 1731. Austin, "Municipal Government," p. 305.

136. *Recopilación de Indias*, 5.3.4.

137. Liehr, *Ayuntamiento y Oligarquía*, t. 1, pp. 96–97.

138. Kicza, *Colonial Entrepreneurs*, pp. 13–14. Poyo, "Immigrants and Integration," p. 87.

139. McKnight, "Law Books," p. 78. *Recopilación de Indias*, 8.7.34, stipulated that "en cada una de nuestras Audiencias, Tribunales de Cuentas, y ordinarios de Hacienda, oficios de gobierno, Archivos de la Ciudad, Villa, o Lugar de las Indias, e Islas, haya, y se guarde esta nuestra Recopilacion de leyes."

140. *Recopilación de Indias*, 5.3.1, 5.10.13. Exact territorial limits varied for diverse municipalities. Royal law (*Recopilación de Indias*, 5.3.19) recognized local custom in establishing such limits. See AGI Guadalajara 110, "Año 1750. Testimonio de diligencias executadas en la Ciu.d de durango sobre la Jurisdición que perteneze a los Alc.es ordinarios de dicha Ciudad." This case involved a squabble between the *alcaldes ordinarios* of Durango and the provincial governor, Juan Francisco de la Puerta, over authority on the outskirts of Durango.

141. Liehr, *Ayuntamiento y Oligarquía*, t. 1, p. 138, notes that the "gobernador-intendente" of Puebla had jurisdiction over *alcaldes ordinarios* in cases involving Indians.

142. *Recopilación de Indias*, 5.3.1. Example of appeal to governor, BA, r. 16 fr. 467, "Año de 1785. Autos Criminales formados por el Alcalde de Segundo Boto

de esta Villa D.n Marcos de Castro, a Pedimento de José Sambrano sobre haberlo erido Grabem.te de el Brazo Yzq.do, y concluhidos en este tribunal por Via de Apelación." 26 February–27 March 1785. Austin, "Municipal Government," p. 317, says that "appeals from the *alcalde's* decisions were usually carried to the governor's court, and then to the viceroy's."

143. *Recopilación de Indias*, 5.3.8.

144. BA, r. 14 fr. 336, Caballero de Croix to Cabello. Arizpe, 19 July 1780; BA, r.14 fr.598, Cabello to Croix. Béxar, 11 October 1780. SANM II:890, Anza to Alcalde Mayor of Taos. Santa Fe, 24 April 1784.

145. SANM II:170, "Caussa criminal contra don fernando de chaues." 20–26 January 1712, for alcalde involved in proceedings.

146. SANM II:170, "Caussa criminal contra don fernando de chaues." 20–26 January 1712, with Alonso Rael de Aguilar as juez.

147. SANMI:1356, Santa Ana v. San Felipe. 5 May 1813. Both José Pino, *alcalde mayor* of Albuquerque, and José María de Arce, from Santa Fe, an officer, served as jueces delegados in this case.

148. One striking exception in the borderlands was Spanish New Orleans, where, because of the vitality of trade and commerce, a number of true professionals existed. See McKnight, "Law Without Lawyers," pp. 52, 55; and McKnight, "Law Books," pp. 74–76.

149. BA, r. 12 fr. 188, Pedro José Tejada v. Cabildo. 13 January–1 February 1778.

150. BA, r. 15 fr. 321, Luis Mariano Menchaca v. Francisco Javier Rodríguez. 31 March–21 November 1783.

151. BA, r. 15 fr. 42, Antonia Rosalía de Armas v. Pedro Granado. 1 March 1782.

152. McKnight, "Law Books," p. 78.

153. SANM II:531a, "Vna petiz.on presentada antte el s.r Vicario y Juez eclesiastico p.r Domingo Luxan, soldado de este real Presidio contra christobal xaramillo hasimismo soldado y Probidenzia que se dio." 9–21 August 1755.

154. SANM II:507a, Felipe Tafoya to Tomás Vélez Cachupín, Santa Fe, 10 [December] 1749, in which he referred to himself as "procurador público de esta villa"; other references to Tafoya as procurador in SANM II:517 (1751–52); SANM I:1351 (1763); SANM I:571 (1766).

155. SANM I:869; SANM I:1351, "Autos Seguidos por los Yndios del Pueblo de S.n Yldefonso contra los Erederos de Juana Lujan y de fran.co Gomez deel Castillo," 4 February 1763.

156. SANM II:516, José Mariano Yturrieta (for Eduarda Yturrieta) v. Nicolás Durán y Chaves. 15 April 1747–15 October 1751.

157. SANM II:453, "Demanda de Fran.ca Salas muger de Gregorio Jaramillo Vecina de la Poblazon de fuen Clara contra el cap.n Joseph Baca Alc.e may.r de dho partido sobre decir hauerla ynjuriado de palabras, a que dio satisfacion dho Alc.e en cuia Vista se probeio el Auto que esta al fin de este Quaderno." 16–27 May 1744.

158. SANM II:463, "Orden, que se da a Joseph Baca Alc.e may.r y cap.n a Guerra de la Villa de Alburquerque, para que notifique a Ysidro Sanchez Vezino de dha Juridicion, que pena de cincuenta p.s y quinze dias de cepo por

la primera vez, no haga escritos, ni coopere a ellos, y por la segunda se estra-
ñara de este Reyno." 3 March 1745.

159. The handwriting in a petition found in SANM II:465a, 16 June 1745, for
example, appears to be that of Isidro Sánchez.

160. ARAG Civil s/c, n.o 4, 1801–20, "Contestación de d.n José de la Peña,"
f. 14. Santa Fe, 4 September 1803; "Constestación de D. Ant.o [Estanislao]
Ruiz," f. 16. San Antonio, 7 October 1803. Appointed to both positions by
Vicario José María Bibian de Ortega, Peña was the *notario público* for the villa
of Santa Fe, as well as the cantor in the Capilla castrense; Ruiz was *notario
público* and *cantor* for the *villa* of Albuquerque, also named by Ortega.

Chapter 5

1. AGN Provincias Internas 254. Informe of Jacobo Ugarte y Loyola, f. 29.
Arizpe, 10 December 1787.

2. For complaints of not using stamped paper (*papel sellado*), required by
law on all official documents, and advice on how to remedy this deficiency, see
ARAG Criminal s/n s/c, "Provincia del N.o México. Jurisdicción de Alburquerque. Año de 1806. Causa criminal formada contra Juan Christóbal García,
por haver dado muerte en riña a Antonio Josef Baca, vecinos de dicha Jurisdicción. Juez el Alcalde de Alburquerque Don Manuel de Arteaga=actuando
p.r receptoria." 3 November 1806–24 January 1810. Examples of inadequate
defense found in ARAG Criminal s/n s/c, "Provincia del N.o México. Jurisdicción de Alburquerque. Año de 1806. Causa criminal formada contra Juan
Christóbal García," ff. 15–15v; for insufficient proof of guilt, ARAG Criminal
s/c n. 4 1818–19, "Villa de S.ta Fee del Nuevo México. Año de 1818. Causa
criminal contra José Eleuterio Martínez, Vecino del Partido del Vado, acusado
de coyto Bestial con una Burra, seguida por el Alcalde del mismo Partido, Don
Vizente Ybarguen de Villanueva." 11 March 1818–13 May 1819.

3. *Siete Partidas. Partida* 3 deals with civil law; *Partida* 7 treats criminal law.

4. On the restructuring of peninsular law under the Bourbons, see Tomás
y Valiente, *Manual*, pp. 367–76.

5. For the accusative dimension of alphonsine criminal procedure, see *Siete
Partidas,* 7.1.14–16.

6. On the growth of royal power and its relationship to the judiciary, see
Tomás y Valiente, *Derecho Penal*, pp. 23–46. On the inquisitive process, see
Alonso Romero, *Proceso Penal*, pp. 91–103.

7. I use the term *inquisitorial* only in the sense of a specific mode of legal
procedure, and not necessarily to connote any association with the Holy Office
of the Inquisition.

8. For a fuller discussion of this vital point, see Alonso Romero, *Proceso
Penal*, pp. 91–95.

9. Alonso Romero, *Proceso Penal*, pp. 290–95. The work of the Cortes of
Alcalá became the basis of the *Ordenamiento de Alcalá* (1348), a fundamental text
of Spanish law.

10. Sala, *Ilustración del Derecho Real*, t. 2, lib. 3, tít. 2, p. 135. Similarly, Carrillo y Sánchez, *Prontuario Alfabético*, p. 158, "Ordinario es aquel, en que se observan todos los trámites y solemnidades establecidas por derecho. Estraordinario es cuando no se procede mediante acción o acusación verdadera, sino de oficio, sin guardar el orden y las solemnidades legales. Sumario, cuando se procede brevemente de plano, sin aparato ni figura de juicio, atendiendo solo a la verdad del hecho"; Alvarez, *Instituciones de Derecho Real*, lib. 4, p. 212, "Estraordinario, cuando se procede sin querella ni acción intentada por parte, sólo de oficio del juez. Sumario, se llama aquel en que se procede breve y sencillamente, sin ningún aparato ni figura de juicio"; Escriche, *Diccionario Razonado*, p. 997, "Juicio sumario, que viene a ser lo mismo que extraordinario, es aquel en que se conoce brevemente de la causa, omitiendo las largas solemnidades establecidas para los juicios comunes, atendiendo solamente a la verdad del hecho."

11. Some authors, among them Joaquín Escriche, label the initial proceedings in a criminal case as the *sumario,* rather than the *sumaria.* To avoid confusion, I have chosen to follow the majority of contemporary authors and magistrates in referring to these initial proceedings as the *sumaria,* and have reserved the term *sumario* for what can best be described as a summary proceeding.

12. While cases that returned to the provinces after review at superior level do indicate a bit more care with judicial procedure at the local level, cases that remained within the confines of the province do not reveal any extraordinary attention to procedural formalities.

13. ARAG s/c n.o 2, criminal 1810, Manuel Salcedo to Real Audiencia de Guadalajara. San Fernando, 9 July 1810. SANM II:1593, Chacón to Real Audiencia. Santa Fe, 28 March 1802.

14. On the *juicio sumario* in Spain, see Alonso Romero, *Proceso Penal*, pp. 287–302.

15. Andrés Cornejo, *Diccionario Histórico, y Forense del Derecho Real de España* (Madrid: Joaquín Ibarra, 1779), p. 365.

16. Juan de Hevia Bolaños, *Curia Philipica* (Madrid: Herederos de la Viuda de Juan García Infanzón, 1761), p. 42.

17. Charles R. Cutter, transcripción y estudio preliminar, *Libro de los Principales Rudimentos Tocante a Todos Juicios, Criminal, Civil y Executivo. Año 1764* (México: Universidad Nacional Autónoma de México, 1994), p. 29.

18. According to a late-colonial-period jurist, José María Alvarez, a criminal case by accusation must adhere to the lengthy *proceso ordinario.* Alvarez, *Instituciones de Derecho Real*, lib. 4, pp. 273–76.

19. Alonso Romero, *Proceso Penal*, p. 186.

20. Pérez y López, *Teatro de la Legislación*, voz "juicios."

21. *Libro de los Principales Rudimentos*, p. 29, for example, refers to this actor as the *"denunciador acusador."* Alonso Romero, *Proceso Penal*, pp. 183–86, notes the blurring tendency in Castile.

22. Juan y Colom, *Instrucción*, lib. 3, p. 177; Cornejo, *Diccionario*, voz "sumaria"; Berní y Catalá, *Práctica Criminal.*

23. Alonso Romero, *Proceso Penal*, pp. 189–95. Trial records from the AGN indicate similar practice.

24. Alonso Romero, *Proceso Penal*, p. 189.

25. Berní y Catalá, *Práctica Criminal*, p. 99.

26. Examples in SANM II:172, "Año de 1712. Caussa Criminal Contra Diego Velasco sobre hauer muerto en su cassa al Sarg.to mig.l de herrera." Examples of midwives in BA, r. 24 fr. 901, "Año de 1794. Causa formada a Juan José Hernández a pedimento de Fran.co Travieso, sobre Estrupo [sic] a María Martina." 16 August–4 September 1794. BA, r. 38 fr. 822, Nemesio Salcedo to Cordero. Chihuahua, 14 October 1808.

27. SANM II:187, Criminal proceedings against Miguel Luján. 20 April 1713–22 October 1714.

28. BA, r. 8 fr. 800, "Causa Criminal contra Ant.o Tellos." 21 August–2 September 1744.

29. SANM II:363a, "Año de 1731. Causa Criminnal fulminada de ofisio de la Real Justisia contra Joseph Naranjo vesino de la Villa Nueva de S.ta Cruz por hauer dado unas herridas a Lorenzo Xaramillo de las q. murió a pocos días de hauerlos reseuido." 1 September 1731–17 July 1734.

30. SANM II:296, Proceedings against Catalina Villalpando. 17 April–10 May 1719.

31. Berní y Catalá, *Práctica Criminal*, pp. 105–7. The *Libro de los Principales Rudimentos*, p. 29, however, indicates that in Mexico City, suspects were allowed to make a statement at this point.

32. Berní y Catalá, *Práctica Criminal*, pp. 110–14.

33. Taylor, *Drinking, Homicide, and Rebellion*, p. 76.

34. Alonso Villadiego de Vascuñana y Montoya, *Instrucción Política y Práctica Judicial* (Madrid: Antonio Marín, 1766), p. 60, states that the investigating magistrate might question "los testigos que halla, aunque sean prohibidos por derecho."

35. SANM II:239c, "Causa Criminal Contra fran.co Jauier Rom.o, Santiago Rom.o, Joseph Vasq.z, y Ju.o Al.o Monrroy por hauer Muerto un buey del yndio lucas de aBenbua." 26 August–20 November 1715, 4 April 1716.

36. See Escriche, *Diccionario*, voz "testigo," 1572.

37. Biblioteca Pública del Estado de Jalisco, Manuscritos 197. "Bocabulario Alfabético de Derecho Civil y Canónigo, arreglado conforme a las leyes y disposiciones vigente en los lugares habitados por los indios," p. 199. Although anonymous and without a date, internal evidence indicates that this piece dates from the mid eighteenth century.

38. Solórzano Pereira, *Política Indiana*, 2.28.34, "les estará mejor a los Indios que no les crea, que ponerles en ocasión de que se perjuren, por la poca firmeza, y estabilidad de su juicio, y deposiciones, y por las sospechas que siempre tendrémos en ellas de falsedad"; 2.28.35, "no se les dé más fé, y crédito, que si sólo uno idóneo se huviere examinado." Similar opinions of Indians held sway in Mexico. See José A. Llaguno, S.J., *La Personalidad Jurídica del Indio y el III Concilio Provincial Mexicano (1585)* (México: Editorial Porrúa, S.A., 1983), p. 118.

39. For example, SANM II:394, "Causa Criminal contra el Capitán Bernavé Vaca Alcalde Mayor de la Jurisdisión de Zuñi por querella de los Yndios de los Pueblos de Acoma, y Laguna sobre unos cambalaches y otras cosas q.e en ella

se contiene." 21 December 1733–26 January 1734. Juan González Bas, *alcalde mayor* and *juez comisionado,* found some of the Indian deponents to be not capable of taking the oath, though he gave no reason. In subsequent proceedings, however, Lieutenant Governor Juan Páez Hurtado accepted testimony from some of the same witnesses who previously had been unacceptable.

40. SANM II:440, "Unas diligencias seguidas contra Manuel Martín y Salvador de Torres." 5–10 June 1741; also SANM II:406a, Francisco Padilla v. Sebastián Gallegos. 29 October 1735–25 February 1736. As a plaintiff, Sebastián Gallegos, a Jumano, was described as "muy capaz," and took the oath "por Dios nuestro señor y la señal de una cruz."

41. SANM II:452, "Ymbenttario de los vienes de María Calabazitta, Yndia del Pueblo de S.to Domingo, ya difunta en la forma que adentro se expresa." 18–23 May 1744.

42. On the status of Indians, see Cutter, *Protector de Indios*, pp. 5—7. Woodrow Borah, *Justice by Insurance: The General Indian Court of Colonial Mexico and the Legal Aides of the Half-Real* (Berkeley: University of California Press, 1983), pp. 80–83, 59–60.

43. See Bustamante, "'The Matter Was Never Resolved'"; Poyo, "Immigrants and Immigration," p. 87. For Mexico City, see Patricia Seed, "Social Dimensions of Race: Mexico City, 1753," *Hispanic American Historical Review* 62 (November 1982): 569–606.

44. *Siete Partidas*, 3.8.

45. Alvarez, *Instituciones de Derecho Real*, l. 4, p. 279. *Libro de los Principales Rudimentos*, p. 31.

46. For example, SANM II:498, "Causa criminal de querella de Joseph Man.l Truxillo Contra Antonio Balberde, y dos hijos suios, todos Vecinos de la Juridición de la Villa de S.ta Cruz de la Cañada, por vnas heridas, que dieron al dho Joseph Man.l Truxillo." 10–30 September 1748.

47. Carrillo, *Prontuario*, p. 109; Escriche, *Diccionario*, p. 609, states "el embargo tiene por objeto asegurar las resultas del juicio, esto es, la satisfacción de la responsabilidad pecuniaria que una persona ha contraido realmente o se cree haber contraido, sea en virtud de obligación civil que dimane de convención o de ley, sea en virtud de algún delito o cuasidelito que hubiese perpetrado."

48. *Siete Partidas*, 3.9.

49. Liehr, *Ayuntamiento y Oligarquía*, t. 1, pp. 149–50.

50. For example, SANM II:299, "Causa Criminal q de oficio de la R.l Justizia se a seguido contra Pedro asensio lopez Joseph Gonzalez y Pedro lopez Vez.s de la villa de alburquerq.e." 27 July–6 November 1719.

51. For this confusion in procedural order on the peninsula, see Alonso Romero, *Proceso Penal*, p. 198. Proper procedure called for the *auto de prisión* to take place at this juncture. Berní y Catalá, *Práctica Criminal*, pp. 108–10.

52. SANM II:590, "Año de 1765. Autos Criminales seguidos contra evsebio chabes vecino de la Lameda por vnos golpes que dió a su suegro Andrés Martín." 3 June–12 July 1765. The *auto de prisión* precedes the *sumaria* but follows the *cabeza del proceso.*

53. The *Reglamento* of 1729, n. 77, stipulated that the military help *"juezes ordinarios"* to apprehend suspects or escapees guilty of *"graves delitos."*

54. SANM II:441, Proceedings v. Antonio Jiménez, Felipe Trujillo, and Luis Quintana. 8 July 1741–28 July 1742.

55. For example, SANM II:178, "Demanda puesta p.r Miguel de Quintana a Joseph Truxillo por auerle Vrtado Vnos yndios el uno sirviente suyo dos Cau.os, etc." 8 August–24 October 1712. For the manner in which to conduct criminal proceedings in *rebeldía,* see *Libro de los Principales Rudimentos*, pp. 53–57.

56. For example, SANM II:480, "Demanda criminal de pedimento de D.n Juan del Pino mercader Viandante, y recidente de este Reyno de la Nueba México contra Dos Yndios Genízaros." 19 June–5 August 1747. BA, r. 8 fr. 288, Juan Leal Goraz v. Patricio Rodríguez Galano. 6–7 September 1734. BA, r. 11 fr. 712, Criminal proceedings against María del Refugio de Jesús María and Francisco de Arocha. 4–28 June 1776. In this instance the suspect was placed "in these *casas reales* where the *cabildo* of this *villa* customarily meets, for lack of another jail."

57. AGN Provincias Internas 100, exp. 1. "Copia de los artículos desde el veinte, que el Comandante Ynspector ha pasado al Varón de Riperdá Gov.or de Texas por lo perteneciente a lo político a continuación de la q.e deve observar en el establecimiento del nuevo Real Reglamento, y notas con que satisface a ellos." Real Campo de N.a S.a de el Carmen, 6 May 1773.

58. The same lack of facilities characterized the jail system on the peninsula under the Habsburgs. See José Luis de las Heras Santos, *La Justicia Penal de los Austrias en la Corona de Castilla* (Salamanca: Universidad de Salamanca, 1991), p. 272.

59. For example, SANM II:517, "Criminales contra Cayetano Pasote calidad lobo, sobre unas heridas y lo demas que dentro se expresa." 12 January 1751–23 November 1752.

60. In colonial Texas, presidios also existed at La Bahía and, sporadically, at Nacogdoches.

61. This individual's nickname probably meant something like "the bullslinger." Francisco J. Santamaría, *Diccionario General de Americanismos* (Méjico: Editorial Pedro Robredo, 1942), voz "cuajar": "En algunas partes de Méjico, echar mentiras. Es anticuado. Hablar por hablar, y hacer a uno perder el tiempo." Also, under "cuajo": "En Méjico, charla ociosa. Embuste o bola."

62. SANM II:480, "Demanda criminal de pedimento de D.n Juan del Pino mercader viandante, y residente de este Reino de la Nueva México contra dos Indios Genízaros, que viven en el paraje de Belén de la Jurisdicción de la Villa de San Felipe de Alburquerque, sobre suponer haberle robado varios géneros de la casa de Don Juan Miguel Alvarez del Castillo en la que dice los tenía." 19 June–5 August 1747.

63. For example, SANM II:406a, Proceedings against Francisco Padilla and Sebastian Gallegos. 29 October 1735–25 February 1736.

64. BA, r. 8 fr. 300, Juan Leal Goraz v. Martín Lorenzo de Armas, Juan Curbelo, and Francisco José de Arocha. 25 November 1735.

65. *Siete Partidas*, 7.29. Carrillo, *Prontuario*, p. 211, "Las cárceles sólo están destinadas para la custodia y no para tormento de los reos." Alonso Romero, *Proceso Penal*, pp. 196–97. De las Heras Santos, *Justicia Penal*, p. 268. Writing in the early seventeenth century, however, Alonso de Villadiego, *Instrucción Política*, p. 201, states "la Carcel no se inventó para pena de los delitos, sino para guarda de los presos, mas con todo en algunos se puede, y debe dar por pena al delinquente . . . y aun ya oy es tanto la Cárcel para pena, como para guarda de los presos."

66. SANM I:1248, Order of Governor Tomás Vélez Cachupín. Santa Fe, 29 March 1753; also SANM I:1251, Bando of Francisco Cuervo y Valdés. Santa Fe, 25 April 1705.

67. ARAG s/c Civil 1809–19. Certificación of citizens of Santa Fe, 25 June 1808.

68. For example, SANM II:515, "Criminales contra Alejandro Mora vecino de Bernalillo sobre resistencia a la Justicia; maltrato de su mujer y de una yndia su sirviente." 23 September 1751–6 November 1752. BA, "Declaración tomada a D. José Antonio Sausedo sobre azotes que dio a un sirviente suio." 8 July–3 October 1809. The defendant had been jailed during the proceedings and this was deemed to be sufficient punishment. Case cited in Faulk, *Last Years of Spanish Texas*, p. 95.

69. Berní y Catalá, *Práctica Criminal*, pp. 110–14. Alonso Romero, *Proceso Penal*, p. 207.

70. For Castilian practice, see Tomás y Valiente, *Derecho Penal*, p. 172.

71. For example, SANM II:187, Criminal proceedings against Miguel Luján. 20 April 1713–22 October 1714.

72. This seems to have been the case in Mexico City as well. A contemporary prompter referred to this phase as the "*declaración.*" *Libro de los Principales Rudimentos*, p 31.

73. SANM II:687, "Diligencias seguidas de oficio de la R.l Justicia sovre vn acto de Bestialidad cometido por un Yndio de Taos." 22 June 1775–11 June 1776. In this case the suspect admitted his guilt in both his *confesión* and in his *declaración*.

74. Juan y Colom, *Instrucción*, lib. 3, p. 211; Gutiérrez, *Práctica Criminal*, t. 1, cap. 7, p. 240; Sala, *Ilustración*, t. 2, lib. 3, p. 324. Carrillo, *Prontuario*, pp. 65–66, calls this phase the "confesión o declaración judicial," in which the defendant might confirm or deny his guilt.

75. For denials of charges, SANM II:239c, "Causa Criminal Contra fran.co Jauier Rom.o, Santiago Rom.o, Joseph Vas.z y Ju.o Al.o Monrroy por hauer Muerto un buey del yndio lucas de aBenbua." 26 August–20 November 1715, 4 April 1716. BA, r. 14 fr. 901, Pedro José Tejada v. Juana Francisca Pérez. 4 January 1782.

76. For a contemporary view on proper procedure for torture, see Villadiego, *Instrucción Política*, pp. 86–88; for judicial torture as practiced in eighteenth-century Mexico, see *Libro de los Principales Rudimentos*, pp. 47–49.

77. Abelardo Levaggi, *Manual de Historia del Derecho Argentino*, t. 2, p. 76, opines that the crown applied torture only rarely in the eighteenth century. On torture as a procedural step in penal law, see Francisco Tomás y Valiente, *La*

Tortura en España (Barcelona: Editorial Ariel, 1973). Indications that torture was practiced in the Real Audiencia de México are found in BN ms. 20311, "Varias Alegaciones Jurídicas que el Lic.do D. Juan Antonio de Torquemada, Abogado de la R.l Audiencia de esta Nueva España, dijo en sus Reales Estrados, en los de su Real Sala de el Crimen, y en los de el Juzgado, y Audiencia Ecclesiástica. Compiladas en este II.o Tomo, los años de [1724] y [1725]," pp. 151–79, "Por parte de D.a Teresa Ruiz" includes the statement: "y para que se revoque la sentencia de vista, de que éste [reo] se halla absuelto, procediendose, a imponerle la pena a tanto exceso correspondiente [a un robo], o al menos a la de tortura, que tiene D.a Teresa pedido en la primera instancia, se le imponga." The preceding passage indicates that torture may have been perceived as a punishment in itself, and not simply a means to elicit a confession. On Torquemada and his judicial arguments, see María Luz Alonso Martín, "Un Jurista Indiano: Juan Antonio Torquemada," in *Justicia, Sociedad y Economía en la América Española (Siglos XVI, XVII y XVIII)* (Valladolid: Universidad de Valladolid, 1983), pp. 205–33. See also the description found in *Libro de los Principales Rudimentos*, pp. 47–49.

78. SANM II:187, Criminal proceedings against Miguel Luján. 20 April 1713–22 October 1714.

Chapter 6

1. Alonso Romero, *Proceso Penal*, p. 225.

2. SANM II:687, "Diligencias seguidas de oficio de la R.l Justicia sovre vn acto de Bestialidad cometido por un Yndio de Taos." 22 June 1775–11 June 1776.

3. *Libro de los Principales Rudimentos*, p. 42.

4. For example, SANM II:673, "Causa Criminal contra las reas M.a Fran.ca y M.a su madre sentenciadas a muerte con parecer de asesor." 22 April 1773.

5. This contrasts with the apparent practice in mid-eighteenth-century Mexico City, where all indigenous defendants were provided with an interpreter. *Libro de los Principales Rudimentos*, p. 31.

6. For example, BA, r. 24 fr. 527, José María Rojo v. Agustín de los Santos. 27 February–8 March 1794; BA, r. 8 fr. 403, "Legajo y Proceso de Littis Seguydo por Dn fran.co fernz. de Rumayor, recidentte en la Villa del Saltillo, Contra disttinttos Ynquilinos de estta Prov.a de Thexas." 11 April–10 May 1736; SANM II:590, "Año de 1765. Autos Criminales seguidos contra evsebio chabes." 3 June–12 July 1765; SANM II:458a, "Causa Criminal Por Querella de Juana Marttín Contra Joseph de Armijo, en razón de el amanseuam.to Con Gertrudis de Segura, mulatta Soltera." 20 July 1744.

7. *Libro de los Principales Rudimentos*, p. 31; Escriche, *Diccionario*, p. 747; Carrillo, *Prontuario*, voz "tacha."

8. SANM II:401, Antonio Tafoya and Carlos Mirabal v. Juan Lorenzo de Valdés. 18 January–14 May 1735.

9. For example SANM II:317a, "Causa Criminal en sumaria contra el

Capp.n Nicolás Ortiz por ynobediente a la R.l Justizia q.e passó antte mi el Capp.n d.n fran.co Bueno de Bohorques alcalde mayor de esta Villa de S.ta fee de que yze Remizión al S.or Th.e Gral." 13–17 July 1723.

10. For example, SANM II:516, "Año de 1751. Diligencias sobre una dote ofrecida por Nicolás durán y chaues a eduarda yturrieta Mujer Lexítima de Luis Durán y Chaues: hijo de Nicolás." 15 April 1747–15 October 1751. For Pueblos, see SANM II:507a, Felipe Tafoya to Tomás Vélez Cachupín, Santa Fe, 10 [December] 1749. These *procuradores* are not to be confused with *cabildo* representatives of the same name.

11. For Pueblo Indians' use of a legal representative, see Cutter, *Protector de Indios*, pp. 73–79. The office of *protector de indios* appears never to have existed in Texas.

12. For example, BA, r. 20 fr. 733, "Año de 1790. Espediente promovido por D.n Juan José de la Santa, y Don Fran.co Bueno . . . contra Don Juan Mar.n de Amondarayn." 8 October 1790–4 June 1793.

13. For example, BA, r. 15 fr. 42, Antonia Rosalía de Armas v. Pedro Granados. 1 March 1782. Pedro José Tejada drafted a petition "a ruego de" Antonia Rosalía de Armas. SANM II:463, "Orden que se da a Joseph baca Alc.e may.r y cap.n a Guerra de la Villa de Alburquerque, para que notifique a Ysidro Sánchez Vezino de dha Juridición, que pena de cincuenta p.s y quinze dias de cepo por la primera vez, no haga escritos, ni coopere a ellos, y por la segunda se estrañará de este Reyno." Santa Fe, 3 March 1745.

14. By way of contrast, the points which *asesores* raised usually cited royal legislation, in addition to recounting the facts involved in a case. See, for example, BA, r. 11 fr. 117, proceeding against Juan Chirinos, 16 January–22 June 1772. Likewise, those who practiced in the *audiencias* of Mexico City and Guadalajara show themselves to be adept at legal reasoning. These lawyers apparently made extensive use of the "doctors" in supporting their positions. See, for example, BN ms. 12460. Juan Antonio de Torquemada, "Varias Alegaciones Jurídicas." A document that shows the degree of sophistication at which audiencia judges conversed is found in AGI Guadalajara 158, "Fvndamentos legales que guarnecen la determinasion de la R.l Aud.a de Guadalax.a." 8 November 1709.

15. Berní y Catalá, *Práctica Criminal*, pp. 120–21.

16. Carrillo, *Prontuario Alfabético*, voz "careo," notes that some jurists disapproved. Escriche, *Diccionario*, voz "careo," appears to favor the *careo*, but cites a number of jurists who do not—"Hay algunos autores que desaprueban el careo, suponiendo que este medio da la victoria al más sereno, astuto, o descarado sobre el tímido, inexperto, o inadvertido." Evidence of its acceptability in Mexico City is in *Libro de los Principales Rudimentos*, p. 31. The *careo* is still a feature of the judicial process in Spain.

17. SANM II:592, "Año de 1766. Autos Criminales seguidos a petición de Toribio Ortiz contra Mauricio Trugillo, sobre el robo de vnas vacas." 20 July 1765–24 January 1766.

18. See note no. 16 above.

19. For example, SANM II:498, "Causa criminal de querella de Joseph Man.l Truxillo contra Antonio Balberde, y dos hijos suios, todos vecinos de la Juridi-

cion de la Villa de S.ta Cruz de la Cañada, por vnas heridas, que dieron al dho Joseph Man.l Truxillo consta de sanidad, y esta determinada esta causa." 10–30 September 1748. In the *careo* between Juana Trujillo and Juan Domingo Valverde, over whether he had deflowered her, neither party budged from their story.

20. BA, r. 36 fr. 235, Concepción de Estrada v. Félix Menchaca. 12 June 1807–4 April 1810. The reason given in the legal documents for the two parties coming to an out-of-court agreement was "para evitar tales displasencias, y daños, y en amor y en obsequio a la paz, buena armonía y parentesco de afinidad" (fr. 311). BA, r. 16 fr. 467, "Año de 1785. Autos Criminales . . . contra la persona de Pedro José Sambrano." 26 February 1785–27 March 1785. The contending parties ended their dispute out of court "por via de paz y concordia hemos venido en componernos" in order to "evitar la gravación de costas judiciales." For Christian charity, SANM II:458a, "Causa Criminal Por Querella de Juana Marttín Contra Joseph de Armijo, en razón de el amanseuam.to Con Gertrudis de Segura, mulatta Soltera." 20 July 1744.

21. Francisco Tomás [y] Valiente, "El Perdón de la Parte Ofendida en el Derecho Penal Castellano (Siglos XVI, XVII, y XVIII)," *Anuario de Historia del Derecho Español* 31 (1961): 55–114. On *avenencias,* p. 59; on lack of guidelines for the implementation of the pardoning process, p. 88.

22. Tomás y Valiente, "El Perdón," notes that any mention of specific price, or even of having bought the pardon disappear from Castilian judicial documents by the beginning of the eighteenth century, and that by the end of the century, the pardoners expressly deny that they had received anything for the pardon.

23. SANM II:239j, "Auto y caueza de Proseso y Caussa criminal q.e se siguió, contra Alonso Por la muerte que hizo al sarg.to fran.co tamaris." 14 December 1715—31 July 1716. Alonso Rael, Jr., also later received a government pardon, or *indulto,* from Governor Félix Martínez in exchange for serving on a military campaign against the Moqui. Upon returning from the campaign, he was absolved of the murder of Tamaris, 4 November 1716. See SANM II:256a.

24. BA, r. 11 fr. 470, Santiago Villaseñor v. José Antonio Brito and José Hernández Juvera. 28 October–1 December 1774.

25. On proper form, contemporary texts are instructive. See Berní y Catalá, *Práctica Criminal,* pp. 118–23; *Nueva Recopilación de Castilla,* libro 4; Alvarez, *Instituciones de Derecho Real,* t. 2, pp. 238–43.

26. Alonso Romero, *Proceso Penal,* p. 260. On the problems that this prohibition poses, see Tomás y Valiente, *Derecho Penal,* p. 182.

27. BN ms. 12460.

28. Quote from Taylor, *Drinking, Homicide, and Rebellion,* p. 76. In a similar vein, Gutiérrez, *When Jesus Came,* pp. 224–25.

29. On the prohibitions regarding the *sentencia fundada,* see Tomás y Valiente, *Derecho Penal,* pp. 181–82.

30. For example, ARAG Criminal 34–7-761. "San Antonio de Béxar. Año de 1801. Prov.a de Coahuila. Causa contra Rafael Gutiérrez, alias quemaculos, por Lad.on, muerte y otros excesos." 26 September 1801–10 October 1810.

31. Aharon Barak, *Judicial Discretion* (New Haven and London: Yale University Press, 1989), p. 7.

32. *Recopilación de Indias,* 5.2.11. Gerónimo de Cevallos, *Arte Real para el Buen Govierno de los Reyes y Príncipes y sus Vasallos* (Toledo: D. Rodríguez, 1623), pp. 71v.–72.

33. BA, r. 10 fr. 570, Proceedings against Vicente Amador, 30 May–16 August 1768. Amador may be the same person who served as *alcalde ordinario* of San Antonio in the 1790s.

34. SANM II:418, "Autos criminales fechos contra Fran.co Padilla por Querella de Juan Antonio sobre Vnas heridas y otros daños." 12 June–12 July 1737. Although an Indian, Juan Antonio referred to himself as a *"vecino"* of San Clemente, thus revealing something of the social fluidity in colonial New Mexico.

35. Tomás y Valiente, *Derecho Penal,* 353–54.

36. Escriche, *Diccionario,* voz "pena," p. 1400; *Partidas,* 7.31.

37. Cevallos, *Arte Real para el Buen Gobierno,* p. 60.

38. BA, r. 14 fr. 921, Proceedings against Juan José Vergara. 4 February–30 June 1782. See also SANM II:13, "Autos criminales contra Ju.o caititi yndio." 22 June 1682.

39. SANM II:467, "Causa criminal de officio de la R.l Justicia contra Manuel Baca Vecino del Puesto de Paxarito Juridición de la Villa de S.n Phelipe de Alburquerque, sobre inobediencia a lo mandado por este superior Govierno, y lo demás que consta en dha causa." 5–18 October 1745.

40. BA, r. 22 fr. 37, Proceedings against Francisco Hernández. 25 January–1 February 1792.

41. Michael Weisser, *Crime and Punishment in Early Modern Europe* (Atlantic Highlands, New Jersey: Humanities Press, 1979), pp. 67, 66.

42. On ridicule as a form of punishment in pre-modern Europe, see Weisser, *Crime and Punishment,* pp. 64–65. The concept of honor in colonial New Mexico is a dominant theme in Ramón Gutiérrez's, *When Jesus Came.* See also, by the same author, "Honor Ideology, Marriage Negotiations, and Class-Gender Domination in New Mexico, 1690–1846," *Latin American Perspectives* 12 (Winter 1985): 81–104. In *Tragic Cavalier,* Félix Almaráz touches lightly upon the idea of honor, which he feels was crucial in the makeup and actions of Texas Governor Manuel Salcedo. For a discussion of the notions of honor in colonial Mexico City, see Patricia Seed, *To Love, Honor, and Obey in Colonial Mexico: Conflicts Over Marriage Choice, 1574–1821* (Stanford: Stanford University Press, 1988), pp. 61–74, 136–57.

43. SANM II:590, "Año de 1765. Autos seguidos contra evsebio chabes." 3 June–12 July 1765. Case described also in Gutiérrez, *When Jesus Came,* pp. 205–6.

44. See discussion of this case in Chapter 2.

45. SANM II:458a, "Causa Criminal Por Querella de Juana Marttín Contra Joseph de Armijo, en razon de el amanseuam.to Con Gertrudis de Segura, mulatta Soltera." 20 July 1744. Juana later dropped her *querella,* saying that "fue violentada, del selo de muguer, no advirttiendo, por entonses con alguna, en los graues daños que de ella se podian seguir . . . y auiendo

considerado que soy chrisptiana, y que el dho mi esposo, no me ha faltado ni me faltta en todo aquello, que le es de obligasion en la manutension y bistuario, y todo quanto alcansa con su trauajo, todo lo gasto. Yo en casa." This and other incidents of women's involvement with the legal system in New Mexico also cited in Rosalind Z. Rock, "'*Pido y Suplico*': Women and the Law in Spanish New Mexico, 1697–1763," *New Mexico Historical Review* 65 (April 1990): 145–59.

46. SANM II:360, "Caussa Criminal Contra Ant.o Yuba, yndio natural del Pu.o de tezuque : y Asensio Povia Yndio natural del Pueblo de Nambe de la naz.n teguas = Sobre hauer cometido el pecado nefando segun la denunziaz.n y declaraz.n de Man.l Truxillo Vezino de la Villa de Santa fee." 25 June–2 August 1731. Cruzat y Góngora ordered Povia down river to San Felipe Pueblo, while Yuba went to the distant western pueblo of Zuni.

47. BA, r. 14 fr. 901, Pedro José Tejada v. Juana Francisca Pérez. 4 January 1782; SANM II:172, "Año de 1712. Causa Criminal contra Diego Velasco." 28 March 1712–24 April 1713.

48. SANM II:498, "Causa criminal de querella de Joseph Man.l truxillo Contra Antonio Balberde, y los hijos suios." 10–30 September 1748.

49. SANM II:105, Tomás Méndez v. Cristóbal Maese. 28 December 1704–15 January 1705.

50. AGI Guadalajara 354, Conde de Revillagigedo to Antonio Valdés. México, 27 March 1790.

51. AGI Guadalajara 354, Conde de Revillagigedo to Antonio Valdés. México, 27 March 1790. Ruth Pike, "Penal Servitude in the Spanish Empire: Presidio Labor in the Eighteenth Century," *Hispanic American Historical Review* 58 (February 1978): 21–40.

52. On the role of the presidio in the far north of New Spain, see Max L. Moorhead, *The Presidio, Bastion of the Spanish Borderlands* (Norman: University of Oklahoma Press, 1975). For a discussion of the evolution of the northern presidio, consult Thomas H. Naylor and Charles W. Polzer, *The Presidio and Militia on the Northern Frontier of New Spain, 1570–1700* (Tucson: University of Arizona Press, 1986), pp. 15–29.

53. BA, r. 11 fr. 665; 793, Proceedings against Francisco, Henrique, Silvestre, and Pedro. 18 December 1775–15 January 1776; 30 November 1776.

54. ARAG Criminal 34–7-761, "San Antonio de Béxar. Año de 1801 . . . Causa contra Rafael Gutiérrez, alias quemaculos." 26 September 1801–10 October 1810.

55. AGI Guadalajara 334, Parecer of Fiscal. Madrid, 8 April 1767. A precedent existed under the *Reglamento* of 1729 (nn. 40, 100), which applied to military jurisdiction and required that criminal cases that merited capital punishment be forwarded for review to the viceroy (as *capitán general*).

56. For example, SANM II:187, Criminal proceedings against Miguel Luján. 20 April 1713–22 October 1714.

57. Taylor, *Drinking, Homicide, and Rebellion*, p. 98, notes this phenomenon in central and southern New Spain. Michael R. Weisser, *The Peasants of the Montes: The Roots of Rural Rebellion in Spain* (Chicago and London: The University of Chicago Press, 1976), p. 78, states that "of more than fourteen hundred sen-

tences pronounced [from 1600–90] in the courtroom of Toledo covering every conceivable social crime, no Montes peasant was ever condemned to the galleys or subjected to any other form of corporal punishment, even in cases of murder and rape."

58. AGI Guadalajara 365, "Lista de negocios despachados, 1798." Guadalajara, 31 December 1798.

59. Levaggi, *Manual de Historia del Derecho Argentino*, t. 2, p. 7. For a discussion of the idea of legal inequality in Spain, see de las Heras Santos, *Justicia Penal de los Austrias*, pp. 19–27.

60. Cited in Gutiérrez, *When Jesus Came*, p. 191; also in Bustamante, "'The Matter Was Never Resolved'," p. 159.

61. SANM II:441, Proceedings against Antonio Jiménez, Felipe Trujillo, and Luis Quintana. 8 July 1741–31 July 1742.

62. SANM II:517, "Criminales contra Cayetano Pasote, calidad lobo, sobre unas heridas y lo demas que dentro se expresa." 12 January 1751–23 November 1752.

63. Both quotes in Levaggi, *Manual de Historia del Derecho Argentino*, t. 2, pp. 105, 279.

64. SANM II:447, Proceedings against Juan Miguel Alvarez del Castillo, Baltasar Baca, and Gregorio de Benavides. 11–24 September 1743.

65. AGI Guadalajara 277, Caballero de Croix to José de Gálvez. Arizpe, 23 October 1781.

66. For example, BA, r. 38 fr. 303, Proceedings against Martín de Jesús. 23 June–24 October 1808. For other parts of New Spain, see AGI Guadalajara 318, "Lista de la qual se manifiesta el estado de los negocios civiles pendientes, y conclusos en esta Aud.a Pub.a. Año de 1813." Of the 93 cases listed under the heading "Causas Conclusas," 24 received indultos. Some of these had been convicted for serious crimes such as murder.

67. BA, r. 38 fr. 196, Proceedings against José Guadalupe Urrutia. 4 June–22 October 1808. It should be pointed out that in some instances communication between the commandant and the provincial governors was remarkably quick. In this case, Urrutia was declared free on 22 October by virtue of a *bando* from Commandant General Salcedo, dated 4 October 1808, a span of only eighteen days.

68. SANM II:256a, Bando of Félix Martínez. Santa Fe, 1 August 1716. On the practice of taking refuge in New Mexico, see Elizabeth Howard West, "The Right of Asylum in New Mexico in the Seventeenth and Eighteenth Centuries," *New Mexico Historical Review* 41 (April 1966): 115–53. In the late eighteenth century, the Bourbon monarchs greatly curtailed the traditional right of asylum. See Farriss, *Crown and Clergy in Colonial Mexico*, and García y García, *El Derecho de Asilo*.

69. Alonso Romero, *Proceso Penal*, p. 287.

70. This became institutionalized with the Cortes de Cádiz, art. 13, cap. 2, decreto of 9 October 1812, cited in Alvarez, *Instituciones de Derecho Real*, t. 4, pp. 224–25.

71. SANM II:655, Fr. Juan Joseph de Ynojosa v. Pedro Pino. Santa Fe, 14–29 September 1770.

72. Michael C. Meyer, *Water in the Hispanic Southwest: A Social and Legal History, 1550–1850* (Tucson: University of Arizona Press, 1984), pp. 163–64, 166. Studies for other parts of New Spain that also demonstrate the flexibility of Spanish colonial water law include Michael E. Murphy, *Irrigation in the Bajío Region of Colonial Mexico* (Boulder and London: Westview Press, 1986), especially pp. 177–97, and Guillermo F. Margadant S., "El Agua a la Luz del Derecho Novohispano. Triunfo de Realismo y Flexibilidad," *Anuario Mexicano de Historia del Derecho* 1 (1989): 113–46.

73. Daniel Tyler, *The Mythical Pueblo Rights Doctrine: Water Administration in Hispanic New Mexico* (El Paso: Texas Western Press, 1990), p. 45, quote on p. 29.

74. SANM II:372, Cristóbal García v. José Montaño. 19 August–12 November 1732.

75. SANM II:379, "Litis que tubieron D.n Ysavel Jorge, Phe Galego y Antt.o Gurulé contra Xptoval García vesinos de la Villa de Alburquerque." 7 January–9 February 1733.

76. Jesús F. de la Teja, "Forgotten Founders: The Military Settlers of Eighteenth-Century San Antonio de Béxar," in Poyo and Hinojosa, eds., *Tejano Origins in Eighteenth-Century San Antonio*, pp. 36–37; Poyo, "Canary Island Immigrants," pp. 43–45, 50–52.

77. SANM II:795, Caballero de Croix to Governor of New Mexico. Arizpe, 21 June 1780.

78. SANM II:837, Caballero de Croix to Juan Bautista de Anza. Arizpe, 21 February 1782.

79. For example, BA, r. 16 fr. 467, "Año de 1785. Autos formados . . . contra la persona de Pedro José Sambrano." 26 February–27 March 1785.

80. See discussion of "el Cuajo" in Chapter 5.

81. Berní y Catalá, *Práctica Criminal*, pp. 128–36; Alvarez, *Instituciones*, t. 2, pp. 244–46.

82. On this propensity to pick and choose the elements most suited to a particular case, see Cutter, *Protector de Indios*, pp. 61–80.

83. On Taos, see Jenkins, "Taos Pueblo and Its Neighbors," pp. 93–95. SANM I:1357, Felipe Sandoval to Governor. Santa Fe, 15 April 1815. Cutter, *Protector de Indios*, pp. 85–86.

84. ARAG Judicial-civil 261-15-3564, "El Común del Pueblo de Cochití diciendo de nulidad a la venta de un Rancho cituado en su fundo legal y reclamando la usurpación de otro." 26 September 1816. On the Juzgado General de Indios see Borah, *General Indian Court*. Incident described in Cutter, *Protector de Indios*, pp. 1–2, 88–93.

Epilogue

1. Faulk, *Last Years of Spanish Texas*, p. 108; Stein and Stein, *Colonial Heritage of Latin America*, p. 81; Gibson, *Spain in America*, p. 109.

Sources

Archival Collections

Archivo General de Indias, Sevilla
Archivo General de la Nación, México
Archivo Histórico Nacional, Madrid
Archivo de Instrumentos Públicos, Guadalajara, Jalisco
Bexar County Archives, San Antonio
   Mission Records
Biblioteca del Estado de Jalisco, México
   Archivo de la Real Audiencia de Guadalajara
   Manuscritos
Biblioteca Nacional, Madrid
Biblioteca Nacional, México
Huntington Library, San Marino, California
   Rare Books
Indiana University, Bloomington
   Lilly Library
Museum of New Mexico, Santa Fe
New Mexico State Archives and Records Center, Santa Fe
   Mexican Archives of New Mexico
   Spanish Archives of New Mexico
   Records of the U.S. Surveyor General
Real Academia de la Historia, Madrid
University of New Mexico General Library, Albuquerque
   Special Collections
University of Texas General Library, Austin
   Barker Texas History Center, Bexar Archives
   Benson Latin American Collection, Mexican Manuscripts

Printed Documents and Contemporary Works

Abel, Annie Heloise. *The Official Correspondence of James S. Calhoun.* Washington, D.C.: Government Printing Office, 1915.

Alessio Robles, Vito, ed. *Diario y Derrotero de lo Caminado, Visto y Observado en la Visita que Hizo a los Presidios de la Nueva España Septentrional el Brigadier Pedro de Rivera*. México: Archivo Histórico Militar Mexicano, 1946.

Alvarez, José María. *Instituciones de Derecho Real de Castilla y de Indias*. New York: Casa de Lanuza, Mendia, and Co., 1827; facsimile reprint, México: Universidad Nacional Autónoma de México, 1982.

Berní y Catalá, José. *El Abogado Instruido en la Práctica Civil de España*. Valencia: Cosme Grancha, 1738.

_____. *Instrucción de Alcaldes Ordinarios, que Comprehende las Obligaciones de Estos, y del Amotacén*. Valencia: Imprenta de Agustín Laborda, 1757.

_____. *Práctica Criminal*. Valencia: Simón Faure, 1749.

Carrillo y Sánchez, Pedro. *Prontuario Alfabético de Legislación y Práctica*. Madrid: Boix Editor, 1840.

Castillo y Bobadilla, Jerónimo. *Política Para Corregidores y Señores Vasallos, en Tiempos de Paz, y de Guerra*. Medina del Campo: Cristóbal Lasso y Francisco García, 1608.

Cevallos, Gerónimo de. *Arte Real para el Buen Govierno de los Reyes y Príncipes y sus Vasallos*. Toledo: D. Rodríguez, 1623.

Colección de los Decretos y Ordenes que Han Expedido las Cortes Generales y Extraordinarias. 2 vols. Cádiz: En la Imprenta Nacional, 1813; facsimile reprint, Madrid: Cortes Generales, 1987.

Colón de Larriátegui, Félix. *Juzgados Militares de España y sus Indias*. Madrid: Repulles, 1797.

Constituciones Synodales . . . de Coria. Salamanca: n.p., 1606.

Cornejo, Andrés. *Diccionario Histórico, y Forense del Derecho Real de España*. Madrid: Joaquín Ibarra, 1779.

Cutter, Charles R., transcripción y estudio preliminar. *Libro de los Principales Rudimentos Tocante a Todos Juicios, Criminal, Civil y Executivo. Año de 1764*. México: Universidad Nacional Autónoma de México, 1994.

Domínguez, Fray Francisco Atanacio. *The Missions of New Mexico in 1776*. Edited by Eleanor B. Adams and Fray Angelico Chavez. Albuquerque: University of New Mexico Press, 1956.

Escriche, Joaquín. *Diccionario Razonado de Legislación y Jurisprudencia*. Paris: Librería de Garnier Hermanos, 1869.

Guardiola y Sáez, Lorenzo. *El Corregidor Perfecto y Juez Exactamente Dotado de las Calidades Necesarias y Convenientes para el Buen Gobierno Económico y Político de los Pueblos*. Madrid: Alfonso López, 1785.

Gutiérrez, José Marcos. *Práctica Criminal de España*. 3 vols. Madrid: Fermín Villalpando, 1824.

Hevia Bolaños, Juan de. *Curia Philipica*. Madrid: Herederos de la Viuda de Juan García Infanzón, 1761.

Humboldt, Alejandro de. *Ensayo Político Sobre el Reino de la Nueva España*. México: Editorial Porrúa, S.A., 1973.

Idea General Sobre la Conducta Política de D. Miguel Ramos de Arizpe, Natural de la Provincia de Coahuila, Como Diputado que Ha Sido por esta Provincia en la Cortes Generales y Extraordinarias, y en las Ordinarias de la Monarquía

Española Desde el Año de 1810 Hasta el de 1812. México: Doña Herculana del Villar y Socios, 1822.

Instrucción Para Formar una Línea o Cordón de Quince Presidios Sobre las Fronteras de las Provincias Internas de este Reino de Nueva España, y Nuevo Reglamento. México: Imprenta del Br. D. José Antonio de Hogal, 1771.

Jovellanos, Gaspar Melchor de. *Obras.* Vol. 46 of *Biblioteca de Autores Españoles.* Madrid: Ediciones Atlas, 1951.

Juan y Colom, Joseph. *Instrucción de Escribanos en Orden a lo Judicial.* 2 vols. Madrid: Antonio Fernández, 1787.

Juan y Santacilia, Jorge and Antonio de Ulloa. *Discourse and Political Reflections on the Kingdom of Peru.* Edited and introduction by John J. TePaske. Translated by John J. TePaske and Bessie A. Clement. Norman: University of Oklahoma Press, 1978.

Kessell, John L., Rick Hendricks, Meredith D. Dodge, Larry D. Miller, and Eleanor B. Adams, eds., *Remote Beyond Compare: Letters of don Diego de Vargas to His Family from New Spain and New Mexico, 1675–1706.* Albuquerque: University of New Mexico Press, 1989.

Kinnaird, Lawrence, ed. *The Frontiers of New Spain: Nicolás Lafora's Description, 1766–1768.* Berkeley: Quivira Society, 1958.

Martínez Marina, Francisco. *Juicio Crítico de la Novísima Recopilación.* Madrid: 1820.

Morfi, Fray Juan Agustín de. *Diario y Derrotero (1777–1781).* Monterrey: Publicaciones del Instituto Tecnológico y de Estudios Superiores de Monterrey, 1967.

_____. *History of Texas, 1673–1779.* 2 vols. Edited and translated by Carlos Eduardo Castañeda. Albuquerque: The Quivira Society, 1935.

Novísima Recopilación de las Leyes de España. Madrid: 1805; facsimile reprint, Madrid: Boletín Oficial del Estado, 1976.

Paula Miguel Sánchez, Francisco de. *Dirección Teórico-Práctica de Alcaldes Constitucionales.* Reprint, Madrid: Instituto de Estudios de Administración Local, 1979.

Pérez y López, Antonio Javier. *Teatro de la Legislación Universal de España e Indias.* 28 vols. Madrid: Manuel González, 1791–98.

Pike, Z[ebulon] M[ontgomery]. *An Account of Expeditions to the Sources of the Mississippi, and the Western Parts of Louisiana, . . . And a Tour Through the Interior Parts of New Spain.* Philadelphia: C. & A. Conrad, 1810; facsimile reprint, n.p.: Readex Microprint, 1966.

Pino, Pedro Bautista. *Exposición Sucinta y Sencilla de la Provincia del Nuevo México.* Cádiz: Imprenta del Estado Mayor General, 1812.

Ramos Arizpe, Miguel. *Memoria Sobre el Estado de la Provincias Internas de Oriente Presentada a las Cortes de Cádiz.* Edited by Vito Alessio Robles. México: Bibliófilos Mexicanos, 1932.

_____. *Report That Dr. Miguel Ramos de Arizpe, Priest of Borbon and Deputy in the Present General and Special Cortes of Spain for the Province of Coahuila, One of the Four Eastern Interior Provinces in the Kingdom of Mexico, Presents to the August Congress on the Natural, Political, and Civil Conditions of the Provinces of Coahuila, Nuevo Leon, Nuevo Santander, and*

Texas of the Four Eastern Interior Provinces of the Kingdom of Mexico. Translated and introduction by Nettie Lee Benson. Austin: University of Texas Press, 1950.

Real Reglamento Para las Milicias Provinciales de Nueva Vizcaya. Madrid: Pedro Marín, 1782.

Recopilación de Leyes de los Reynos de las Indias. 4 vols. Madrid: Julián de Paredes, 1681; facsimile reprint, Madrid: Ediciones Cultura Hispánica, 1973.

Reglamento Para Todos los Presidios de las Provincias Internas de Esta Gobernación . . . Hecho por el Exc.mo Señor Marqués de Casa-Fuerte. México: Herederos de la Viuda de Miguel de Rivera Calderón, 1729.

Riezgo, Juan Miguel. *Memoria Sobre las Proporciones Naturales de las Provincias Internas Occidentales: Causas de que Han Provenido sus Atrasos, Providencias Tomadas con el Fin de Lograr su Remedio, y las que por Ahora se Consideran Oportunas para Mejorar su Estado, e ir Proporcionando su Futura Felicidad.* México: Imprenta de D. José Ramos Palomera, 1822.

Rodríguez de León Pinelo, Antonio. *Tratado de Confirmaciones Reales.* Madrid: Juan González, 1630; facsimile reprint, Caracas: Biblioteca de la Academia Nacional de la Historia, 1979.

Rodríguez de San Miguel, Juan N. *Pandectas Hispano-Megicanas.* 2 vols. Méjico: Librería de J. F. Rosa, 1852; facsimile reprint, México: Universidad Nacional Autónoma de México, 1991.

Sala, Juan. *Ilustración del Derecho Real de España.* 2 vols. Valencia: Joseph de Orga, 1803.

Las Siete Partidas del Sabio Rey don Alonso el Nono. 3 vols. Salamanca: Andrea de Portonaris, 1555; facsimile reprint, Madrid: Boletín Oficial del Estado, 1974.

Solórzano Pereira, Juan de. *Política Indiana.* Madrid: 1647; reprint, Madrid and Buenos Aires: Compañía Ibero-Americana de Publicaciones, S.A., 1930.

Thomas, Alfred Barnaby. *Forgotten Frontiers: A Study of the Spanish Indian Policy of Don Juan Bautista de Anza, Governor of New Mexico, 1777–1787.* Norman: University of Oklahoma Press, 1932.

_____. *Teodoro de Croix and the Northern Frontier of New Spain, 1776–1783.* Norman: University of Oklahoma Press, 1941.

Ventura Beleña, Eusebio. *Recopilación Sumaria de Todos los Autos Acordados de la Real Audiencia y Sala del Crímen de esta Nueva España.* México: Don Felipe de Zúñiga y Ontiveros, 1787; facsimile reprint, México: Universidad Nacional Autónoma de México, 1991.

Villadiego de Vascuñana y Montoya, Alonso de. *Instrucción Política y Práctica Judicial.* Madrid: Antonio Marín, 1766.

Vizcaíno Pérez, Vicente. *Tratado de la Jurisdicción Ordinaria Para Dirección y Guía de los Alcaldes de los Pueblos de España.* Madrid: Viuda de Ibarra, 1796.

Books and Articles

Adams, Eleanor B. and France V. Scholes. "Books in New Mexico, 1598–1680," *New Mexico Historical Review* 17 (July 1942): 226–70.

_____. "Two Colonial New Mexico Libraries, 1704, 1706," *New Mexico Historical Review* 19 (April 1944): 135–67.

Adamson, Walter L. *Hegemony and Revolution: A Study of Antonio Gramsci's Political and Cultural Theory.* Berkeley: University of California Press, 1980.

Ahlborn, Richard Eighme. "The Will of a New Mexican Woman in 1762," *New Mexico Historical Review* 65 (July 1990): 319–55.

Alemparte R., Julio. *El Cabildo en Chile Colonial (Orígenes Municipales de las Repúblicas Hispanoamericanas).* Santiago: Ediciones de la Universidad de Chile, 1940.

Almaráz, Félix D., Jr. *Tragic Cavalier: Governor Manuel Salcedo of Texas, 1808–1813.* Austin: University of Texas Press, 1971.

Alonso Martín, María Luz. "Un Jurista Indiano: Juan Antonio Torquemada," in *Justicia, Sociedad y Economía en la América Española (Siglos XVI, XVII, y XVIII).* Valladolid: Casa-Museo de Colón and Seminario Americanista de la Universidad de Valladolid, 1983.

Alonso Romero, María Paz. *El Proceso Penal en Castilla (Siglos XIII–XVIII).* Salamanca: Ediciones Universidad de Salamanca, 1982.

Altman, Ida and James Lockhart, eds. *The Provinces of Early Mexico: Variants of Spanish-American Regional Evolution.* Los Angeles: University of California Press, 1973.

Anes, Gonzalo. *El Antiguo Régimen: Los Borbones.* Madrid: Alianza Editorial, 1975.

Aragón, Janie Louise. "The People of Santa Fé in the 1790s," *Aztlán* 7 (Fall 1976): 391–417.

Archer, Christon I. *The Army in Bourbon Mexico, 1760–1810.* Albuquerque: University of New Mexico Press, 1977.

Arnold, Morris S. *Unequal Laws Unto a Savage Race: European Legal Traditions in Arkansas, 1686–1836.* Fayetteville: University of Arkansas Press, 1985.

Austin, Mattie Alice. "The Municipal Government of San Fernando de Béxar, 1730–1800," *Southwestern Historical Quarterly* 8 (April 1905): 277–352.

Baade, Hans W. "Número de Abogados y Escribanos en la Nueva España, La Provincia de Téxas y La Luisiana," in José Luis Soberanes Fernández, ed., *Memoria del III Congreso de Historia del Derecho Mexicano (1983).* México: Universidad Nacional Autónoma de México, 1984.

Bakewell, Peter J. *Silver Mining and Society in Colonial Mexico: Zacatecas, 1546–1700.* Cambridge: Cambridge University Press, 1971.

Bancroft, Hubert H. *History of Arizona and New Mexico, 1530–1888.* San Francisco: The History Company, 1889.

Barak, Aharon. *Judicial Discretion.* New Haven and London: Yale University Press.

Barnes, Thomas C., Thomas H. Naylor, and Charles W. Polzer. *Northern New Spain: A Research Guide.* Tucson: University of Arizona Press, 1981.

Barragán Barragán, José. *Temas del Liberalismo Gaditano.* México: Universidad Nacional Autónoma de México, 1978.

Barrero García, Ana María. "La Literatura Jurídica del Barroco Europeo a Través de la Obra de Solórzano Pereira," *Revista Chilena de Historia del Derecho* 15 (1989): 65–85.

Baxter, John O. *Las Carneradas: Sheep Trade in New Mexico, 1700–1860.* Albuquerque: University of New Mexico Press, 1987.

Bayle, Constantino. *Los Cabildos Seculares en la América Española.* Madrid: Sapienta, S.A. de Ediciones, 1952.

Beers, Henry Putney. *Spanish and Mexican Records of the Southwest.* Tucson: University of Arizona Press, 1979.

Benavides, Adán, Jr. "Loss By Division: The Commandancy General Archive of the Eastern Interior Provinces," *The Americas* 43 (October 1986): 203–19.

Beneyto Pérez, Juan. *Historia de la Administración Española e Hispanoamericana.* Madrid: Aguilar, 1958.

Berry, Charles R. "The Election of the Mexican Deputies to the Spanish Cortes, 1810–1822," in Nettie Lee Benson, ed., *Mexico and the Spanish Cortes, 1810–1822: Eight Essays.* Austin: University of Texas Press, 1966.

Bloom, Lansing B., transcriber. "Ynstrucción a Peralta Por Vi-Rey," *New Mexico Historical Review* 4 (April 1929): 178–87.

Bolton, Herbert E. *Coronado, Knight of Pueblos and Plains.* Albuquerque: University of New Mexico Press, 1949.

———. "The Mission as a Frontier Institution in the Spanish American Colonies," in John Francis Bannon, ed., *Bolton and the Spanish Borderlands.* Norman: University of Oklahoma Press, 1964.

———. *Texas in the Middle Eighteenth Century: Studies in Spanish Colonial History and Administration.* Austin and London: University of Texas Press, 1970.

Borah, Woodrow, coordinator. *El Gobierno Provincial en la Nueva España, 1570–1787.* México: Universidad Nacional Autónoma de México, 1985.

———. *Justice by Insurance: The General Indian Court of Colonial Mexico and the Legal Aides of the Half-Real.* Berkeley: University of California Press, 1983.

Brading, D.A. "Government and Elite in Late Colonial Mexico," *Hispanic American Historical Review* 53 (August 1973): 389–414.

Bravo Lira, Bernardino. "El Derecho Indiano y sus Raices Europeas: Derecho Común y Propio de Castilla," *Anuario de Historia del Derecho Español* 58 (1988): 5–80.

Burkholder, Mark A. "The Council of the Indies in the Late Eighteenth Century: A New Perspective," *Hispanic American Historical Review* 56 (1976): 404–23.

Bustamante, Adrian. "'The Matter Was Never Resolved': The *Casta* System in Colonial New Mexico, 1693–1823," *New Mexico Historical Review* 66 (April 1991): 143–63.

Campbell, T.N. "Coahuiltecans and Their Neighbors," *Handbook of North American Indians.* Vol. 10, *The Southwest.* Washington, D.C.: The Smithsonian Institution, 1979.

Carroll, H. Bailey and J. Villasana Haggard, eds., *Three New Mexico Chronicles.* Albuquerque: The Quivira Society, 1942.

Casado Fuente, Ovidio. *Don Francisco Cuerbo y Valdés, Gobernador de Nuevo*

México, Fundador de la Ciudad de Alburquerque. Oviedo: Instituto de Estudios Asturianos, 1983.

Castañeda, Carlos E. *Our Catholic Heritage in Texas.* 7 vols. Austin: Von Boeckmann-Jones Company, 1936–58.

Céspedes del Castillo, Guillermo. "La Visita como Institución Indiana," *Anuario de Estudios Americanos* 3 (1946): 984–1025.

Chance, John K. *Race and Class in Colonial Oaxaca.* Stanford: Stanford University Press, 1978.

Chapman, Charles Edward. *The Founding of Spanish California: The Northwestward Expansion of New Spain, 1687–1783.* New York: 1916; reprint, New York: Octagon Books, 1973.

Chavez, Fray Angelico. *Archives of the Archdiocese of Santa Fe, 1678–1900.* Washington, D.C.: Academy of Franciscan History, 1957.

———. "Genízaros," in Alfonso Ortiz, ed., *Handbook of North American Indians.* Vol. 9, *The Southwest.* Washington, D.C.: Smithsonian Institution, 1979.

———. *Origins of New Mexico Families.* Santa Fe: The Historical Society of New Mexico, 1954.

Chevalier, François. *Land and Society in Colonial Mexico: The Great Hacienda.* Translated by Alvin Eustis. Edited by Lesley Byrd Simpson. Berkeley and Los Angeles: University of California Press, 1963.

Chipman, Donald E. *Spanish Texas, 1519–1821.* Austin: University of Texas Press, 1992.

Cruz, Gilbert R. *Let There Be Towns: Spanish Municipal Origins in the American Southwest, 1610–1810.* College Station: Texas A&M Press, 1988.

Cuello, José. "Beyond the 'Borderlands' is the North of Colonial Mexico: A Latin-Americanist Perspective to the Study of the Mexican North and the United States Southwest," in Kristyna P. Demaree, ed., *Proceedings of the Pacific Coast Council on Latin American Studies* 9 (1982): 1–24.

Cutter, Charles R. "Indigenous Communities and Spanish Colonial Law," *Indiana Academy of the Social Sciences: Proceedings, 1992,* 3rd series, 27 (1992): 1–9.

———. "El Indio Fronterizo ante la Justicia Española: La Creación de una Hegemonía Consensual," in *IX Congreso del Instituto Internacional de Historia del Derecho Indiano: Actas y Estudios.* Madrid: Universidad Complutense, 1991.

———. "La Magistratura Local en el Norte de la Nueva España: El Caso de Nuevo México," *Anuario Mexicano de Historia del Derecho* 4 (1992): 29–39.

———. *The Protector de Indios in Colonial New Mexico, 1659–1821.* Albuquerque: University of New Mexico Press, 1986.

———. "La Real Audiencia del Norte de la Nueva España: Historia de un Proyecto Frustrado," in *Memoria del X Congreso del Instituto Internacional de Historia del Derecho Indiano.* México: Universidad Nacional Autónoma de México, 1995.

Davis, W. W. H. *El Gringo: New Mexico and Her People.* New York: Harper, 1857; reprint, Lincoln: University of Nebraska Press, 1982.

de la Hera, Alberto. "La Legislación del Siglo XVIII sobre el Patronato Indiano," *Anuario de Historia del Derecho Español* 40 (1970): 287–311.
de la Teja, Jesús F. "Forgotten Founders: The Military Settlers of Eighteenth-Century San Antonio de Béxar," in Gerald E. Poyo and Gilberto Hinojosa, eds., *Tejano Origins in Eighteenth-Century San Antonio*. Austin: University of Texas Press, 1991.
de las Heras Santos, José Luis. *La Justicia Penal de los Austrias en la Corona de Castilla*. Salamanca: Universidad de Salamanca, 1991.
Díaz Rementería, Carlos J. "La Costumbre Indígena en el Perú Hispánico," *Anuario de Estudios Americanos* 33 (1976): 189–215.
Dobkin, Betty Eakle. *The Spanish Element in Texas Water Law*. Austin: University of Texas Press, 1959.
Domínguez Compañy, Francisco. "La Condición del Vecino," in *Estudios Sobre las Instituciones Locales Hispanoamericanas*. Caracas: Biblioteca de la Academia Nacional de la Historia, 1981.
Domínguez Ortiz, Antonio. *El Antiguo Régimen: Los Reyes Católicos y los Austria*. Madrid: Alianza Editorial, 1983.
_____. *Carlos III y la España de la Ilustración*. Madrid: Alianza Editorial, 1981.
Ebright, Malcolm. "New Mexican Land Grants: The Legal Background," in Charles L. Briggs and John R. Van Ness, eds., *Land, Water, and Culture: New Perspectives on Hispanic Land Grants*. Albuquerque: University of New Mexico Press, 1987.
_____. *Spanish and Mexican Land Grants and the Law*. Manhattan, Kansas: Sunflower University Press, 1989.
Egido, Teófanes. "El Regalismo y las Relaciones Iglesia-Estado en el Siglo XVIII," in *Historia de la Iglesia en España*. Madrid: Editorial Católica, 1979.
Elliot, J. H. *The Count-Duke of Olivares*. New Haven: Yale University Press, 1988.
_____. *Imperial Spain, 1469–1716*. New York: The New American Library, Inc., 1966.
_____. *Spain and its World, 1500–1700: Selected Essays*. New Haven: Yale University Press, 1989.
Epstein, Steven. *Wills and Wealth in Medieval Genoa, 1150–1250*. Cambridge, Massachusetts: Harvard University Press, 1984.
Espinosa, J. Manuel. *Crusaders of the Rio Grande: The Story of Don Diego de Vargas and the Reconquest and Refounding of New Mexico*. Chicago: Institute of Jesuit History, 1942.
Farriss, N[ancy] M. *Crown and Clergy in Colonial Mexico, 1759–1821: The Crisis of Ecclesiastical Privilege*. London: The Athlone Press, 1968.
_____. *Maya Society Under Colonial Rule: The Collective Enterprise of Survival*. Princeton: Princeton University Press, 1984.
Faulk, Odie B. *The Last Years of Spanish Texas, 1778–1821*. The Hague: Mouton and Co., 1964.
Fisher, John R. *Government and Society in Colonial Peru: The Intendant System, 1783–1814*. London: Athlone, 1970.
Fisher, Lillian Estelle. *The Intendant System in Spanish America*. Berkeley: University of California Press, 1929.

Gallegos, Bernardo P. *Literacy, Education, and Society in New Mexico, 1693–1821.* Albuquerque: University of New Mexico Press, 1992.

García-Gallo, Alfonso. *Estudios de Historia del Derecho Indiano.* Madrid: Instituto Nacional de Estudios Jurídicos, 1972.

———. *Manual de Historia del Derecho Español.* 2 vols. Madrid: Alfonso García-Gallo, 1984. 10th edition.

———. *Metodología de la Historia del Derecho Indiano.* Santiago de Chile: Editorial Jurídica de Chile, 1971.

García y García, Tomás de Aquino. *El Derecho de Asilo en Indias.* Madrid: Editorial Reus, 1930.

Gibson, Charles. *Spain in America.* New York: Harper, 1966.

Góngora, Mario. *Studies in the Colonial History of Spanish America.* Cambridge: Cambridge University Press, 1975.

González, María del Refugio and Teresa Lozano. "La Administración de Justicia," in Woodrow Borah, coordinator, *El Gobierno Provincial en la Nueva España, 1570–1787.* México: Universidad Nacional Autónoma de México, 1985.

González Alonso, Benjamín. *El Corregidor Castellano (1348–1808).* Madrid: Instituto de Estudios Administrativos, 1970.

Greenleaf, Richard E. "The Inquisition in Eighteenth-Century New Mexico," *New Mexico Historical Review* 60 (January 1985): 29–60.

Gregg, Josiah. *Commerce of the Prairies.* Norman: University of Oklahoma Press, 1954.

Gutiérrez, Ramón A. "Honor Ideology, Marriage Negotiations, and Class-Gender Domination in New Mexico, 1690–1846," *Latin American Perspectives* 12 (Winter 1985): 81–104.

———. *When Jesus Came, the Corn Mothers Went Away: Marriage, Sexuality, and Power in New Mexico, 1500–1846.* Stanford: Stanford University Press, 1991.

Hackett, Charles Wilson, ed. and trans. *Pichardo's Treatise on the Limits of Louisiana and Texas.* 4 vols. Austin: University of Texas Press, 1931–34.

Hall, G. Emlen. *Four Leagues of Pecos: A Legal History of the Pecos Grant, 1800–1933.* Albuquerque: University of New Mexico Press, 1984.

——— and David J. Weber. "Mexican Liberals and the Pueblo Indians, 1821–1829," *New Mexico Historical Review* 59 (January 1984): 5–32.

Hammond, George P. and Agapito Rey. *Don Juan de Oñate: Colonizer of New Mexico, 1595–1628.* 2 vols. Albuquerque: The University of New Mexico Press, 1953.

———, ed. and trans., *Narratives of the Coronado Expedition, 1540–1542.* Albuquerque: The University of New Mexico Press, 1940.

———. *The Rediscovery of New Mexico, 1580–1594: The Explorations of Chamuscado, Espejo, Castaño de Sosa, Morlete, and Leyva de Bonilla and Humaña.* Albuquerque: The University of New Mexico Press, 1966.

Haring, C. H. *The Spanish Empire in America.* New York: Oxford University Press, 1947.

Herr, Richard. *The Eighteenth-Century Revolution in Spain.* Princeton: Princeton University Press, 1958.

Hinojosa, Gilberto M. "The Religious-Indian Communities: The Goals of the Friars," in Gerald E. Poyo and Gilberto M. Hinojosa, eds., *Tejano Origins in Eighteenth-Century San Antonio.* Austin: University of Texas Press, 1991.

———. and Anne A. Fox. "Indians and Their Culture in San Fernando de Béxar," in Gerald E. Poyo and Gilberto M. Hinojosa, eds., *Tejano Origins in Eighteenth-Century San Antonio.* Austin: University of Texas Press, 1991.

Iguíniz, Juan B. *Los Gobernantes de Nueva Galicia: Datos y Documentos para sus Biografías.* Guadalajara: Unidad Editorial, 1981.

Jackson, Jack. *Los Mesteños: Ranching in Spanish Texas, 1721–1821.* College Station: Texas A&M University Press, 1986.

Jenkins, Myra Ellen. "The Baltasar Baca 'Grant': History of an Encroachment," *El Palacio* 68 (Spring, Summer 1961): 47–64, 87–105.

———. "Spanish Land Grants in the Tewa Area," *New Mexico Historical Review* 47 (April 1972): 113–34.

———. "Taos Pueblo and its Neighbors, 1540–1847," *New Mexico Historical Review* 41 (April 1966): 85–114.

Jiménez Pelayo, Agueda. "La Importancia de la Tierra y los Montes para los Pueblos de Indios de la Nueva Galicia," *Revista Encuentro* 17 (Octubre–Diciembre 1987): 49–66.

John, Elizabeth A. H. *Storms Brewed in Other Men's Worlds: The Confrontation of Indians, Spanish, and French in the Southwest, 1540–1795.* College Station: Texas A&M Press, 1975.

Jones, Oakah L., Jr. *Los Paisanos: Spanish Settlers on the Northern Frontier of New Spain.* Norman: University of Oklahoma Press, 1979.

———. *Pueblo Warriors and Spanish Conquest.* Norman: University of Oklahoma Press, 1966.

Kagan, Richard L. *Lawsuits and Litigants in Castile, 1500–1700.* Chapel Hill: University of North Carolina Press, 1981.

Kamen, Henry. *Spain, 1469–1714: A Society of Conflict.* London: Longman, 1983.

———. *Spain in the Later Seventeenth Century.* London: Longman, 1980.

Keen, Benjamin. *A History of Latin America.* Boston: Houghton Mifflin Company, 1992.

Kessell, John L. *Kiva, Cross, and Crown: The Pecos Indians and New Mexico, 1540–1840.* Washington, D.C.: National Park Service, 1979.

———. "Spaniards and Pueblos: From Crusading Intolerance to Pragmatic Accommodation," in David Hurst Thomas, ed., *Columbian Consequences.* Vol. 1, *Archaeological and Historical Perspectives on the Spanish Borderlands West.* Washington, D.C.: Smithsonian Institution Press, 1989.

Kicza, John E. *Colonial Entrepreneurs: Families and Business in Bourbon Mexico City.* Albuquerque: University of New Mexico Press, 1983.

Langum, David J. *Law and Community on the Mexican California Frontier: Anglo-American Expatriates and the Clash of Legal Traditions, 1821–1846.* Norman and London: University of Oklahoma Press, 1987.

_____."The Legal System of Spanish California: A Preliminary Study," *Western Legal History* 7 (Winter/Spring 1994): 1–23.

Lears, T. J. Jackson. "The Concept of Cultural Hegemony: Problems and Possibilities," *American Historical Review* 90 (June 1985): 568–93.

Levaggi, Abelardo. "El Concepto del Derecho Según los Fiscales de la Segunda Audiencia de Buenos Aires (1784–1810)," in *Actas del VIII Congreso del Instituto Internacional de Historia del Derecho Indiano*. Santiago: Revista Chilena de la Historia del Derecho, 1987.

_____. "El Derecho Indiano y Derecho Romano en el Siglo XVIII," *Anuario Histórico Jurídico Ecuatoriano* 5 (1980): 269–309.

_____. "El Derecho Romano en la Formación de los Abogados Argentinos del Ochocientos," *Derecho* 40 (1986): 17–33.

_____. *Manual de Historia del Derecho Argentino*. 3 vols. Buenos Aires: Ediciones Depalma, 1991.

_____. *El Virreinato Rioplatense en las Vistas Fiscales de José Márquez de la Plata*. 3 vols. Buenos Aires: Universidad del Museo Social Argentino, 1988.

Levene, Ricardo. *Historia del Derecho Argentino*. 5 vols. Buenos Aires: Editorial Guillermo Kraft, Ltda., 1945.

_____. "Las Indias No Eran Colonias," *Boletín de la Academia Nacional de Historia* 25 (1951): 596–626.

Liehr, Reinhard. *Ayuntamiento y Oligarquía en Puebla, 1787–1810*. México: Sep/Setentas, 1976. Olga Hentsche, trans.

Lira, Andrés. *Comunidades Indígenas Frente a la Ciudad de México: Tenochtitlan y Tlatelolco, sus Pueblos y Barrios, 1812–1919*. México and Zamora: El Colegio de México and El Colegio de Michoacán, 1983.

Llaguno, José A., S.J. *La Personalidad Jurídica del Indio y el III Concilio Provincial Mexicano (1585)*. México: Editorial Porrúa, S.A., 1983.

López Bohórquez, Alí Enrique. *La Real Audiencia de Caracas en la Historiografía Venezolana*. Caracas: Biblioteca de la Academia Nacional de la Historia, 1986.

_____. *Los Ministros de la Audiencia de Caracas (1786–1810)*. Caracas: Biblioteca de la Academia Nacional de la Historia, 1984.

Lozano Armendares, Teresa. *La Criminalidad en la Ciudad de México, 1800–1821*. México: Universidad Nacional Autónoma de México, 1987.

Luján Muñoz, Jorge. "Acerca de la Llegada y Aplicación de la Recopilación de la Leyes de Indias en el Reino de Guatemala, 1681–1699," in *Memoria del Simposio Hispanoamericano Sobre las Leyes de Indias*. San José, Costa Rica: Imprenta Nacional, 1984.

_____. *Los Escribanos en las Indias Occidentales, y en Particular en el Reino de Guatemala*. Guatemala: Instituto Guatemalteco de Derecho Notarial, 1977.

McAlister, Lyle. *The "Fuero Militar" in New Spain, 1764–1800*. Gainesville: University of Florida Press, 1957.

McKnight, Joseph W. "Law Books on the Hispanic Frontier," *Journal of the West* 27 (July 1988): 74–84.

_____. "Law Without Lawyers on the Hispano-Mexican Frontier," *The West Texas Historical Association Year Book* 66 (1990): 51–65.

MacLachlan, Colin M. *Spain's Empire in the New World: The Role of Ideas in Institutional and Social Change.* Berkeley: University of California Press, 1988.

Madden, Marie R. *Political Theory and Law in Medieval Spain.* New York: Fordham University Press, 1930.

Malagón-Barceló, Javier. *La Literatura Jurídica Española del Siglo de Oro en la Nueva España.* México: Biblioteca Nacional de México, Instituto Bibliográfico Mexicano, 1959.

Manzano Manzano, Juan. "El Proceso Recopilador de las Leyes de Indias Hasta 1680: Estudio Preliminar," in *Recopilación de Leyes de los Reynos de las Indias.* Madrid: Julián de Paredes, 1681; facsimile reprint, Madrid: Cultura Hispánica, 1973.

Margadant S., Guillermo F. "El Agua a la Luz del Derecho Novohispano. Triunfo de Realismo y Flexibilidad," *Anuario Mexicano de Historia del Derecho* 1 (1989): 113–46.

_____. *Introducción a la Historia del Derecho Mexicano.* México: Editorial Esfinge, S.A., 1986.

_____. "El Plan de Pitic," *Boletín Mexicano de Derecho Comparado* 21 (Mayo–Agosto 1988): 699–715.

Mariluz Urquijo, José María. *Ensayo Sobre los Juicios de Residencia Indianos.* Sevilla: Escuela de Estudios Hispano-Americanos de Sevilla, 1952.

Meinig, D. W. *Imperial Texas: An Interpretive Essay in Cultural Geography.* Austin and London: University of Texas Press, 1969.

Merryman, John Henry. *The Civil Law Tradition: An Introduction to the Legal Systems of Western Europe and Latin America.* 2nd. ed. Stanford: Stanford University Press, 1985.

Meyer, Michael C. *Water in the Hispanic Southwest: A Social and Legal History, 1550–1850.* Tucson: University of Arizona Press, 1984.

_____. and William L. Sherman. *The Course of Mexican History.* New York and Oxford: Oxford University Press, 1991.

Moore, John Preston. *The Cabildo in Peru Under the Bourbons: A Study in the Decline and Resurgence of Local Government in the Audiencia of Lima.* Durham: Duke University Press, 1966.

_____. *The Cabildo in Peru Under the Habsburgs: A Study in the Origins and Powers of the Town Council in the Viceroyalty of Peru, 1530–1700.* Durham: Duke University Press, 1954.

Moorhead, Max L. *The Apache Frontier: Jacobo Ugarte and Spanish-Indian Relations in Northern New Spain, 1769–1791.* Norman: University of Oklahoma Press, 1968.

_____. *New Mexico's Royal Road: Trade and Travel on the Chihuahua Trail.* Norman: University of Oklahoma Press, 1958.

_____. *The Presidio, Bastion of the Spanish Borderlands.* Norman: University of Oklahoma Press, 1975.

Morazzani de Pérez Enciso, Gisela. *La Intendencia en España y América.* Caracas: Consejo de Desarrollo Científico y Humanístico, 1966.

Mörner, Magnus. *Race Mixture in the History of Latin America.* Boston: Little, Brown, and Company, 1967.

Muro Romero, Fernando. "El 'Beneficio' de Oficios Públicos con Jurisdicción en Indias. Notas Sobre Sus Orígenes," *Anuario de Estudios Americanos* 35 (1978): 1–67.

_____. *Las Presidencias-Gobernaciones in Indias (Siglo XVI)*. Sevilla: Escuela de Estudios Hispano-Americanos de Sevilla, 1975.

Murphy, Michael E. *Irrigation in the Bajío Region of Colonial Mexico*. Boulder and London: Westview Press, 1986.

Myers, Sandra L. *The Ranch in Spanish Texas, 1691–1800*. El Paso: Texas Western Press, 1969.

Navarro García, Luis. *Don José de Gálvez y la Comandancia General de las Provincias Internas del Norte de la Nueva España*. Sevilla: Escuela de Estudios Hispano-Americanos de Sevilla, 1964.

_____. *Intendencias en Indias*. Sevilla: Escuela de Estudios Hispano-Americanos de Sevilla, 1959.

_____. *Las Provincias Internas en el Siglo XIX*. Sevilla: Escuela de Estudios Hispano-Americanos, 1965.

Naylor, Thomas H. and Charles W. Polzer, S.J. *Pedro de Rivera and the Military Regulations for Northern New Spain, 1724–1729: A Documentary History of His Frontier Inspection and the Reglamento of 1729*. Tucson: The University of Arizona Press, 1988.

_____. *The Presidio and Militia on the Northern Frontier of New Spain, 1570–1700*. Tucson: University of Arizona Press, 1986.

A New Pronouncing Dictionary of the Spanish and English Languages. New York and London: D. Appleton and Company, 1900.

Newcomb, W. W., Jr. "Karankawa," *Handbook of North American Indians*. Vol. 10. Washington, D.C.: Smithsonian Institution, 1979.

Nuttall, Zelia. "Royal Ordinances Concerning the Laying Out of New Towns," *Hispanic American Historical Review* 5 (May 1922): 249–54.

O'Gorman, Edmundo. *Historia de las Divisiones Territoriales de México*. México: Editorial Porrúa, S.A., 1966.

Orozco, Wistano Luis. *Los Ejidos de los Pueblos*. Reprint of 1914 edition, México: Ediciones "El Caballito," 1975.

Ortiz, Alfonso, ed. *Handbook of North American Indians*. Vol. 9, *The Southwest*. Washington, D.C.: Smithsonian Institution, 1979.

Ots Capdequí, José María. *El Estado Español en las Indias*. México: Fondo de Cultura Económica, 1946.

_____. *Historia del Derecho Español en América y del Derecho Indiano*. Madrid: Aguilar, 1969.

_____. *Instituciones*. Barcelona: Salvat Editores, S.A., 1959.

Paláu y Dulcet, Antonio. *Manual del Librero Hispanoamericano*. Barcelona: A. Paláu, 1947.

Parry, J. H. *The Audiencia of New Galicia in the Sixteenth Century*. Cambridge: Cambridge University Press, 1948.

_____. *The Sale of Public Office in the Spanish Indies Under the Hapsburgs*. Berkeley: University of California Press, 1953.

Phelan, John L. *The People and the King: The Comunero Revolution in Colombia, 1781*. Madison: University of Wisconsin Press, 1978.

Pike, Ruth. "Penal Servitude in the Spanish Empire: Presidio Labor in the Eighteenth Century," *Hispanic American Historical Review* 58 (February 1978): 21–40.

Poyo, Gerald E. "The Canary Island Immigrants of San Antonio: From Ethnic Exclusivity to Community in Eighteenth-Century Béxar," in Gerald E. Poyo and Gilberto M. Hinojosa, eds., *Tejano Origins in Eighteenth-Century San Antonio*. Austin: University of Texas Press, 1991.

———. "Immigrants and Integration in Late Eighteenth-Century Béxar," in Gerald E. Poyo and Gilberto M. Hinojosa, eds., *Tejano Origins in Eighteenth-Century San Antonio*. Austin: University of Texas Press, 1991.

Priestley, Herbert Ingram. *José de Gálvez, Visitor-General to New Spain, 1765–1771*. Berkeley: University of California Press, 1916.

Rees Jones, Ricardo. *El Despotismo Ilustrado y los Intendentes de la Nueva España*. México: Universidad Nacional Autónoma de México, 1983.

Ríos-Bustamante, Antonio José. "New Mexico in the Eighteenth Century: Life, Labor and Trade in la Villa de San Felipe de Albuquerque, 1706–1790," *Aztlán* 7 (Fall 1976): 357–89.

Ripodas Ardanaz, Daisy. "Los Indios y la Figura Jurídica del Rey Durante el Quinientos," in *Justicia, Sociedad y Economía en la América Española (Siglos XVI, XVII y XVIII)*. Valladolid: Casa-Museo de Colón and Seminario Americanista de la Universidad de Valladolid, 1983.

Rock, Rosalind Z. "'Pido y Suplico': Women and the Law in Spanish New Mexico, 1697–1763," *New Mexico Historical Review* 65 (April 1990): 145–59.

Rodríguez, Mario. *The Cádiz Experiment en Central America, 1808–1821*. Berkeley: University of California Press, 1978.

San Martino de Dromi, María Laura. *Intendencias y Provincias en la Historia Argentina*. [Buenos Aires]: Editorial Ciencias de la Administración S.R.L, n. d.

Sánchez Albornoz, Nicolás. *The Populations of Latin America*. Berkeley: University of California Press, 1974.

Sánchez-Arcilla Bernal, José. *Las Ordenanzas de las Audiencias de Indias (1511–1821)*. Madrid: Dykinson, S.L., 1992.

Sánchez Bella, Ismael, et al. "El Proyecto de Recopilación de Leyes de León Pinelo," in *IX Congreso del Instituto Internacional de Historia del Derecho Indiano: Actas y Estudios*. Madrid: Universidad Complutense, 1991.

Santamaría, Francisco J. *Diccionario General de Americanismos*. 3 vols. Méjico: Editorial Pedro Robredo, 1942.

Scardaville, Michael C. "(Habsburg) Law and (Bourbon) Order: State Authority, Popular Unrest, and the Criminal Justice System in Bourbon Mexico City," *The Americas* 50 (April 1994): 501–25.

Schäfer, Ernesto. *El Consejo Real y Supremo de las Indias*. 2 vols. Sevilla: Escuela de Estudios Hispano-Americanos, 1935–47.

Scholes, France V. "Church and State in New Mexico," *New Mexico Historical Review* 11 (January 1936): 9–76.

_____. "Civil Government and Society in New Mexico in the Seventeenth Century," *New Mexico Historical Review* 10 (April 1935): 71–111.

_____. "Royal Treasury Records Relating to the Province of New Mexico, 1596–1683," *New Mexico Historical Review* 50 (January and April 1975): 5–23, 139–64.

_____. *Troublous Times in New Mexico, 1659–1670.* Albuquerque: The University of New Mexico Press, 1942.

Seed, Patricia. "Social Dimensions of Race: Mexico City, 1753," *Hispanic American Historical Review* 62 (November 1982): 569–606.

_____. *To Love, Honor, and Obey in Colonial Mexico: Conflicts Over Marriage Choice, 1574–1821.* Stanford: Stanford University Press, 1988.

Simmons, Marc. "Settlement Patterns and Village Plans in Colonial New Mexico," in David J. Weber, ed., *New Spain's Far Northern Frontier: Essays on Spain in the American West, 1540–1821.* Albuquerque: University of New Mexico Press, 1979.

_____. *Spanish Government in New Mexico.* Albuquerque: The University of New Mexico Press, 1968.

Stein, Stanley J. and Barbara H. Stein. *The Colonial Heritage of Latin America.* New York: Oxford University Press, 1970.

Stern, Steve J. *Peru's Indian Peoples and the Challenge of Spanish Conquest: Huamanga to 1640.* Madison: The University of Wisconsin Press, 1982.

Stradling, R. A. *Europe and the Decline of Spain: A Study of the Spanish System, 1580–1720.* London: Allen & Unwin, 1981.

Tanzi, Héctor José. "El Conocimiento del Derecho en la Legislación de Indias," in *III Congreso del Instituto Internacional de Historia del Derecho Indiano, Actas y Estudios.* Madrid: Instituto Nacional de Estudios Jurídicos, 1973.

Tau Anzoategui, Víctor. "Los Bandos de Buen Gobierno de Buenos Aires en la Epoca Hispánica," in *Justicia, Sociedad y Economía en la América Española (Siglos XVI, XVII, y XVIII).* Valladolid: Casa-Museo de Colón and Seminario Americanista de la Universidad de Valladolid, 1983.

_____. "La Costumbre Como Fuente del Derecho Indiano en los Siglos XVI y XVII: Estudio a Través de los Cabildos del Río de la Plata, Cuyo y Tucumán," in *III Congreso del Instituto Internacional de Historia del Derecho Indiano, Actas y Estudios.* Madrid: Instituto Nacional de Estudios Jurídicos, 1973.

_____. "La Doctrina de los Autores como Fuente del Derecho Castellano-Indiano," *Revista de Historia del Derecho* 17 (1989): 351–408.

_____. *La Ley en América Hispana: Del Descubrimiento a la Emancipación.* Buenos Aires: Academia Nacional de la Historia, 1992.

_____. "La Ley 'Se Obedece Pero no Se Cumple.' En Torno a la Suplicación de las Leyes en el Derecho Indiano," *Anuario Histórico Jurídico Ecuatoriano* 6 (1980): 55–110.

_____. "La Noción de Ley en América Hispana durante los Siglos XVI a XVIII," *Anuario de Filosofía Jurídica y Social* 6 (1986): 193–232.

Taylor, William B. *Drinking, Homicide, and Rebellion in Colonial Mexican Villages.* Stanford: Stanford University Press, 1979.

———. *Landlord and Peasant in Colonial Oaxaca.* Stanford: Stanford University Press, 1972.

Tjarks, Alicia Vidaurreta. "Comparative Demographic Analysis of Texas, 1777–1793," *Southwestern Historical Quarterly* 77 (January 1974): 291–338.

Tomás y Valiente, Francisco. *El Derecho Penal de la Monarquía Absoluta (Siglos XVI-XVII–XVIII).* Madrid: Editorial Tecnos, 1969.

———. *Gobierno e Instituciones en la España del Antiguo Régimen.* Madrid: Alianza Editorial, 1982.

———. *Manual de Historia del Derecho Español.* 4th ed. Madrid: Editorial Tecnos, 1983.

———. "El Perdón de la Parte Ofendida en el Derecho Penal Castellano (Siglos XVI, XVII, y XVIII)," *Anuario de Historia del Derecho Español* 31 (1961): 55–114.

———. *La Tortura en España.* Barcelona: Editorial Ariel, 1973.

Twitchell, Ralph Emerson. *The Leading Facts of New Mexico History.* 5 vols. Cedar Rapids, Iowa: The Torch Press, 1911–17.

———. *The Spanish Archives of New Mexico.* 2 vols. Cedar Rapids, Iowa: The Torch Press, 1914.

Tyler, Daniel. *The Mythical Pueblo Rights Doctrine: Water Administration in Hispanic New Mexico.* El Paso: Texas Western Press, 1990.

———. *Sources for New Mexican History, 1821–1848.* Santa Fe: Museum of New Mexico Press, 1984.

Van Kleffens, E.N. *Hispanic Law Until the End of the Middle Ages.* Edinburgh: Edinburgh University Press, 1968.

Vance, John Thomas. *The Background of Hispanic-American Law.* Washington, D.C.: The Catholic University of America, 1937.

Viñas Mey, Carmelo. *El Régimen Jurídico y de Responsabilidad en la América Indiana.* Madrid: Publicaciones de la Revista de las Españas, n.d.

Wallerstein, Immanuel. *The Modern World-System: Capitalist Agriculture and the Origins of the European World-Economy in the Sixteenth Century.* New York: Academic Press, 1974.

Weber, David J. "John Francis Bannon and the Historiography of the Spanish Borderlands: Retrospect and Prospect," *Journal of the Southwest* 29 (Winter 1987): 331–63.

———. *The Mexican Frontier, 1821–1846: The American Southwest Under Mexico.* Albuquerque: University of New Mexico Press, 1982.

———, ed. and intro., *New Spain's Far Northern Frontier: Essays on Spain in the American West, 1540–1821.* Albuquerque: University of New Mexico Press, 1979.

———. *The Spanish Frontier in North America.* New Haven and London: Yale University Press, 1992.

Weddle, Robert S. *Wilderness Manhunt: The Spanish Search for La Salle.* Austin: University of Texas Press, 1973.

Weisser, Michael R. *Crime and Punishment in Early Modern Europe*. Atlantic Heights, New Jersey: Humanities Press, 1979.

_____. *The Peasants of the Montes: The Roots of Rural Rebellion in Spain*. Chicago and London: The University of Chicago Press, 1976.

West, Elizabeth Howard. "The Right of Asylum in New Mexico in the Seventeenth and Eighteenth Centuries," *New Mexico Historical Review* 41 (April 1966): 115–53.

Williams, Raymond. "Base and Superstructure in Marxist Cultural Theory," *New Left Review* 82 (November–December 1973): 3–16.

Yalí Román, Alberto. "Sobre Alcaldías Mayores y Corregimientos en Indias: Un Ensayo de Interpretación," *Jahrbuch für Geschichte von Staat, Wirtschaft und Gesellschaft Lateinamerikas* 9 (1972): 1–39.

Zorraquín Becú, Ricardo. "Los Distintos Tipos de Gobernador en el Derecho Indiano," in *III Congreso del Instituto Internacional de Historia del Derecho Indiano, Actas y Estudios*. Madrid: Instituto Nacional de Estudios Jurídicos, 1973.

_____. *La Función de Justicia en el Derecho Indiano*. Buenos Aires: Imprenta de la Universidad, 1948.

_____. *La Organización Judicial Argentina en el Período Hispánico*. Buenos Aires: Editorial Perrot, 1981.

Index

About the Book and Author

The Legal Culture of Northern New Spain, 1700–1810
Charles R. Cutter

Spain's colonial rule rested on a judicial system that resolved conflicts and meted out justice. But just how was this legal order imposed throughout the New World? Re-created here from over six hundred civil and criminal cases are the procedural and ethical workings of the law in two of Spain's remote colonies—New Mexico and Texas in the eighteenth century.

Professor Cutter challenges the traditional view that the legal system was inherently corrupt and irrelevant to the mass of society, and that local judicial officials were uninformed and inept. Instead he found that even in peripheral areas the lowest-level officials—the *alcalde* or town magistrate—had a greater impact on daily life and a keener understanding of the law than previously acknowledged by historians. These local officials exhibited flexibility and sensitivity to frontier conditions, and their rulings generally conformed to community expectations of justice. By examining colonial legal culture, Cutter reveals the attitudes of settlers, their notions of right and wrong, and how they fixed a boundary between proper and improper actions.

"A superlative work."—Marc Simmons, author of *Spanish Government in New Mexico.*

Charles R. Cutter is a professor of history at Purdue University and the author of *The Protector de Indios in Colonial New Mexico* (UNM Press).